GW00400915

THE GLOBAL
HR MANAGER

Editors

Professor Pat Joynt is professor of management development at Henley Management College and professor of international management at the Bodø Graduate School of Business in Northern Norway. As a consultant, he has worked with such organisations as General Motors, Siemens, Volvo and PowerGen. He is the author of eight books and has contributed chapters to 18 other books. He has published over 80 articles in various management journals and is on the editorial boards of eight international journals.

Bob Morton CIPD is the head of HRD for Northern Europe for Ciba Specialty Chemicals PLC. He has worked internationally in all areas of human resources from employee relations through to organisational development and has held a variety of senior HR posts in the UK, USA and Switzerland. He is the IPD's Vice-President International. He has also served as an external examiner for the IPD and is a visiting lecturer on international human resources to MBA and Masters programmes. He is a frequent contributor to national and international conferences.

THE GLOBAL
HR MANAGER

edited by
Pat Joynt and Bob Morton

**INSTITUTE OF PERSONNEL
AND DEVELOPMENT**

Typeset by Fakenham Photosetting Limited, Fakenham
Printed in Great Britain by the Short Run Press, Exeter

British Library Cataloguing-in-Publication Data
A catalogue record for this book is available from the British Library

ISBN 0-85292-815-7

**INSTITUTE OF PERSONNEL
AND DEVELOPMENT**

IPD House, Camp Road, London SW19 4UX
Tel: 020 8971 9000   Fax: 020 8263 3333
Registered office as above. Registered Charity No. 1038333
A company limited by guarantee. Registered in England No. 2931892

CONTENTS

Contributors   vii
Foreword   xi

1   **Introduction: Crossing the Seven Cs**   1
    Pat Joynt and Bob Morton

Competition (global)
2   **The New Frontier of Global HR**   12
    J. Stewart Black and Dave Ulrich

Culture
3   **Organisational Culture and International
    HRM**   39
    Rob Goffee and Gareth Jones

Communications
4   **The HR Manager as Global Business
    Partner**   59
    Terence Brake

Competencies
5   **International Recruitment, Selection and
    Assessment**   87
    Paul Sparrow

Compensation
6   **International Compensation**   115
    Stephen J. Perkins and Chris Hendry

Careers
7   **International HR: Career Management**   144
    Yochanan Altman

8   **Sustaining Constructive Relationships
    across Cultural Boundaries**   156
    Ann Parkinson

Collaboration

9 **International Teamworking**   179
   Linda Holbeche

10 **Developing International Management
   Teams through Diversity**   207
   Malcolm Higgs

11 **International HRM: an Asian Perspective**   233
   Sek-hong Ng and Malcolm Warner

   Afterword   258
   Pat Joynt and Bob Morton

Index   **259**

CONTRIBUTORS

Yochanan Altman is a research professor of international HRM at the University of London Business School. In 1999–2000 he is also visiting professor at the University of Paris and the University of Vienna. He consults widely with multinational companies and new international start-ups. His particular interests are careers and management development. He is the editor of *The Journal of Managerial Psychology* and the author of five books and over 40 articles in academic and professional journals.

J. Stewart Black PhD is a professor at the University of Michigan and executive director of the school's Asia Pacific Human Resource Partnership – a consortium involving 30 large, multinational firms with significant operations in Asia. He is also managing director of the Center for Global Assignments in San Diego, California. He has authored or co-authored eight books and over 70 articles and chapters on various aspects of international HR and leadership. He regularly consults with firms on issues of globalisation.

Terence Brake is an author, facilitator and international business consultant. He is also a frequent contributor to business journals and newspapers, as well as a renowned keynote speaker at international conferences. In 1994 he was awarded the American Society for Training and Development's International Professional Practice Area Research Award. He is senior executive vice-president in Transnational Management Associates (TMA), a leading executive development consultancy based in London, Paris, Singapore and Princeton, USA.

Rob Goffee is an internationally respected authority on organisational transformation. A professor of organisational behaviour and subject chair at London Business School, he has published six books and more than 40 articles. He is a frequent contributor to newspapers and magazines and has spoken frequently on TV and radio on business issues. With Gareth Jones, he runs Creative Management

Associates (CMA), instituting large-scale cultural change at such companies as Johnson and Johnson, Glaxo-Wellcome, Shell, Unilever and Apple.

Chris Hendry is centenary professor in organisational behaviour and head of the department of HRM and organisational behaviour at City University Business School. He was previously associate director of the Centre for Corporate Strategy and Change at Warwick Business School, and is the author of 12 research monographs, some 40 articles and book chapters, and three books.

Malcolm Higgs PhD is a member of Henley Management College's human resource and organisational behaviour faculty. He moved to Henley from a role as principal partner in Towers Perrin's London human resource management practice. Prior to joining Towers Perrin, Malcolm had eight years' consulting experience with the Hay Group and Arthur Young, covering a diverse range of human resource management assignments. Publications include a book and a range of papers on leadership, team development and executive assessment. He is a member of the British Psychological Society and a chartered occupational psychologist.

Linda Holbeche is director of research at Roffey Park Management Institute. She is also programme director for the strategic leadership programme and is actively involved in board-level development and management development programmes, working with an extensive range of clients from all sectors. She has produced several major research publications and numerous articles, and her book *Motivating People in Lean Organisation*s (1997) was shortlisted for the 1997 Management Consultancy Association's Book Prize. Prior to joining Roffey Park, Linda was manager of management development for Europe, the Middle East and Africa at American Express.

Gareth Jones is BT professor of organisational development at Henley Management College and visiting professor of organisational behaviour at INSEAD in France. Immediately prior to joining Henley he was senior vice-president, human resources, at Polygram International. He is the co-author, with Rob Goffee, of the widely acclaimed *Harvard Business Review* article 'What holds the modern company together?'

Sek-hong Ng PhD is a graduate from the University of Hong Kong and a postgraduate from the London School of Economics and Political Science, where he obtained an MSc in industrial relations and later a doctorate in industrial sociology. He is now a reader at the School of Business at the University of Hong Kong, teaching and researching in industrial relations, labour law and human resources. He has published widely in the field of Asian IR and HRM.

Ann Parkinson PhD has a practitioner background in human resources and total quality – culminating in her role as personnel strategy manager for British Telecom plc – which has led her to a 'plural' career in consultancy and lecturing in human resources while completing her doctorate. Recent consultancy clients include IBM(UK), Barclays Funds Ltd, BUPA, SPT (Czech Telecom), MATAV (Hungarian Telecom), ST (Slovak Telecom), CfBT (careers service), MHF, and Jackdaws (charities). She is part-time/associate faculty at Henley Management College and Imperial College, University of London, and a guest lecturer in human resources for MBA programmes at Cranfield Business School and the University of West of England.

Stephen J. Perkins is director of the Strategic Remuneration Research Centre and a visiting fellow at City University Business School. Author of *Internationalization – The people dimension* (1997) and co-author of a new IPD guide on international reward and recognition (in press), he has advised a range of leading private and state-owned enterprises internationally on organisation change and associated people strategy. His current research interests major on the interactions between global business strategy and 'high value-added knowledge-workers'.

Paul Sparrow PhD is professor in international human resource management at Sheffield University Management School. From 1982 to 1984 he was a freelance consultant, following which he became a research fellow at Aston University and a senior research fellow at Warwick Business School. In 1988 he joined PA Consulting Group, returning to academia in 1991 when he took up a lectureship in organisational behaviour at Manchester Business School. He moved to Sheffield University to take up a readership in 1995 and then a chair in 1997. He has written many articles and numerous books. He is editor of the *Journal of Occupational and Organisational Psychology* and a deputy director of the Institute of Work Psychology.

Dave Ulrich is professor of business administration at the University of Michigan. He has published over 90 articles and book chapters, and has co-authored numerous books. He is the editor of *Human Resource Management* journal and serves on the editorial board of four others. He has been listed by *Business Week* as one of the world's 'top ten educators' in management and the top educator in human resources, and has consulted and done research with over half of the Fortune 200.

Malcolm Warner is professor and fellow of Wolfson College, Cambridge, and the Judge Institute of Management Studies, University of Cambridge. He is the editor-in-chief of the *International Encyclopædia of Business and Management Studies* (1996).

FOREWORD

The stimulus for this book came from discussions with practitioners working in international people management who, during our conversations, came up with a common need for a cohesive and accessible source of the latest thinking, research and practice in the international human resource management (IHRM) field.

The catalyst for its production was an entertaining and stimulating flight with Pat Joynt back to the UK from Budapest and a subsequent discussion with Fran Wilson, the manager, international, for the IPD. We had talked many times during my vice-presidency of international of the need to have such a book in the IPD's catalogue. So here it is!

It should appeal to practitioners and students alike, because it combines excellent research with best practice in the IHRM field. We have attracted some of the world's leading researchers and practitioners in IHRM. The contributions cover a very broad canvas and, because of that, the book is intended to provide not only some very pertinent and practical frameworks but also to be a source of stimuli to think and find out more in depth where needed.

Bob Morton

Chapter 1

Introduction: Crossing the Seven Cs

Pat Joynt and Bob Morton

Globalisation has become one of the buzz-words in business and academia. Definitions vary, but there is one certainty among the confusion: the conduct of business *is* increasingly global.

> **"At least two in six of all products sold anywhere in the world cross international boundaries on their way to market"**

The volume of international business continues to expand dramatically from year to year. At least two in six of all products sold anywhere in the world cross international boundaries on their way to market. It is estimated that between one-third and one-half of the UK economy is involved with international trade. In Germany it is over 50 per cent. The advent of the Internet and e-commerce is further increasing the flow of goods and services and, most importantly, is also increasing the speed at which knowledge – and therefore competitive advantage – can be transferred across the globe.

Companies are organising across these borders. The seamless organisation is now with us, especially in the field of technology, where work is routinely moved across time and geographical zones without interruption and where 'virtual' organisations are being created. Continuous development is increasingly the norm in the software industry in order to optimise expensive resources, gain speed of development and be the first to market – one of the ultimate competitive advantages. This is not confined to 'high-tech' industries. More traditional industries have not only modernised their production lines and supply chains in the pursuit of the 'lean' organisation but now have the capacity to move production very rapidly to different parts of the world in order to gain competitive advantage in terms of costs and speed of distribution. Resources of all types now flow relatively freely across national borders.

One of these resources is people. Millions of people live abroad working for their companies. It is estimated that over two million Americans live and work abroad. As long ago as 1991 it was estimated that there were two million European Community (EC) citizens (including their families, this means over five and a half million people) working and living in EC countries other than their home ones. In 1991 there were also approximately eight million 'guest workers' from outside the EC who worked within its borders. At least one in six UK employees is working for a Japanese company, and increasing investment in the UK is taking place from south-east Asia (eg Korea), despite the economic roller-coaster that the Asian region has been riding over the past 18 months. The UK still has a lower unit cost of production, a better infrastructure and greater stability than most of the rest of Europe, and there are estimates that the number of people in the UK employed by foreign companies, directly or indirectly, will rise to three in six by 2005.

What does this mean for people management professionals?

As more and more companies operate internationally, the impact on various business functions becomes more pronounced. Practitioners in each business function must develop the skills, knowledge and experience in the international arena that will help their companies succeed in this demanding and often volatile environment. This is particularly true for the human resource management (HRM) function. Effective people management is essential, especially for small to medium-sized firms, because international expansion and operation place additional stress on resources, particularly people.

People management in the UK is therefore taking place in an increasingly international context. The implications for HRM are that internationalisation is a reality, and people management practices need to acknowledge and work within this context and reflect a broader perspective. The advent of the seamless organisation means that people management policies and practices have to facilitate the process of working across time, distance and culture not only in a practical, operational sense but also in creating a new mind-set in managers of thinking and operating internationally.

The internationalisation of people management can take many forms. From the perspective of HR practices, HR managers can find themselves involved in international people management issues in any of the following situations:

- ⊕ the operation of parent-company firms overseas
- ⊕ government agencies and non-profit organisations
- ⊕ the operation of foreign firms in the home country
- ⊕ the employment of foreign citizens.

> **"The reality today is that most companies consciously or unconsciously experience one or more aspects of international people management"**

In addition, an HR manager could be employed in a role that combines these situations. Each situation creates challenges for people management. One of the fundamental challenges is to identify and train HR managers who, although they were raised and experienced in one culture, can effectively interact with and manage people raised in one or more different cultures. A further challenge is to develop effective personnel policies and practices in each of the business environments in which the employer operates. HR managers must integrate and co-ordinate activities taking place in diverse environments with people of diverse backgrounds. The reality today is that most companies consciously or unconsciously experience one or more aspects of international people management, and the successes and failures of these companies are directly related to how well they handle such challenges.

The development of IHRM or 'global HRM' has aroused debate. It is described by some as 'more fiction than fact'. Some suggest that it is at an infancy stage, and yet others believe there is already a substantial 'body of knowledge and practice' that provides an important starting-point for studying IHRM. There are widely differing views as to the state of research into IHRM, and the rhetoric often does not match the reality of practice.

The information available through literature searches and surveys in multinational firms suggests that IHRM differs from domestic HRM in a number of factors. These include:

- being responsible for a greater number of functions and activities
- requiring a broader perspective
- greater involvement in employees' lives
- having to change emphasis, because the employee mix of parent- and host-country nationals varies at different locations and over time, distance and cultures
- greater exposure to problems and difficulties
- coping with a greater number of external influences
- having to consider greater overall complexities in decision-making.

Given this background, the purpose of this book is:

- firstly to help people-professionals to operate effectively in this international environment by providing examples of and insights into leading international people management and development practices and research
- secondly to provide the basis for people-professionals to compare their current dilemmas and challenges with what is happening in the field of IHRM, so providing frameworks and approaches that they can use to think through their own situations and develop their own insights.

Case-study

In order to illustrate the complexities, variations, depth and diversity of the world of international people management, imagine that an executive training course in managing people is nearing completion. The trainer opens the journal *Strategy and Business* and begins to read about a case involving GloCorp. GloCorp was the first international firm to reach a stunning $500 billion in annual revenue. The firm cannot hire people fast enough and, already engaged in seven major lines of business, is contemplating others.

Three-quarters of its revenue flow from 200 alliances, and its head-quarters have changed three times in the last two decades. The top team works out of the 'global core', which involves only about 200 employees. Success is driven by people, knowledge-sharing and a coherent business model which involves empowerment, financial allocation and a system that operates independently of organisation charts and hierarchies.

The trainer looks up and notices that many of the executives in front of her have a puzzled look on their faces. From all their reading they do not remember the name GloCorp – and there is a good reason for that. GloCorp does not exist! The authors of the article, Pasternack and Viscio, call GloCorp the 'centerless corporation'. As we approach the end of this century, it is fascinating to imagine how the world will look in the next millennium. Elements of GloCorp exist in many organisations today, and many of the ideas of this new inter-national – or global – organisation are described in detail in the chapters that follow.

But let's return to the training group a few weeks later. The 'teach-ing' part of the course has finished, and the managers are in the process of preparing a paper and a presentation on a topic of their choice. Both the paper and the presentation have interesting elements, as we shall see.

The paper is limited to 2,000 words, with additional appendices. This is just over 10 pages, but many complain that this is not enough if one is to present a hot topic on managing people. The response of the trainer is that most executives never read a report that runs longer than 10 pages. 'If you can't say it in 10, then ...'. The report also has a one-page executive summary.

We join the seminar as the first group begins their 20-minute pres-entation. The topic is 360-degree feedback, and they begin by reviewing the theory and applying a benchmark process to such international organisations as GE, AT&T, Digital, W. H. Smith and

Nabisco. The group has also taken the time to talk to Professor Beverly Alimo-Metcalfe at the University of Leeds about her views on the effectiveness of 360-degree feedback for appraisal, personal development and teamwork. The group concludes that 360-degree feedback should not be used just as a tool for appraisal: it is an excellent tool for developing individuals and teams. The feedback system should have clearly defined objectives, they argue, and should be carefully designed and implemented. The other members of the seminar are eager to put their questions, and the next 20 minutes fly by.

The second group has selected motivation and leadership. Their unique approach has been to sample motivation factors from six of the organisations represented in the group. Organisation diversity is apparent, because the organisations comprise a UK research-based pharmaceutical firm; a UK subsidiary of a Canadian-based software company; a major UK financial services provider; a major telecommunications equipment manufacturer with 80,000 employees; a UK-based engineering and construction company that is part of a major German corporation; and, finally, a global leader in travel and in the travel automation distribution industry. One of their major conclusions is that 'consideration of the individual employee's needs and characteristics is necessary for effective motivation to action; hence the reliance on line managers, who are closer to the individual employees'.

The third group had a real challenge: knowledge management. Let's look at their executive summary:

Executive summary

The relatively new discipline of knowledge management (KM) has arisen as a result of the on-going search by companies for competitive advantage in association with the progressive development of ever-more powerful information technology systems. Knowledge management, like other aspects of management, is eclectic in nature. For success to be achieved, it requires the ability to operate effectively across functional, technical and cultural boundaries, with an emphasis on being able to elicit both tacit and explicit knowledge.

From research undertaken in 1997 by Sklyrme and Amidon at the Business Intelligence Unit (BIU), a number of factors have been identified that contribute to a successful knowledge-based culture. Four companies that have started on the route to knowledge management were benchmarked against the BIU model. The results indicated that the two communications companies and the service company would need to continue to build on existing good practices through incremental change to achieve the desired state defined by the model. The manufacturing company, however, would need to implement a radical change in its business culture.

Some factors of the model, such as culture and individual learning, were difficult to benchmark. However, the findings of this study, from the literature review and benchmarking exercises, confirmed that, although there are common elements in a successful knowledge-based culture, there are many routes by which it can be achieved, and the involvement and commitment of the whole company is essential.

Role-playing was a central strategy of the fourth group, who opened their session with a discussion between Professor Hammer, the guru in the process re-engineering field, and Professor Davenport, the expert in process redesign. Change efforts are very common in most organisations today, and the need to understand this process, especially the people aspect of it, is central for any HR practitioner. Later, during the group's discussion with the class, the role of consultants became the central theme, followed by the crucial role of IT in many of today's major business changes.

The 'balanced scorecard' was the theme for the next presentation. Traditional finance measures were complemented with crucial indicators for:

- the customer perspective – how do customers see us?
- innovation and learning – how do our employees feel?
- internal perspective – are we productive and effective?

Other items included the 'balance' between tangible and intangible measures, long-term goals against short-term goals, and lag measures against lead measures. The presentation focused on role-play, top executives from Ericsson in Sweden and British Telecom plc presenting their companies' experiences with the scorecard.

The agenda for the fifth group was performance appraisal systems. One member of the group works for General Electric (GE), noted for its innovations in this area. A gap analysis was undertaken to identify significant differences from the GE system in the other executives' companies. The conclusions were most interesting:

- ⊕ The appraisal systems of the seven organisations surveyed differ in varying degrees from the GE system. The most similar are those at Nortel and CIRIA. The most different is that of Hitachi Credit.
- ⊕ There is a relationship between some of the appraisal characteristics and some organisational characteristics. These relationships are not very strong, however.
- ⊕ Smaller organisations can have elements of appraisal that are 'better' than those of world-class organisations.
- ⊕ This study has made the participating organisations more aware of the factors to consider when designing appraisal systems.

And now, the final presentation. Imagine yourself working with the new KLM and Alitalia joint sales company in Zurich. Both airlines merged about a year ago. The Zurich office is an interesting casestudy on the complexities of culture, organisational as well as national. Most of the KLM employees come from second-generation Dutch families living near Zurich. Most of the Alitalia employees are second-generation Italians. They now work together for a firm that aspires to be *one*. Let's look at the conclusions of the groups' report:

> As Schein points out, it can be difficult to move outside one's own paradigm in assessing cultural differences of any sort. Whilst being cognisant of that and aware of the fact that our primary researcher is an employee of one of the participating companies, we have drawn the following conclusions.
>
> First, the cultural differences were not as marked as one might have expected from two organisations, one having been privatised for a relatively short period and the other still entirely owned by the national government, bearing in mind the national differences between Italy and the Netherlands in Hofstede's own studies. This was particularly the case in the questionnaire responses. We believe there are a number of reasons for this.
>
> Drawing first on Trompenaars' three levels of culture, there is a significant difference between national culture and corporate culture. National culture is a function of influences experienced early in life, whereas corporate culture is a function (to an extent) of one's own choice of organisation, and the influences therein on an adult.

Furthermore, again drawing on Trompenaars, there is a high likelihood that professional culture has a unifying influence on behaviour within the airline industry as a whole, and this is reflected in our results.

The second major reason that may allow for the similar results is the fact that both airlines have multinational staff with many second-generation Dutch and Italians born and raised in Switzerland.

Having noted that the corporate cultural differences were perhaps smaller than anticipated, they were nevertheless evident. This was particularly so in the interviews. Specific differences based on Hofstede's six-dimensions model have been outlined above and there are a number of questions that arise.

First, will the cross-cultural issues be a help or hindrance to the new company? The answer to this lies in the way in which they are managed. The key, as Hofstede points out, is 'to minimise friction losses and preserve unique cultural capital'. It is imperative that culture, like other major influences on business success or failure, is driven by everyone at all levels in the organisation. In essence, this means that the new company management must recognise that the embryonic organisation has the opportunity to develop its own cultural mosaic in which each element preserves its unique value, if carefully managed.

Managers, teams and employees have to confront cultural differences, learn from them and derive means of utilising them creatively in order to benefit from their potential added value.

This leads to the more fundamental question of whether culture or multiculturalism can be considered a competitive advantage. The answer to this is a definite yes. As we have already seen, the culture of a corporation influences organisational structure, practices, strategy and HR management. More importantly, corporate culture is the one competitive advantage which is truly sustainable, because it cannot easily be copied. On the other hand, mismanagement can lead to the risk of severe competitive disadvantage.

Ultimately, whilst the differences in corporate culture between KLM and Alitalia were not found to be as great as might have been expected, it is important that they are recognised by the new management team and by the organisation as a whole. The process of melding the two will not be without its problems, but the results, if managed well, will add significantly to the capital of the new organisation.

The seven Cs

Welcome to the real world of international human relations as seen through the eyes of executives 'on the ground'! The short descriptions above illustrate the complexities, variations, depth and diversity of the subject we are about to review in the following chapters. The central question facing the international HR manager, as Black and Ulrich say in Chapter 2, is how to surf the waves of globalisation rather than just ride them out. This is the exciting, occasionally stormy journey crossing the seven Cs of International HRM. Our journey is charted as follows:

- ⊕ Competition (global) – capability follows strategy (*Chapter 2*)
- ⊕ Culture – national and organisational – getting the values right (*Chapter 3*)
- ⊕ Communications – global networking/use of technologies (*Chapter 4*)
- ⊕ Competencies – recruiting and selecting core capabilities (*Chapter 5*)
- ⊕ Compensation – right pay for the right person in the right place at the right time (*Chapter 6*)
- ⊕ Careers – the psychological contract between the individual and the organisation (*Chapters 7 and 8*)
- ⊕ Collaboration – ensuring managers from different nationalities work effectively together (*Chapters 9 and 10*).

IHRM is a relatively new field which is still largely developmental and emergent. Although some aspects of IHRM are supported by considerable research and documented practice in the field (for instance, in the context of expatriate management), other aspects have yet to receive the same attention. This book therefore encompasses a broader perspective than simply expatriate management in an attempt to offer the sort of contingent approach, frameworks and shared experiences the editors believe essential for effective IHRM.

References and further reading

BARTLETT C. *and* GHOSHAL S. *Managing across Borders: The transnational solution.* 2nd edn. Cambridge, MA, Harvard Business School Press, 1998.

BRISCOE D. R. *International Human Resource Management.* New Jersey, Prentice Hall, 1995.

DOWLING P. J. *International Human Resource Management: Managing people in a multinational context.* South Western College Publishing, 1999.

FLOOD P. C., GANNON M. J. *and* PAAUWE J. *Managing without Traditional Methods.* Reading, MA, Addison Wesley, 1996.

HARZING A.-W. *and* RUYSSEVELDT J. V. *International Human Resource Management.* London, Sage, 1995.

RHINESMITH S. H. *A Managers' Guide to Globalization.* Irwin Professional Publishing, 1996.

SHENKAR O. *Global Perspectives of Human Resource Management.* New Jersey, Prentice Hall, 1995.

The help of the Henley Management College Masters Programme 30 with this chapter is gratefully acknowledged.

Chapter 2

The New Frontier of Global HR

*J. Stewart Black and
Dave Ulrich*

Introduction

In recent years, a nascent theory of organisation has emerged. Rather than defining organisations through their morphology, a growing group who study and observe organisations are seeing organisations as bundles of capabilities (Ulrich and Lake, 1990; Stalk *et al*, 1992). This transition shifts the focus from rules, procedures, policies, levels of management and other hierarchical mechanisms to a focus on:

- core competencies (Prahalad and Hamel, 1990; Gallon, Stillman and Coates, 1995)
- agility (Dyer and Shafer, 1998)
- culture (Barney, 1986)
- high-performing work practices (Becker, Huselid, Pickus and Spratt, 1997; Delaney and Huselid, 1996).

An effective organisation is not defined by the number of layers of management, systems in place or headcount, but by the ability of the organisation to respond to business demands. The age-old adage 'structure follows strategy' is being replaced with 'capability follows strategy' (Ulrich, 1997).

The logic of this converging and emerging view of organisation is portrayed in Figure 1. As suggested in this figure, as an organisation shifts its strategy from cell 1 to cell 4, it must also redefine required capabilities (cell 5) and HR investments (cell 6) to align with the emerging strategy.

For example, Intel had a product development strategy for years, with organisation capabilities focused on speed to market with new

Figure 1
STRATEGY/CAPABILITY/ORGANISATION ASSESSMENT

	Current	**Future**
Strategy	1	4
Organisation capability	2	5
Organisation action (HR investments)	3	6

products. After the crisis of the pentium chip – a small mathematical error that an Intel chip produced was highlighted by the media, and Intel's response concentrated on the technical specification at the expense of the customer, with subsequent loss of credibility – Intel's management realised that their strategy should not just be product, but customer, or brand. So they began to find ways to build the brand (Intel Inside) that would attract and retain customers. This strategic shift required a new set of capabilities for Intel's success, such as building customer intimacy, leveraging brand across products, forming alliances with distributors, and quality. Embedding these new capabilities enabled Intel to turn its strategy into practice. Once these new capabilities were identified, Intel executives and HR professionals could make HR investments (cell 6) that drove these capabilities. For example, they began:

- to hire individuals with a customer focus
- to develop training and development experiences focused on customers
- to create incentive programs that encouraged customer-oriented behaviours.

The HR practices bundled together (Becker *et al*, 1997) to deliver critical organisational capabilities.

A capability focus entails rethinking the organisational implications for delivering on global strategies. Imagine a team working to shape the strategy for doing or increasing business in a particular new country. As this team prepares its strategy of product offerings, markets and distribution channels, it must make organisational choices to accomplish the strategy. Traditionally, the organisational choices focus on decisions where work is done (eg 'Do we do research and development (R&D), production, marketing, advertising, or distribution within a country or across multiple countries?') and crafting HR practices that enable the firm to enter the market (eg 'How do we pay people in this market?' 'How do we form alliances to gain market presence?' or 'Where do we find people to work in this market?'). The capability focus suggests that the initial organisational question to be raised to accomplish a global strategy is not about where work is done or how to shape an HR practice in order to be global, but how to identify and instil organisational capabilities that allow the global strategy to be sustained. Once capabilities are identified, the HR practices may be crafted to ensure the creation and endurance of those capabilities. In the team charged with developing a global strategy, either the line manager or HR professionals (or both) must ask 'What capabilities are required to compete in this global market?'

This chapter aims to answer this question by:

- reviewing current views of the global firm
- defining capabilities for global integration and local adaptation
- suggesting implications for executives and scholars trying to figure out how to create an effective global organisation.

Current views of the global firm

A comprehensive and exhaustive review of the typologies and models of globalisation and its relationship to firm strategy and structure would be a chapter in itself. Consequently, we shall not undertake that task. Rather we shall focus on a particular approach that has had a significant impact on both theory and practice. Bartlett and Ghoshal (1995) argue that, increasingly, companies are pushed simultaneously towards both global integration and local responsiveness. The popular phrase 'Think global, act local' has become the mantra of this particular view of the global world of organisations.

Essentially, this approach argues that there are powerful forces push-ing organisations towards greater global integration. These include the benefits gained from worldwide volume, such as efficiencies based on economies of scale, leverage of high-cost distribution networks, and greater returns on expensive R&D activities.

For example, in a variety of industries the minimally efficient pro-duction scale is beyond that which could be supported in a single market. If we look at Boeing, the break-even point for the new 777 is approximately 300 planes, each costing in excess of $100 million. This requires total sales of $30 billion! Boeing has no choice but to try to develop planes that will have global appeal in order to get an acceptable return on its investment. The high level of R&D and such scale economies as these push organisations towards globalisation and towards concentration on, and integration upstream of, such activities as product development and manufacturing.

By contrast, differences among countries and customer preferences are two key factors that push towards localisation. 'Localisation' in this context refers to the pressure to differentiate activities on a local basis. Firms are pushed in the direction of localisation when benefits gained from location-specific differentiation and adaptation are sig-nificant and such factors as economies of scale are small.

For example, Procter & Gamble (P&G) recently faced pressures of localisation for a laundry detergent it developed. Although P&G wanted to develop one detergent, Visor, for all of Europe and to cap-ture the efficiencies of a single development, manufacturing and marketing effort, it found significant differences between specific countries in Europe. These differences pushed away from globalis-ation and towards localisation. P&G found that Germans generally prefer front-loading washers and believe that boiling whites is the only way to clean them, whereas the French prefer top-loading washers and do not believe you have to boil whites to get them clean.

This created several problems. First, the detergent was designed to work best at cleaning whites in cold, not boiling, water – cold water is more easily available, after all. Second, the detergent did not get distributed so well among clothes when poured into a front-loading washing machine as when poured on top of the clothes from a

"The greater the differences between one country and another, and the more significant these differences are relative to the nature of a product or service, the greater the need for localisation"

top-loading machine. In short, Visor worked well in France but not in Germany. Yet, as P&G discovered, it is not easy to change deeply – and widely – held beliefs such as those in Germany about cleaning whites. It is also not easy to get an entire nation to change from front-loading washing machines to top-loading ones. Naturally, German firms making front-loading machines did not support the change. As this case points out, the greater the differences between one country and another, and the more significant these differences are relative to the nature of a product or service, the greater the need for localisation.

Obviously, forces can simultaneously push towards both globalisation and localisation, requiring firms to be globally integrated and locally responsive. In the case of P&G, the development costs for a powerful cold-water detergent were relatively high, that is, it took scientists long hours of expensive research and lab work to develop an effective cold-water detergent. Furthermore, the manufacturing process for the detergent was continuous. In other words, the final product was delivered after a long continuous process of mixing various chemicals in different states and at different temperatures until the desired chemical reactions and bonding for the final product were achieved. This means that the process cannot be stopped at discrete points, and partially finished products cannot be shipped to different countries for final processing. Both these factors push towards globalisation, or (to put it another way) towards the concentration of development and manufacturing activities and the sale of the product without much modification on a worldwide basis.

On the other hand, the significant differences in beliefs and laundry practices between Germany and France pushed towards localisation.

Much of the returns would be lost if P&G had to make on the one hand a hot-water detergent for Germany that could be effectively applied from the front of a washing machine and on the other a different one for France. The transnational solution was to see if there was a way both to think global *and* act local.

In the case of P&G, it first developed a plastic ball into which detergent could be poured and which could then be thrown into the clothes inside a front-loading machine. The plastic ball was designed to dispense the detergent gradually though small holes as it bounced around in the clothes while they were being washed. This solved the front-loading versus top-loading machine difference. The differences in beliefs about the importance of boiling water were much more difficult to solve, because they had been passed from generation to generation and would not be easy to change.

P&G's local advertising staff and consultants developed commercials in which a mother introduced the new detergent and its excellent cold-water cleaning powers to her daughter. At first, these commercials stressed the cleaning power relative to coloured clothes and only later focused on whites. This approach was quite successful.

Although this type of solution is not always possible and rarely easy, organisations that face pressures of both globalisation and localisation need structures that incorporate a fair amount of integration, especially in terms of cognitive orientation. They need people who have a 'matrix of the mind' – people who can think about how to realise global efficiencies and at the same time not overlook local differences. It can also lead to complex organisational structures in which discrete activities within a firm are broken up along the continuum from global integration to local responsiveness.

Figure 2 depicts a common structure for a global beverage company. In this example, product development might be more centralised in an effort to try to capture global scale economies. In essence, P&G was trying to capture scale economies and leverage concentrated R&D investments relative to its cold-water detergent. It wanted a global cold-water formula because (as stated earlier) cold water is more readily available around the world for washing clothes than hot water. But P&G wanted one formula, not 50.

Figure 2

DISTRIBUTION OF GLOBAL AND LOCAL ACTIVITIES WITHIN A FIRM

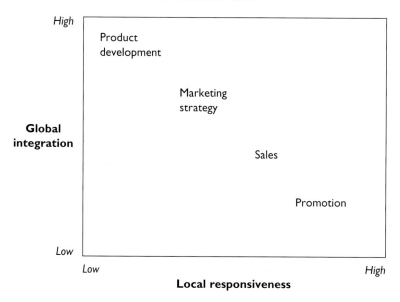

Marketing strategy might be organised on a regional basis to account for major regional differences. Sales strategy might be organised on a country basis to account for differences in distribution channels or traditional promotion practices (for example, in Japan and Korea discount coupons do not exist as a product promotional tool). Promotion campaigns might be organised on a national basis or, within a country, on a regional basis to suit different media (print, TV, radio) and different local-customer preferences.

From our consulting experience and research, the notion of simultaneous pressures for both global integration and local adaptation rings true. However, when executives attempt to apply this general notion (ie 'Think global, act local') in building organisations to support their global strategy, they often find it inadequate to deal with the complexities of turning their strategy into action. This is because even though an organisation may experience dual pressures overall for global integration and local responsiveness, it is not the case that all aspects of the organisation experience these pressures equally. As we have illustrated in the example above, there may be great pressure for a globally integrated brand strategy, but differences by region may require regional (rather than global) marketing strategies. In terms of promotions, there may be so many significant differences at local level that successful promotion campaigns are all about local responsiveness. To deal with the complex realities of globalisation better, HR executives require a more detailed framework that can help them understand the various capabilities required in order to untangle the specific pressures that particular activities face.

Capabilities for global strategy

We propose that, for a global strategy to be implemented, there is a set of capabilities that must be created. As we have organised them, each set represents important tensions to be managed effectively for global business success. From our perspective, the overall capability of managing tensions correlates with the overall dynamics of thinking globally and acting locally. Thus, the overall capability is that of being able to think simultaneously in two different directions.

However, at a more detailed level, this requires certain capabilities that enable a firm to acquire global leverage, while others ensure that a firm can maximise its local adaptation. In a meeting where global strategy is being debated and proposed, identifying the capabilities required both to compete globally and adapt locally helps focus investments of management time and HR practice.

We suggest six capabilities that enable firms to integrate and concentrate global activities appropriately and also to separate and adapt local activities effectively. They are summarised in Figure 3 and are explained below.

Determining the core v determining the non-core

As we mentioned earlier, in reality it is not the case that exactly the same thing is simultaneously globally integrated and locally adapted. In fact, we would argue that this is no more feasible than it is for one person to be in Tokyo and Paris at the same moment. Instead, our observation is that some things are globally integrated, whereas others are locally adapted. Consequently, the first critical capability is being able to determine what is core to the organisation

Figure 3

CAPABILITIES FOR GLOBAL INTEGRATION AND LOCAL ADAPTATION

Global integration	Local adaptation
Determine the core ...	Determine the non-core ...
Achieve consistency ...	Allow flexibility
Build global brand equity ...	Honour local customs
Get leverage and scale ... bigger is better	Get focus ... smaller is better
Share knowledge and learning	Experiment and create new knowledge
Engender a global perspective	Ensure local accountability

and should be integrated and standardised throughout its worldwide operations, and what is not core.

Issues core to the business generally relate to principles that give the firm a global identity. For example, Disney has identified a set of core principles on which its theme parks function. When Walt Disney created the first theme park in Anaheim, California, he did so in order to provide a clean, safe and fun experience for families. The experience he set out to create was in stark contrast to the seedy carnivals of the time. This core principle remains the same throughout all of Disney's theme parks, whether it be the oldest one in Anaheim or a proposed one in Hong Kong.

‘‘The world is just too big and too diverse to entertain the notion that every policy or practice, let alone product or process, can be the same everywhere’’

Just as senior executives must determine what is core and therefore common across the firm's worldwide operations, they must also determine what is non-core and therefore open to local adaptation.

The world is just too big and too diverse to entertain the notion that every policy or practice, let alone product or process, can be the same everywhere. You might think, though, that if you have determined what is core then you have automatically defined what is non-core. However, there is a great risk in taking this approach – that people will spend time and energy debating whether specific policies or practices should be subsumed under the core. Let's return to our Disney example to help illustrate this.

Because of the firm's belief that alcohol and a safe, fun experience for the family did not mix, Disney banned alcohol from being served in any of its theme parks. However, guests at Disney's park in Paris complained about the rule. Essentially, the top management team in Paris had to decide whether the assumption that the consumption of alcohol would get in the way of a clean, safe and fun family experience applied to Europe.

Identifying policies, practices and so on that are clearly non-core can eliminate the time and energy that would otherwise go into debating, 'politicking' and arguing over the issues. Clearly, not everything can – or even should – be classified from the outset as core or non-core. Some issues will be grey or only be decided on a case-by-case basis.

However, effective global competitiveness requires the ability to determine the tails of the distribution, that is, the ability to identify the core and non-core issues. To some extent, we might think about this general capability as being able to distinguish means from ends. For Disney, the end was a clean, safe, fun experience for the family. Not serving alcohol was a means to this end. However, it had been a means so long that in the minds of many executives it had been transformed into an end in itself. Success on this particular issue for Disneyland Paris came only when executives were able effectively to distinguish between means and ends and recognise that regional and country differences required adaptation to reach the desired global ends. Consequently, although alcohol is still not served in the majority of Disney theme parks (including the park in Tokyo), beer and wine are now served in Paris.

Achieving consistency v allowing flexibility

A second required capability is that of achieving consistency while also allowing flexibility. In achieving consistency, the first step is to determine what is core to the organisation, which we have just discussed. Still, it makes little difference whether Disney determines that clean, safe, family fun is a part of its core values if Disney cannot achieve consistency around that core across its worldwide operations.

This capability centres on understanding what guides people's behaviour when no one is looking. But the world is too big a place for any corporation to be able to afford to monitor employee behaviour constantly and then to correct anything undesirable in it.

In achieving consistency, several specifics are required. First, executives must be able to help employees to understand the core. People cannot consistently honour what they do not understand. This understanding is, typically, achieved only when there is an explanation of both *what* the core is and *why* the core is. Neither the 'what' nor the 'why' can lead to understanding unless the words come to life through stories and examples. However, understanding will not alone guarantee consistency. In addition to understanding, executives must be able to engender a high level of commitment to the core. In other words, both the head (understanding) and heart (commitment) must be engaged. With understanding and commitment, employees are well on their way to consistent behaviour concerning the core.

Disney achieves this consistency through two principal HR activities. First, in all its parks the world over it selects individuals who already believe in Disney's core values of clean, safe, family fun. Disney carefully interviews job candidates to determine whether they are already disposed towards providing guests with friendly service and towards believing in the importance of cleanliness. In fact, Stephen Burke, who was sent over to help fix the problems at the troubled European park in 1993, determined that one of the problems was that park employees ('cast members') had been selected whose dispositions were not consistent with Disney's core values. One of the first things he changed was to increase the care with which cast members were selected. In addition, Burke increased the intensity of the detailed orientation Disney provided for all new cast members. These orientation sessions were the first and most critical opportunity for the company to explain its core values. In combination, the selection and training efforts were effective in creating the requisite understanding and commitment to achieve the desired consistency.

Clearly, for those issues identified as non-core, flexibility and adaptation must be allowed. In particular, this requires general tolerance of differences. Of course this is easier to say than do, and our experience and research show that such tolerance is rather a rare commodity. In fact, one of the greatest obstacles to effectiveness for managers working outside their native country and culture is a lack of tolerance of differences (Black, Gregersen, Mendenhall and Stroh, 1999). However, a simple tolerance of differences is only the beginning. True flexibility within the organisation requires managers to develop capabilities actually to generate variety.

For example, P&G found in Asia that its standard shampoo bottles just did not appeal to local consumers. Yet, in the mind of many corporate executives at headquarters, the bottle (its shape, size and colour) was part of the overall brand. P&G found greater success in Asia when it abandoned its traditional bottles and put shampoo in single-use packets. Interestingly, Colgate-Palmolive learned a similar lesson in Latin America with its toothpaste. The traditional family-size tubes were just not selling well. It was only when Colgate-Palmolive brought out significantly smaller tubes that sales took off.

Building global brand equity v honouring local customs

The third element of the framework involves the capabilities required to manage the dual tensions between building global brand equity and honouring local customs. If a company is going to be globally integrated with a common core that is consistent throughout its worldwide operations, then it needs the ability to build global brand equity. The logic for this statement rests on a simple but profound assumption. Our assumption is that a key criterion behind the determination of what is core to the organisation is what is important to customers. From our perspective, it is customers who ultimately determine whether the consistency we discussed above has value. For example, it does Disney little good to identify clean,

safe, family fun as core if customers do not value that kind of experience. If customers and their needs are critical to determining what is
core, then building equity in the minds of customers relative to that
core is equally critical.

For example, Richard Branson is dedicated to building a firm brand
equity in the Virgin brand. He believes that Virgin must have an
identity, or 'stand for' something, in customers' minds. The Virgin
brand has four key dimensions:

- a positive buying experience
- experiencing outstanding service
- seeing continuous improvement in products or service
- receiving economic value for the transaction.

Branson has applied this firm brand to records, airlines, cola and
railways. This global firm brand is based on the assumption that a
customer experiencing Virgin anywhere in the world will have a
similar overall experience and will value this overall experience and
the four distinct elements mentioned above.

Despite the need for building global brand equity, now and for the
foreseeable future, differences in local customs will persist. These differences affect everything from how laundry is done to how contracts
are negotiated. So while advances in global media coverage, transportation and communication create benefits for building global
brand equity, actual differences in standards of living, economic
conditions, consumer preferences and the like create benefits from
tailoring products, services and processes to local customs. This
requires capabilities in not only observing local customs but in
understanding their origins and drivers. Only in doing this can firms
have any hope of assessing which differences across local markets are
likely to persist and which may be more amenable to harmonisation
over time.

Unilever began enjoying real success in India with its laundry soaps
after it spent time studying local washing habits. Many people in
India still wash their laundry against rocks or washboards while
standing in rivers. Unilever's traditional boxed laundry soap just
made no sense and would not work in these conditions. Also, few
households could afford the large boxes even if the soap did work.

Success for Unilever came when executives recognised that because both of economic conditions and cultural traditions most people's laundry habits were not going to change quickly. After recognising this, they changed the form of the soap from powder to small bricks and then sold them for a few pennies each. People could hold the small soap bricks in their hands as they scrubbed their laundry on the rocks or washboards. Although they had to purchase these bricks much more often than their counterparts in developed countries would purchase boxed laundry soap, executives came to recognise that their Indian customers did not view this as an important inconvenience.

Getting leverage (bigger is better) v getting focus (smaller is better)

The fourth set of capabilities centre on issues of size. Executives must be capable of balancing the dynamics of leverage and focus. You only have to look at the record number and size of recent international mergers to get a sense of the leverage that executives expect from being bigger. In most cases, 'bigger' translates into 'greater geographical coverage'. Both economies of scale and scope are forces behind getting bigger. Much of the strategic rationale behind the merger of Citicorp and Travelers is based on economies of scope. Both companies are expecting to leverage existing distribution channels by pushing more products through them.

To some extent this is also part of the rationale for the recent Daimler–Chrysler merger. Although Dodge and Mercedes Benz models are not expected to occupy space in the same showroom, the companies do expect to leverage other elements of the distribution channel, including logistics and transportation. In addition, they are expecting to leverage economies of scale by using common components across a variety of models. They hope to cut costs by using their size to get better deals from suppliers and by harmonising their IT systems. Their greater size should also allow them both to reduce the combined total spent on research and development and also to leverage what is invested and generated across a larger product and sales base.

In their search for global efficiencies and economies, firms often forget that they are competing with local firms. In their bigness, multinational firms often forget that many of these local firms must succeed at home to survive – they have no foreign-market options. As a consequence, local competitors, when threatened, often turn fierce in a fight for their life.

❝❝Even if a local firm does have access to foreign markets, it may nonetheless take as acts of war forays into its home turf by alien firms❞❞

Although they may lack many of the advantages of global firms, they have advantages of their own. They often know the inner workings of the relevant government and have close personal relationships with powerful officials. They have years of experience serving local customers and have often built up significant loyalty as well as understanding of and insights into their customers. Even if a local firm does have access to foreign markets, it may nonetheless take as acts of war forays into its home turf by alien firms. Consequently, global firms need the ability to focus on a market with near-laser precision.

Many would characterise the competitive engagement between Kodak and Fuji in Japan as little short of war. For Fuji, Kodak's success in Japan represents a serious threat. Having beaten the other Japanese competitors such as Sakura, its home market provides Fuji with a valuable profit sanctuary. Fuji makes significant profits at home that it can use to finance its expansion and competitive skirmishes around the world. It is little wonder, then, that Fuji has used all its political connections, market savvy and distribution relationships to stop Kodak from getting too large a beachhead and 'invading' Japan.

Sharing learning v creating new knowledge
The fifth set of capabilities centres on knowledge. Global success requires both an ability to leverage learning across a firm's worldwide operations and an ability to create new knowledge wherever incubation conditions exist.

As we mentioned, economies of scale leverage existing production assets towards greater productivity, and economies of scope leverage existing distribution channels towards greater sales. Similarly, economies of learning leverage existing knowledge about productivity, sales, management, competitors, suppliers, systems and so on and gain the cost-savings and revenue-enhancing benefits of the knowledge across the firm's worldwide operations. In fact, the larger the organisation, the greater the potential cost and revenue benefits from sharing knowledge. Consequently, maintaining a competitive position as the firm globalises requires developing the ability to share knowledge throughout the firm's far-flung operations.

Many organisations have found that the key to this is overcoming the 'not invented here' syndrome. As the saying goes, 'All politics is local.' There is nothing more critical to politics than power. 'Foreign ideas' (ie anything not invented here) are often perceived as a threat to local power. Local supervisors, managers or executives resist incorporating best practice from outside for fear of an erosion of their power base. To the extent that knowledge, technical answers or solutions of any type are a source of power, then these sources of power coming in from the outside can be interpreted as threatening. Most of the time, people do not openly admit that they are resisting the adoption of 'best practice' or other shared learning because they feel threatened. Rather, they often couch their resistance in such phrases as 'Oh, *x* is a great idea for others, but the situation here is different. X just wouldn't work here because of *abc*.' Successful companies have found that the key to leveraging learning is overcoming the 'not invented here' syndrome and providing a variety of different means by which learning is shared across the global organisation, and celebrating those that effectively incorporate and leverage these lessons.

General Electric (GE) creates many forums for sharing global knowledge. It:

- uses written and live case-studies in its development programmes from many countries
- deploys best-practice teams to codify best practice that can then be shared
- uses groupware technology to connect people from different countries to share ideas

⊕ transfers people from one country to another either permanently or on temporary assignments to transfer knowledge.

These activities allow good ideas generated within one country to be shared with others.

Although sharing learning across a global organisation is no small task, for many firms it is actually easier than creating new knowledge on a worldwide basis. To hold down costs, more and more firms are concentrating R&D centres in a few targeted locations. This makes great economic sense. However, many organisations experience a natural and negative consequence – undistributed knowledge creation. When knowledge-creation centres such as R&D labs for the entire global organisation are strategically located in only one or two places, people often tend to be a bit lazy and think that those are the only places where great ideas can be generated, and that the people working there are those primarily charged with innovation. Yet the world is too large and contains too many bright and capable people for anyone to believe that key innovations can happen in only a few places among a few people. Thus, although organisations should foster the ability to take in and use knowledge generated elsewhere and avoid the negative consequences of the 'not invented here' syndrome, they should also foster the ability to generate new ideas in any place. They need capabilities aimed at developing in employees the motivation to generate new ideas and the willingness and desire to generalise them.

For example, GE's appliance division in Canada created some innovative mechanisms to reduce inventory by building a data link with buyers. Why (it might be asked) should an innovation in inventory management come out of Canada? Why not? This reply is the attitude that senior GE executives in Canada fostered. Once the idea was created, it was quickly deployed throughout the country. Because of the idea's success, executives in Canada suggested that it might be worthy of identification as an example of global best practice and be shared around the world.

GE executives within countries are constantly encouraged to find innovative ways to accomplish their stretch goals and not wait for new ideas to come out of corporate. When these ideas succeed, executive champions lead their transferred ideas to other locations.

Engendering global perspective v ensuring local accountability
This last capability brings us full circle. Global success requires the capability of viewing the organisation from both a space-shuttle and a ground-level perspective, leading to a sense of belonging to the worldwide entity and at the same time a fervent feeling of accountability for one's own plot of land.

Clearly, whatever aspects of the company are going to be integrated must be seen in their global entirety. From the space shuttle, the world is mostly water and therefore having ships to sail on makes great sense. However, at ground level in the Sahara desert ships seem of little use. Likewise, from a global perspective certain strategies and structures make perfect sense. However, standing on a specific plot of land that sense is often seen as nonsense. This is important, because despite the rhetoric on global business, only a handful of people actually have truly global responsibilities. The vast majority of a firm's executives, managers, supervisors and workers carry out activities at a local level and therefore have more limited accountabilities. They simply cannot afford to be gazing off into global space. However, to carry out their more limited responsibilities most effectively they need to feel connected to the worldwide organisation.

Engendering global perspective is extremely difficult. Although global thinking and globalisation are all the rage in the media, fewer than 25 per cent of all US CEOs have lived or worked in a foreign country (Black *et al*, 1999). Fewer than 11 per cent of all US heads of HR have international experience (Black *et al*, 1999). It is very difficult to have a global view when you have not seen the world. Although international assignments are not the only way to gain global perspective, they are according to a recent study the most powerful (Black, Morrison, and Gregersen, 1998). In a study of over 130 senior executives in 50 firms across Europe, North America and Asia, eight out of ten said that an international assignment was the most powerful developmental experience in shaping their global perspective. Still, international assignments are expensive and cannot be given to everyone that needs a global perspective. So what else can be done?

IBM provides an interesting example. Just before Louis Gerstner took over at IBM, the outgoing CEO, John Ackers, had proposed dividing IBM up into 13 operating units (mainframes, storage, PCs etc) and letting each unit compete much like an independent company. But Gerstner set forth a strategy and structure that was the exact opposite. He believed that IBM was stronger as an integrated company. The new strategy focused on integrated solutions for customers, including global solutions for global customers. He created new groups called 'industry solution units' that were designed to be global and integrated in nature and focus their efforts on targeted industry customers.

The underlying notion was that whereas banks might need different solutions from those of oil and gas companies, banks in Japan need solutions similar to banks in New York. Furthermore, many of the banks in Japan or New York required integrated software and hardware solutions for their worldwide operations. This strategy and the resulting structure required IBMers to work together globally as they never had before. In the past, strategy and structure (and therefore employees' perspectives) were largely country-based.

However, helping employees, especially middle managers, to stretch their minds beyond the provincial boundaries of a single country to include a global perspective was a major challenge. Among the various initiatives IBM undertook, one of its executive education programmes is worth special attention.

First, IBM worked with an outside partner to design and deliver a programme with the objective of helping participants put their minds around the world. Of the nearly 1,000 participants in the programme, IBM made sure that almost one-half came from outside the USA. In most programmes of 25 to 30 participants, 10 to 15 nationalities were represented. IBM also actually held some of the programmes outside the USA to help many of the North Americans gain a more international, if not global, perspective. In addition, during the 10-day programme at least three senior executives would work with the groups as instructors. Classroom time was spent on cases and conceptual material that helped participants to understand and to think about the global environment and IBM's strategy in that context.

But traditional classroom time was only a small part of the overall design. Participants were also given projects to work on during the programme. By design, these projects required participants to think from a more global perspective. Finally, participants were divided into teams and engaged in an interactive, computer-based global business simulation. Each team made decisions, from sourcing raw materials to allocating advertising dollars across multiple products and international markets. With six or seven teams competing in an interactive and intense global business simulation, participants quickly (and sometimes painfully) learned lessons about exchange rate fluctuations and pricing decisions, local manufacturing and global product mix, worldwide brand image and regional customer preferences and so on. Although none of these aspects of the programme magically produced global leaders, they did go a long way towards enhancing a more global perspective of both IBM and its competitive environment.

Clearly, a global perspective and sense of belonging are critical, but a persistent problem with far-flung global operations is that people can easily experience a diffusion of responsibility. The basic dynamics of this are illustrated with a simple experiment. If a single bystander witnesses a person in distress or needing help, nearly eight out of ten times that lone bystander will offer assistance. However, as you increase the number of bystanders, the probability that any one of them will offer assistance declines, and declines sharply. When you have approximately 10 bystanders, the probability that anyone of them will offer assistance drops to under 20 per cent.

"Firms must create a sense of local accountability and ownership in their people"

The point is that firms can create the capability to share every shred of valuable knowledge across all four corners of the world and not gain much benefit because no one feels responsible for implementing these learnings or best practices. Consequently, firms must create a sense of local accountability and ownership in their people. This is a great balancing act. On the one hand, firms need to create a sense of belonging to the entire global organisation and the capability for individuals to tap into needed resources, wherever in the firms' worldwide operations they may lie. At the same time, firms have to engender a sense of ownership and accountability at the most local level.

For example, Shell is a global, integrated oil firm. It assigns global accountability for overall firm results, and the officers at corporate set direction for the whole enterprise. However, within the broad directives local managers are accountable and responsible for their operations. For example, when the price of oil dropped from around $25/barrel to about $13/barrel, Shell Canada faced a real crisis. They had set performance goals based on the higher oil price and consequently had to make local changes to meet their performance goals. To meet these global requirements, Shell leaders in Canada drew on global experts in drilling, technology and exploration to find ways to reduce costs. They also made trade-offs on where to invest resources (eg oil shale v in-ground reserves) to meet financial goals. Canadian leaders were accountable both to the global expectations and the local decisions required to meet them.

Implications for delivering the global strategy

If the above six capabilities are critical for becoming a firm that wins at globalisation and localisation, then, as we see it, the role of the HR professional is to:

⊕ raise, define, and clarify the capabilities required to win globally
⊕ invest, design, and deliver HR practices that ensure these capabilities.

Raise, define, and clarify required capabilities

An HR professional participating in the creation of a global strategy has the responsibility to focus on the capabilities required to win. This effort may be done in stages, but the ultimate objective is be at the table influencing the discussion and decisions about what human capabilities are required to deliver the desired results.

First, the HR professional may engage the global strategy team in a profile and assessment of which capabilities are more critical for the particular global strategy. Figure 4 is a diagnostic that the HR professional (or line manager) may raise in the global strategy discussion.

Figure 4
PROFILING CRITICAL CAPABILITIES

For this business to succeed, where should we rank on each capability?

GLOBAL INTEGRATION	IMPORTANCE	LOCAL ADAPTATION
	High Neutral High	
Determine the core	A B C D 4 3 2 1	Determine the non-core
Achieve consistency	A B C D 4 3 2 1	Allow flexibility
Build global brand equity	A B C D 4 3 2 1	Honour local customs
Get leverage and scale ... bigger is better	A B C D 4 3 2 1	Get focus ... smaller is better
Share knowledge and learning	A B C D 4 3 2 1	Experiment and create new knowledge
Engender a global perspective	A B C D 4 3 2 1	Ensure local accountability

For example, a firm wanting to create a stronger global presence might go through the six diagnostic questions to determine which capabilities are most critical for the firm to succeed in the particular business. If the answers tend towards the globalisation side (in Figure 4, the letters), then the firm should invest in HR actions that encourage co-ordination, integration, and standardisation; if towards the localisation side (the numbers), a focus on local requirements would prevail. If both, then it is important for the HR executive to help the team to identify the specific nature of the dual pressures. As we have already argued, although it is entirely likely that a given organisation might feel pressures for both globalisation and localisation, it is unlikely that a specific activity would simultaneously experience both. Teasing apart the specific pressures and relative capabilities concerning specific activities is one of the more difficult but valuable contributions HR executives can make to the strategic globalisation process.

Second, the HR professional may encourage the global strategy team to identify which of the six capabilities is most critical for the business to succeed and which requires more investment. For example, a business with strong local market presence but an inability to share ideas would probably focus on the knowledge and learning capability as the most salient capability for going forwards. This would then have implications for the HR investments necessary to build global learning into the firm.

Third, in managing the paradoxes inherent in these capabilities the firm should create a forum where dialogue continually occurs. For example, the trade-offs between global brand equity and local customs may never have a definitive answer, but a forum for this dialogue should be predictable and on-going. By profiling and raising the issues of capabilities to win, HR professionals craft a language and forum where global v local trade-offs may be debated and resolved.

Fourth, paradoxes embedded in global v local capabilities may be sequentially managed. For example, when entering a new market with a new product, the focus may be on flexibility, learning local customs, being focused, creating new knowledge, and local accountability. However, over time, the localisation capabilities may need to be adapted to gain global leverage.

"How well are we doing at achieving consistency, managing global brands, gaining scale, learning, and global perspective?"

Finally, HR professionals may create measurement systems to track how well each of the desired capabilities is being delivered. Some of these tracking mechanisms may be relatively generic questions, such as 'How well are we doing at achieving consistency, managing global brands, gaining scale, learning, and global perspective?' These general questions, when raised consistently in global strategy settings, may help the global team to keep a focus on how to maintain a global strategy and effectively manage the tensions between globalisation and localisation pressures. Alternatively, the HR professional may prepare more rigorous assessments of each capability and try to watch out for a lack in any desired capability. For example, the executive might measure the extent to which new ideas are moved from country to country and then track the countries that experiment well but do not share well.

Invest in, design, and deliver HR practices

HR professionals have the expertise to invest in HR practices that build desired capabilities. HR professionals might use the worksheet in Figure 5 to be disciplined about investing in HR practices to build critical capabilities. Once the critical capabilities required to be a successful global firm have been identified, the HR professional may examine the menu of HR investments (ie the rows in Figure 5) to determine which practices would have the most impact on the given capability. As individual practices are identified, investments may be made to design and deliver programmes in line with those practices. In so doing, it is imperative that the HR practices are not only aligned with the capabilities but integrated with each other. For example, if hiring local employees becomes important for adapting to local customs, then the training, compensation and communication practices must also encourage this capability.

Conclusion

At this point, no one debates whether the *tsunami* of globalisation is here. It is here, and it is not going away. It has already completely engulfed such industries as semiconductors, commercial aircraft construction and telecommunications. The central question (and confusion) concerns how to surf this wave, not whether just to ride it out. Given the nature of globalisation, this confusion and uncertainty is natural. If globalisation simply meant integration and worldwide standardisation, or if it meant separation and adaptation, people would not be confused or debate what to do. We all know how to standardise; we all know how just to adapt. What we have difficulty with is doing both at the same time.

While the 'Think global, act local' framework has been helpful in making explicit the dual pressures of business today, it has left many executives, and perhaps HR executives in particular, short of answers and concrete approaches for delivering results. For many of the executives we work with, the framework is too general.

Consequently, what we have attempted to do is to add some detail to that general picture, to try to bring some focus and clarity. We believe that there are six specific capabilities, dualistic in nature, that are critical to global success. Although the importance or sequence

Figure 5

HR INVESTMENTS FOR GLOBAL INTEGRATION AND LOCAL ADAPTATION

HR investment domain (illustrative practices)	Critical capability 1	Critical capability 2	Critical capability 3
STAFFING			
Hiring new people from the outside			
Orienting new employees			
Sourcing new talent			
Contracting with outside talent			
Retaining talent			
DEVELOPING			
Designing and delivering training			
Systematically rotating talent			
Building succession plans			
Using career development			
PERFORMANCE MANAGEMENT			
Setting individual/team goals			
Designing financial and non-financial rewards			
Designing and delivering benefit programmes			
Removing poor performers			
COMMUNICATION			
Crafting communication plans			
Holding communication forums			
GOVERNANCE			
Shaping organisation structure			
Building dynamic teams			
Clarifying decision-making logic			
Setting policies			

of a given set may vary from firm to firm or industry to industry, we have presented examples from a variety of companies and industries because the general challenge to HR executives seems to be similar, regardless of industry or nationality.

In the end, HR executives need to do more than attend global strategy meetings: they need to add value by encouraging dialogue on capabilities required for globalisation and localisation, profiling which capabilities are critical, and then invest in HR practices that ensure those capabilities.

References

BARNEY J. 1986. 'Organisational culture: Can it be a source of sustained competitive advantage?' *Academy of Management Review.* 11 (3). pp656–65.

BARTLETT C. *and* GHOSHAL S. 1995. 'Changing the role of top management: beyond systems to people'. *Harvard Business Review.* May–June. pp132–41.

BECKER B. E., HUSELID M. A., PICKUS P. S. *and* SPRATT M. F. 1997. 'HR as a source of shareholder value: research and recommendations'. *Human Resource Management Journal.* Vol. 36, No. 1. pp39–48.

BLACK, J. STEWART, GREGERSEN H. B., MENDENHALL M. E. *and* STROH L. K. 1999. *Globalizing People through International Assignments.* Boston, MA, Addison-Wesley.

BLACK, J. STEWART, MORRISON A. J. *and* GREGERSEN H. B. 1998. 'Developing leaders for the global frontier'. *Sloan Management Review.* Fall.

DELANEY J. *and* HUSELID M. 1996. 'The impact of human resource practices on perceptions of organisational performance'. *Academy of Management Journal.* 39. pp949–69.

DYER L. *and* SHAFER R. 1998. 'Creating organisational agility: implications for strategic human resource management', in P. Wright, L. Dyer, J. Boudreau and G. Milkovich (eds), *Research in Personnel and Human Resources Management*, Greenwich, CT, JAI Press.

GALLON M., STILLMAN H. *and* COATES D. 1995. 'Putting core competency thinking into practice'. *Research-Technology Management.* May–June. pp20–28.

HUSELID M. A. 1995. 'The impact of human resource management practices on turnover, productivity, and corporate financial performance'. *Academy of Management Journal.* Vol. 38, No. 3. pp635–72.

LADO A. *and* WILSON M. 1994. 'Human resource systems and sustained competitive advantage: a competency-based perspective'. *Academy of Management Review.* 19. pp699–727.

PRAHALAD C. K. *and* HAMEL G. 1990. 'The core competence of the corporation'. *Harvard Business Review.* May–June. pp79–91.

STALK G., EVANS P. and SHULMAN L. E. 1992. 'Competing on

capabilities: the new rules of corporate strategy'. *Harvard Business Review*. 70 (2). pp57–69.

ULRICH D. 1997. *Human Resource Champions: The next agenda for adding value and delivering results*. Cambridge, MA, Harvard Business Press.

ULRICH D. *and* LAKE D. 1990. *Organisational Capability: Competing from the inside/out*. New York, Wiley.

Organisational Culture and International HRM

Rob Goffee and Gareth Jones

Introduction

In this chapter we explore the implications of different cultural contexts for employment relationships and HR strategies within international corporations. We begin by reviewing the literature on national cultural differences. Although this reveals a range of attitudinal and value-based differences, the connections with organisational behaviour in general and HR strategy in particular remain problematic. Certainly, discussions of the impact of culture cannot be left at the level of national, regional or ethnic differences; for international businesses these must be augmented by analyses of organisational culture. We address this issue by developing a model that distinguishes different social architectures and the environmental contingencies with which they are associated. It is our contention that these distinctive architectures shape the psychological contract and the nature and focus of HR strategies. In this context, skilful HR executives can develop the attributes of the anthropologist – sensing the complexities of local cultures inside the international corporation and avoiding the trap of cultural stereotyping.

Cultural diversity in context

Much of the contemporary interest in cultural diversity – and its associated research initiatives – has its origins in the USA. Indeed, it is perhaps ironic that those who wish to rid organisation and management theory of its North American bias are drawn overwhelmingly from, and, presumably, continue to carry the cultural assumptions of, that continent. Nevertheless, diversity in one form or another has become an important economic, social and political issue within many industrialised economies in the 1990s. What was once ignored, wished away or minimised must, it seems, at least be acknowledged – even if only reluctantly. Others would go further and argue that, where possible, cultural diversity should be actively 'managed'.

A number of factors have stimulated recent interest:

⊕ In the West, labour market migration patterns have led to the growth of culturally heterogeneous urban areas and regions. In-migration to Los Angeles over the past 20 years, for example, has produced a city where there is no longer a majority population, while in California as a whole a mixture of 'ethnic groups' now constitutes half the population (Adler, 1991, p224). 'Domestic multiculturalism', both within the USA and elsewhere, has provoked a variety of policy responses. Some have simply attempted – with varying levels of effectiveness – to regulate migration flows. Such controls are likely to increase, particularly, perhaps, along the borders of a unified Europe. Other policies – concerned with population stocks rather than flows – have been designed to counter economic inequality by promoting equal opportunities and controlling discrimination in such areas as education, housing and employment.

⊕ 'Multiculturalism' in the industrial economies of the old socialist bloc, on the other hand, has been driven by different forces and has therefore taken on rather different forms. There the powerful resurgence of regional, ethnic and religious affiliations has played its part in the downfall of state socialist political regimes and appears set to fragment further several European and Soviet nation states. The precise outcome of these shifts remains highly uncertain, although it seems likely that a closer alignment will emerge between distinct religious and ethnic populations and their representative political structures.

⊕ Against this background there has been the growth of international economic activity. The implications for business organisations are perceived to be profound. Mitroff, for example, claims that:

> For all practical purposes, all business today is global. Those individual businesses, firms, industries and whole societies that

clearly understand the new rules of doing business in a world economy will prosper; those that do not will perish.

Mitroff, 1987, p ix

Although this assessment may be exaggerated, the 'new rules' for emerging global corporations appear to have significant implications in terms of business strategy (Prahalad and Doz, 1987), organisational structure (Bartlett and Ghoshal, 1989) and human resource management (HRM) (Evans, 1989). Certainly, international businesses demand more international managers – adaptable and cosmopolitan in outlook – and so the management of diversity has come to be regarded as an increasingly significant executive attribute.

Investigating cultural diversity

A review of research into cultural diversity indicates differences in definitions of culture. Culture has been described as 'historically created designs for living' (Krocher and Kluckhohn, 1952), 'the collective programming of the mind' (Hofstede, 1991), or a 'pattern of basic assumptions' (Schein, 1985) shared by members of particular social groups or categories. Despite such differences, there is general agreement that culture is:

- learned
- shared
- transgenerational
- patterned
- adaptive (Luthans, 1985).

Further, culture is typically seen as encompassing a complex interaction between members' values, attitudes and behaviour (Adler, 1991).

So defined, culture may be manifested at a variety of levels. Hofstede, for example, acknowledges that 'people unavoidably carry several layers of mental programming within themselves' (1991, p10) and lists the following levels:

- national
- regional and/or ethnic and/or religious and/or linguistic
- gender
- generational

⊕ social class
⊕ organisational or corporate.

A large body of research reveals patterned differences according to the variables referred to by these levels. However, it is the contention of this paper that recent discussions of cultural diversity have tended to focus largely upon differences at the national level and, to a somewhat lesser extent, at the regional, ethnic, religious and linguistic level. Further, much research that purports to discuss *culture* concentrates in fact primarily upon analysis of attitudes and values, from which various behaviour patterns are inferred. Such inferences, as much social science research has shown, are often ill-founded: the relationship between *expressed* values and attitudes and *observable* (organisational) behaviours or actions is problematic and cannot be assumed.

In a recent textbook summary of national differences, for example, Adler reviews a range of cultural orientations and suggests that 'each … reflects a value with behavioural and attitudinal implications' (1991, p19). A range of examples is used to contrast typical *practices* in the USA with those common in other national cultures; these are then 'explained' by reference to underlying *value orientations*. 'Activity orientation', which contrasts 'doing' (achieving results) with 'being' (living for the moment), is thus linked with contrasting behaviours in different national contexts.

As Adler (1991, p30) explains, 'doers' maximise work whereas 'be-ers' minimise it. Therefore salary increases motivate doers to work more hours because of the rewards; but they motivate be-ers to work fewer hours, because they can earn enough money in less time and still enjoy their lives. For example, some US expatriate managers (doers) found that raising salaries for Mexican workers (be-ers) actually decreased the total hours that their employees wanted to work. Similarly, Canadians in Malaysia found that workers wanted extra time with their family and friends more than the chance to earn overtime bonuses.

Although such 'explanations' as Adler's may have persuasive initial appeal, they do little to account for the significant (and growing?) number of Americans who behave like Mexicans or Malaysians, and vice versa! Only analyses that integrate, for example, occupational, organisational and social class levels can help to explain *this* kind of diversity.

Managerial attitudes

Another type of research focuses more specifically upon attitudinal differences among managers. In one widely quoted study, Laurent (1983) compares the attitudes of managers in various Western European countries, the USA, Indonesia and Japan. His questionnaire is designed to differentiate managers' views of organisations as:

- ⊕ political systems
- ⊕ authority systems
- ⊕ role formalisation systems
- ⊕ hierarchical relationship systems.

His results indicate distinctive patterns for managers in each of these countries. Only 18 per cent of US managers, for example, agree that 'The main reason for a hierarchical structure is so that everybody knows who has authority over whom', compared with 50 per cent of Italians and 86 per cent of Indonesians. Only 22 per cent of Swedes feel there is a problem with 'bypassing the hierarchical line in order to have efficient work relationships', compared with 46 per cent of Germans and 75 per cent of Italians. Again, only 10 per cent of Swedes feel a manager should 'have at hand precise answers to most of the questions that his subordinates may raise about their work', in contrast to 53 per cent of French and 78 per cent of Japanese managers. Such responses indicate significant differences in conceptions of work organisations, their management and the nature of the managerial role.

These data are clearly important, but their implications for managerial actions are not entirely unproblematic. Two general points may be raised. The first, methodological, point is whether the survey techniques used by Laurent tap into behavioural differences or rather the stated *preferences* for particular actions. The second, substantive, point is that the connections between values, attitudes, perceptions and actions must be crucially affected by structures of constraint.

Hofstede's (1991) widely cited research also uncovers some pronounced variations. In a very large survey of 116,000 managers employed around the world within one US multinational, he distinguishes patterns in work-related values and attitudes according to four dimensions:

- ⊕ power-distance
- ⊕ uncertainty avoidance
- ⊕ individualism/collectivism
- ⊕ masculinity/femininity.

Taken together, these dimensions apparently explain more of the country differences reported than such factors as organisation, profession, age or gender. But it is worth remembering that these dimensions account for just 49 per cent of country differences: 'Whether explaining half of the differences is a lot or not depends on one's degree of optimism' (Hofstede, 1991, p252). Furthermore, it should be remembered that the differences reported relate, as do Laurent's, to attitudes and values, not *behaviour*. Finally, Hofstede (1991, p17) points out that 'Gender, generation and class cultures can only partly be classified by the four dimensions found for national cultures ... Countries are integrated social systems.' Because categories like gender, generation or class are only *parts* of social systems, not all dimensions apply to them; they must therefore be described in their own terms, based on special studies of such cultures.

❝Clearly, members of different cultures attribute different meanings to apparently similar verbal and non-verbal behaviours❞

Micro-level research

Another type of research focuses on the micro-level of the individual, interpersonal relationships and small-group interactions. Some of this work concentrates upon work situations, managerial activity and organisational behaviour; other research takes a wider perspective which incorporates a range of social situations. A central concern within this tradition relates to the difficulties of cross-cultural communication (Samovar and Porter, 1976) and the differing ways in which messages may be encoded, transmitted and decoded. Clearly, members of different cultures attribute different meanings to apparently similar verbal and non-verbal behaviours. What is perceived by some, for example, as overly aggressive is considered by others to be entirely appropriate; mild humour in one context is biting sarcasm in another. Behaviour, then, requires translation, which in turn requires cultural insight. Understanding of this process has been assisted by research into:

- ⊕ perception (Lau and Jelinek, 1995)
- ⊕ social imagery (Burger and Bass, 1979)
- ⊕ learning patterns and the construction of stereotypes (Ratui, 1983)
- ⊕ small-group interactions (Steiner, 1972).

Although a lot of this micro-level research has been based upon observation of actual behaviour, there remain grounds for caution in translating its findings to the work organisation context.

First, differences in the minutiae of social mannerisms may be of interest, but their impact upon critical managerial actions and performance is often assumed rather than demonstrated. Second, research that explores cross-national variations in micro-social behaviour encourages, unintentionally perhaps, the view that national cultural differences dominate those that may derive from such factors as class, gender, religion, or even age. (The typical method is to assume an agreed North American norm and then measure 'deviations' from it.) Third, behaviours viewed under 'ahistorical' laboratory condition – frequently among inexperienced college students – may have only a tenuous relationship with those enacted among the members of actual work organisations with distinctive histories and cultures.

Conclusions

We may sum up our arguments thus far in the following way. Although there may be persuasive evidence for attitudinal and value-based differences between the members of distinct national cultures, the connection with *organisational behaviour* remains problematic. How do expressed preferences and ideals in terms of, for example, management style and organisational structure connect with day-to-day social action within patterns of social and economic constraint?

Even where *behavioural* differences have been observed across different national cultures, which of these have significance for the functioning of work organisations? Finally, has the emphasis upon international differences distracted attention from the powerful cultural impact of different corporate social architectures?

Corporate social architecture

Interest in corporate 'glue' has grown in response to increasing pressures for disintegration in international corporations. This is largely because processes of decentralisation, de-layering and devolution towards complex sets of differentiated centres that are often on different continents – and focused upon distinctive products, customers, regions, suppliers or competences – have made the task of integration more demanding (Bartlett and Ghoshal, 1998; Goffee and Jones, 1998). Differentiation – an inevitable concomitant of scale and complexity – must be balanced with a need for corporate integration. But this relationship between integration and differentiation is not a matter of 'either/or'. So, for example, designers of the modern 'transnational' attempt to combine the autonomy and flexibility of the local business with the cross-unit integration necessary to compete globally.

How can such flexible co-ordination be achieved? Reliance upon conventional, formal mechanisms for organisational integration – hierarchies, structures, systems – seems to have run its course. Increasingly, they are replaced by lateral integration processes: teams, project groups, interpersonal events and networks of one kind or another, as well as a range of development processes and value-shaping activities that promote 'appropriate' attitudes and behaviour (Evans, 1989).

In the 1990s, then, the language and imagery of corporate integration have become distinctive. 'Culture' or 'nervous systems' are the preferred metaphors, with internal organisational architecture described in terms of 'networks' or 'clusters', characterised by relationships of collaboration, intuition, interdependence and reciprocity.

But what is the precise nature of these relationships? Are all networks the same? How might 'reciprocity' vary in different work

contexts? There is little in the modern literature of work organisations to help to answer these questions. However, there is a long
tradition of analysis in the social sciences – particularly sociology –
that can provide insight. In the rest of this chapter we draw upon the
sociological tradition to analyse two conceptually distinct types of
social relations – those of sociability and solidarity (Goffee and Jones,
1998). We use this as a means for understanding the distinctive
social architectures of large-scale corporations, and in particular their
implications for HR strategies and practices.

Key concepts
Sociability v solidarity

Sociability is an aspect of social life central to much sociological
analysis. It refers to affective, non-instrumental relations between
individuals who may regard one another as friends. Friends tend to
share certain ideas, attitudes, interests and values and to be inclined
to associate on equal terms. So defined, friendship groups frequently
constitute a primary unit in sociological analysis of status groups and
of social class. In its pure form, sociability represents a type of social
interaction that is valued for its own sake. It is frequently sustained
through continuing face-to-face relations typically characterised by
high levels of unarticulated reciprocity; there are no prearranged
'deals'. The attitude is 'We help each other, with no strings
attached.'

Solidarity, by contrast, describes task-centred co-operation between
unlike individuals and groups. It does not, in other words, depend
upon close friendship or even personal acquaintance; nor is it necessarily sustained by continuous social relations. Solidarity can be
demonstrated instrumentally and discontinuously – as and when the
need arises. In contrast to sociability, then, its expression can be both
intermittent and contingent.

Although sociability and solidarity may be distinguished conceptually in this way, many discussions of organisational life confuse the
two. Clearly, social interaction at work may be constituted of the
sociability of friends; the solidarity of colleagues; both of these, or
(sometimes) neither. Equally, when colleagues socialise outside
work, this may represent an extension of workplace solidarity rather

than an expression of intimate or close friendship. Few descriptions of organisational social life explicitly address these distinctions, although some provide sufficient ethnographic material to enable an informed guess – and we draw on these later.

Clearly, to co-operate in the instrumental pursuit of common goals it is not necessary for individuals to like one another. Indeed, solidarity may often be exhibited among those who actively dislike each other. Equally, intimate forms of sociability may actually be less likely among those who 'must' act solidaristically as work colleagues.

The intensity of sociability may vary directly with, independently of or inversely to the intensity of solidarity. As a starting-point, it is useful to distinguish organisations as exhibiting high or low levels of sociability and solidarity. In effect, this suggests four distinctive corporate forms:

- the networked
- the mercenary
- the fragmented
- the communal (Goffee and Jones, 1996).

The examples we use below are intended to illustrate each type of organisation and are drawn from recent field research. For the purposes of illustration, the unit of analysis is the firm, but the model can be applied at various levels – the division or business unit, the function or the team, for example.

Networked organisations

Networked organisations exhibit high levels of sociability but relatively low levels of solidarity. Such organisations are often characterised by long service, a 'family ethos' and work patterns regularly punctuated by social events and rituals of one kind or another. These help to sustain a strong sense of intimacy, loyalty and friendship among managers. Patterns of sociability within the workplace often extend beyond, via leisure and sporting clubs and informal social contacts among families.

Levels of solidarity, however, are low. Ties of affection do not automatically translate into high levels of intra-organisational

Figure 1

FOUR ORGANISATIONAL ARCHETYPES

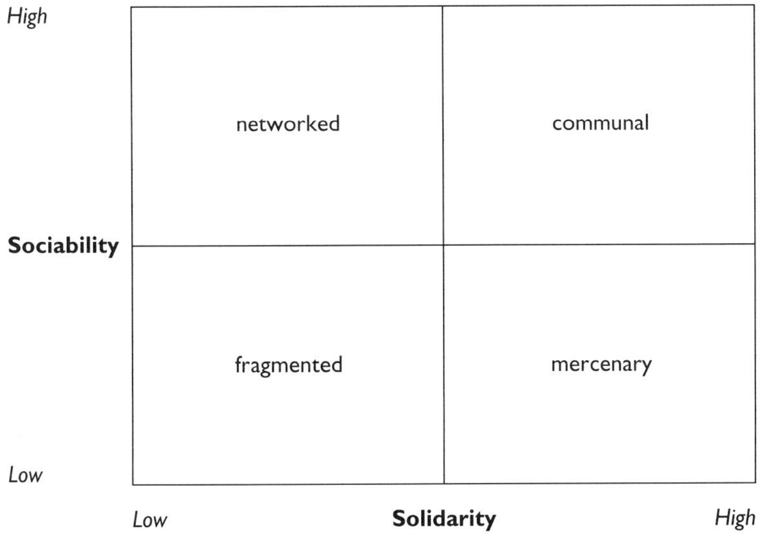

co-operation. Indeed, although social networks are characterised by well-established friendships, the culture of networked organisations can often be described as 'gossipy' and 'political'. Indeed, it is a mistake to assume that well-developed patterns of sociability necessarily form the basis for solidaristic co-operation. In fact, the reverse may be true. Close friendships, for example, may limit possibilities for the open expression of difference, which is a necessary condition for developing and maintaining a shared sense of purpose.

At the level of the firm, the networked form may be indicated where:

⊕ knowledge of local markets is a critical success factor
⊕ corporate success is an aggregate of local success (interdependencies are minimal)
⊕ there are few opportunities for learning between divisions or units
⊕ strategies are long term (sociability maintains strategic intent when short-term calculations of interest would not).

Mercenary organisations

In mercenary organisations a heightened sense of competition and a strong desire to succeed – or at least to 'protect territory' – is often a central feature of corporate culture. The dominant values are built around competitive individualism and personal achievement, but these do not preclude co-operative activity where this demonstrably produces benefits both for individuals and their organisations. In other words, colleagues display a solidarity that does not depend upon close friendships or ties of affection. Day-to-day relationships in such organisations are rarely characterised by high levels of collective co-operation – quite the reverse may be true. As we have pointed out, solidarity may be both *intermittent* and *contingent*.

The mercenary form is indicated where the:

- ⊕ capacity to act swiftly in a highly co-ordinated way is a critical source of competitive advantage
- ⊕ economies of scale and competitive advantage can be gained from creating corporate centres of excellence which can impose processes and procedures on operating units
- ⊕ nature of the competition is clear – external enemies help to build internal solidarity
- ⊕ corporate goals are clear and measurable and there is little need for consensus-building.

Fragmented organisations
But what of organisations that exhibit low levels both of sociability and solidarity – fragmented organisations?

Organisations that rely heavily on outsourcing and homeworking and those that rely largely upon the contribution of individual, non-interdependent experts and professionals may be predominantly fragmented. The major contingencies that indicate the fragmented form are:

- ⊕ where innovation is produced primarily by individuals, not groups
- ⊕ where standards are achieved primarily through input (eg professional qualifications) rather than process controls
- ⊕ where there are few learning opportunities between individuals (or where professional pride prevents knowledge transfer)
- ⊕ low levels of work interdependence.

Can these fragmented organisations survive or succeed? Although it seems unlikely, there is evidence that, at least in some contexts, these 'disintegrated' corporate communities can indeed survive and grow.

Communal organisations

Although, then, it is clearly possible for corporations to survive and prosper in the absence of sociability and solidarity, it is perhaps not surprising that some see the *communal* organisation – with high levels of both qualities – as the ideal. Solidarity alone may suggest an excessively instrumental organisational orientation. In effect, co-operation may be withdrawn the moment that it is not possible for members to identify shared advantage. In such organisations, scope for 'goodwill', 'give and take' and general 'flexibility' may be absent. By contrast, organisations characterised primarily by sociability may lose their sense of purpose. Critics claim that such organisations tend to be overly tolerant of poor performance, and possibly complacent. No doubt, the communal organisation has considerable appeal. Indeed, this model informs much of the literature on innovative high-performing organisations.

''Friendships can undermine collective interests''

However, it may be an inappropriate and unattainable ideal in many business contexts. Businesses able to achieve the communal form frequently find it difficult to sustain. There are a number of possible explanations for this. High levels of sociability and solidarity are often formed around particular founders or leaders whose departure may weaken either or both forms of social relationship. Similarly, the communal corporation may be difficult to sustain in the context of growth, diversification and internationalisation. More profoundly, there may be an in-built tension between relationships of sociability and solidarity, which makes the communal corporation inherently unstable. In effect, friendships can undermine collective interests, or vice versa.

The communal form is indicated where:

- innovation requires elaborate teamworking across functions and locations
- there are measurable synergies and opportunities for teamworking across organisational subunits

⊕ strategies are long-term and emergent rather than the sum of measurable milestones

⊕ the business environment is dynamic and complex – requiring multiple interfaces with the environment and a high capacity for internal information synthesis.

Culture conflict

Of course, many organisations occupy more than one of the quadrants in Figure 1. This raises issues of interface management. In highly innovative pharmaceutical companies, for instance, we might expect the research and development (R&D) function to be communal, but the sales and marketing function to be mercenary. In such organisations a perennial question is 'How and why, in the innovation process, should marketing be involved?' Turf battles often follow, as the communal R&D function protects its cherished 'values' from the perceived 'ruthlessness' of the mercenary marketeers. Similar interface issues arise in companies with cultural products – music, books, television programming. Again, we find here frequent clashes between functions and activities with different social architectures. In international companies these conflicts may arise between different regions or country-based businesses, but they do so from an interplay between national and corporate culture differences.

International human resource management (IHRM)

Where now the psychological contract?

In the context of IHRM, what are the implications for employment relationships and HR strategies within international corporations? A useful conceptual starting-point for this discussion is the psychological contract: the exchange that, explicitly or implicitly, is negotiated when individuals join, remain with and perform in organisations. The psychological contract can vary according to a variety of factors, including age, experience, career orientation and, of course, organisational context. How, then, might the distinctive organisational architectures that we have described help us to predict differences in the psychological contract?

In the networked form we would expect the psychological contract to be predominantly implicit – with substantial elements of the relationship neither written down nor precisely articulated. Close social ties between individuals are likely to have been built up gradually over time, providing the basis for relatively high levels of interpersonal trust. Heavy emphasis may be placed upon the nurture of relationships that are flexible and long-term – with the tacit assumption that actions may have consequences that emerge much later.

This type of 'relational' contract is most effective when all parties recognise that they are participants in a sort of repeated game. Forms of deferred remuneration such as lifetime employment, seniority-based promotion and generous pension schemes all serve this purpose. Although many managers have come to see such an arrangement as outmoded, it is often a serious error to do so.

Networkers v mercenaries

It is within the networked form that the traditional contract of employment security in exchange for loyalty and obedience has come under severest attack. Under pressure to reduce costs, demonstrate 'value' from acquisitions and focus on core capabilities, many employers have acted opportunistically to exploit the discretion granted by relational contracts in order to gain short-term competitive advantage. As a result, long-term trust relationships have been undermined. We have seen these processes at work in (for example) large-scale retail clearing banks, many global manufacturers, the oil industry and the public sector.

In effect, organisational change processes in many larger, well-established corporations in the 1990s have involved a deliberate attempt to move from (in our terms) a network towards a mercenary social architecture – high in solidaristic pursuit of clearly defined, shared interests ('strategic intent') but rather low in terms of sociability. In these contexts we would expect the psychological contract to be more explicit, specific and transaction- or project-related.

Large-scale corporate restructuring – downsizing, de-layering and so on – are an attempt to do more with less: to reduce labour costs but maximise work intensity or 'effort'. At the same time there has been an increasing emphasis upon the monitoring and measurement of 'performance' – particularly for such groups as managers and professionals, who were previously free of external controls of that kind – and the linking of reward packages to such measures. The nature of 'rewards' has also shifted, processes of restructuring serving to undermine two significant (and often implicit) rewards – job security and promotion. These are being replaced with differing mixes of intrinsic (challenge, growth, autonomy) and extrinsic (money, share options) alternatives. Whatever the mix, there has been a trend in the direction of rewards more clearly contingent upon current, measurable contribution. The mercenary psychological contract is closely defined and, apparently, 'equal' parties stay together merely for as long as it serves their respective interests.

But gains in terms of clarity and mutual responsibility (rather than dependence) must be set against losses in terms of flexibility, informal information flows and more open-ended preparedness to help – all of which can characterise the network form at its best. It is also clear that the intended transition from networked to mercenary is not always successfully achieved. Whereas the latter form's explicit contract of 'interests' may be entirely consistent with the expectations of certain occupational groups – eg those employed within highly competitive investment banks or consultant surgeons in hospitals – it can appear as a peculiarly soulless place for those more used to high sociability workplaces.

Going communal

The psychological contract of the communal form has often been promoted as the ideal in much of the prescriptive management literature. In this context there is a powerful alignment of individual and organisational behaviour. Employees become fully immersed in their work and workplace; there are high levels of 'identification'. Here reciprocity is generalised: individuals give with no immediate expectation of return but instead for the good of the organisation. By contrast, reciprocity is *balanced* in the networked form (a return is expected, but not immediately); *negotiated* in the mercenary form (the exchange is both more immediate and explicit); and *negative* in the fragmented form (members attempt to get help without giving anything in return).

Communal relationships may be more sustainable in non-profit or smaller organisations; there are few examples of larger international business corporations that have maintained this form over time (Hewlett Packard and Johnson and Johnson may represent high-profile exceptions). By contrast, the example of Apple illustrates the high risks of disillusionment in this contract when ideals are seen to be transgressed or simply not delivered.

Going fragmented

Finally, what is the nature of the psychological contract in the fragmented form? We have identified two distinctive patterns. The first is where the organisation can be conceived of as a constellation of highly autonomous individuals, often with high levels of expertise. Here the contract involves the exchange of similarly high levels of independence in return for exceptional individual performance – think, for example, of some consulting companies, many law firms or tax specialists, or some academic institutions. A second pattern is evident where organisations have spiralled unintentionally and inappropriately into the fragmented form. Arguably, the psychological contract here has completely broken down – leaving us with the spectacle of the war of all against all. Companies in this condition may well find life to be nasty, brutish and short.

The nature of HR strategies will also vary fundamentally with the context of the corporate social architecture. The issues that dominate the HR agenda capture these differences.

Networked form

Here the key issues are:

- the development of remuneration practices that sustain equity rather than market-testing or widening the gap between fixed and variable rewards
- recruiting compatible people who are predisposed to like each other
- training that is as much concerned with marketing shared norms as with developing technical or cognitive competences
- leadership development processes that focus upon refining interpersonal skills, and enhancing individuals' ability to 'read' the organisation and to influence others through the network
- in international companies, the development of cross-cultural awareness and appropriate communication skills.

These HR strategies are evidenced by such companies as Unilever, Heineken and Philips.

Mercenary form

Here the key issues include:

⊕ the careful measure of performance – there is a persistent attempt to refine metrics and tie them to reward systems
⊕ rigorous processes to lose employees who 'fail' and to capture from competitors talent that succeeds
⊕ the critical challenge to tie in high-performers, making it difficult for them to walk away and expensive for competitors to acquire
⊕ leadership development typically via tournaments or contests often set up by the HR function.

Many or all of these issues are evident in the HR practices of such companies as Citicorp, PepsiCo and Mars.

Fragmented form

In this form the key issues are:

⊕ the recruitment and retention of the best individuals in relevant fields, with little attention as to how they might work together; therefore, expertise in labour market scanning is a critical HR capability
⊕ the provision of 'world-class' support services and resources to nurture individual talent – but with minimal 'interference' from the organisation
⊕ the attempt to codify, retain and protect 'tacit' knowledge generated by individual employees
⊕ finding and supporting the rare individuals who are able and willing to lead in this challenging context.

Examples of this form include law firms, consultants, business schools and some new virtual organisations.

Communal form

Key issues are:

⊕ the maintenance of values that give organisational cohesion; at the same time the most sophisticated HR professionals ensure continuing and constructive critiques of such values

- the development of recruitment, induction and appraisal processes that ensure value compatibility – often, leverage is obtained by presentation of the organisation to the labour market based on its key values
- leadership development that ensures that the 'disciples' who often populate communal organisations acquire the competences necessary to lead as well as to follow.

These issues dominate the HR agendas of Hewlett Packard, Johnson and Johnson, Apple in its early days, and many high-growth entrepreneurial firms.

Conclusion

Thus far, we have argued that culture and cultural differences are critical to the proper understanding of organisations. However, we have further agreed that the existing literature on cross-cultural behaviour is vitiated by two problems. The first is an exaggerated emphasis on attitudes and values as opposed to behaviours. The second problem is the exaggeration of differences at the national level as opposed to other varieties of cultural difference – gender, class, region and generation, for example. We have tried to illustrate this point by showing that differences in organisational social architecture – analysed in terms of patterns of sociability and solidarity – have significant consequences for understanding the psychological contract and the dominant themes of HR strategies.

"Think like a man of action and act like a man of thought"

We are left with something of a paradox. Culture is important to HR management but is complex and not amenable to simple cross-national study. Its multi-layered, many-faceted nature requires the successful HR executive (and many others) to think like an anthropologist and to be constantly in the business of striving to understand cultural nuance – the meanings that individual and collective actions have in their cultural context. Such endless enquiry may lead you to Henri Beysin's oft-quoted advice: 'Think like a man of action and act like a man of thought.'

References

ADLER N. J. 1991. *International Dimensions of Organisational Behaviour*. 2nd edn. Boston, MA, PWS-Kent.

BARTLETT C. A. *and* GHOSHAL S. 1998. *Managing across Borders*. Boston, MA, Harvard Business School Press.

BURGER P. *and* BASS B. M. 1979. *Assessment of Managers: An international comparison*. New York, Free Press.

EVANS P. (ed.) 1989. *Human Resource Management in International Firms*. London, Macmillan.

GOFFEE R. *and* JONES G. 1996. 'What holds the modern company together?' *Harvard Business Review*.

GOFFEE R. *and* JONES G. 1998. *What Holds the Modern Company together?* London, HarperCollins.

HOFSTEDE G. 1991. *Cultures and Organisations*. London, McGraw-Hill.

KROCHER A. L. *and* KLUCKHOHN F. 1952. 'Culture: a critical review of concepts and definitions'. *Peabody Museum Papers*. Vol. 47, No. 1. p181.

LAU J. B. *and* JELINEK M. 1995. 'Perception and management', in A. B. Shani and J. B. Lau (eds), *Behaviour in Organisations: An experiential approach*. pp213–20. Richard D. Irwin.

LUTHANS F. 1985. *Organisational Behaviour*. 4th edn. Maidenhead, McGraw-Hill.

MITROFF I. I. 1987. *Business Not As Usual*. San Francisco, CA, Jossey-Bass.

PRAHALAD C. K. *and* DOZ Y. L. 1987. *The Multinational Mission*. New York, Free Press.

RATUI I. 1983. 'Thinking internationally: a comparison of how international executives learn'. *International Studies of Management and Organisation*. Vol. XIII, Nos 1–2. Spring–summer. pp139–50.

SAMOVER L. A. *and* PORTER R. E. (eds) 1976. *Intercultural Communication: A reader*. Belmont, CA, Wandsworth Publishing.

SCHEIN E. H. 1985. *Organisational Culture and Leadership*. San Francisco, CA, Jossey-Bass.

STEINER I. D. 1972. *Group Process and Productivity*. New York, Academic Press.

Chapter 4

The HR Manager as Global Business Partner

Terence Brake

Success in the global economy derives not just from meeting high standards for competition in world contests, but also from strong relationships – networks that link to global markets and networks that build collective local strength. In the future, companies that flourish will be best partners to their customers, suppliers, employees, and allies in joint ventures. Their leaders will know how to create productive partnerships that span companies, sectors, countries, or communities. Companies need collaborative advantage ...

Rosabeth Moss Kanter[1]

Introduction

Winston Churchill said, 'We are shaping the world faster than we can change ourselves, and we are applying to the present the habits of the past.' We live and work in a turbulent global economy, and this new world poses radically different challenges for us. At the centre of these is the globalisation of business.

The world has seen at least two major movements towards globalisation. The first, in the mid-nineteenth century, was facilitated by such technologies as the steamship, telegraph, railroad and telephone. The second movement started soon after the Second World War but gained rapid momentum after the collapse of communism in the late 1980s. It involves both quantitative and qualitative shifts in economics, politics, technology and culture. Key enablers in this second period have been reduced telecommunication costs, computerisation, digitalisation and modern, high-speed transportation systems.[2]

❝By 2001, 70 per cent of McDonald's operating income is expected to come from overseas sales❞

Over the last 40 years we have seen a 1,500 per cent increase in world trade; currently, $1.3 trillion dollars are exchanged by world currency traders every day. In short, we are witnessing an increased economic interdependence across borders. Motorola, for example, has a presence in more than 100 countries, and more than 40 per cent of its revenue comes from outside the USA. By 2001, 70 per cent of McDonald's operating income is expected to come from overseas sales. Eighty per cent of Coca-Cola's revenue is already generated from foreign sales. Few industries, if any, will be untouched by globalisation.

What must our organisations do to be competitive in this global environment? What role should HR play in building and sustaining global competitiveness? Which habits do we need to break, and which ones need to be developed?

The performance challenge

A subtitle to this chapter might have read 'Beating the laughter challenge!' Let me explain. In August 1998, I flew into London from Spain for breakfast with the CEO, the head of HR, and the director of training and development of a UK-based company. The head of HR took the lead in explaining his company's business, the global challenges they faced and what they wanted to achieve at an upcoming senior manager conference. This briefing was extremely articulate and comprehensive – so much so that the CEO quipped, 'Not bad for an HR guy!' We all broke into laughter. The CEO was tapping into the stereotype of the HR manager as a somewhat marginal business figure. How do we change this? Only by making a positive difference to the item at the top of the business agenda – world-class (or just better) performance.

Given the hyper-competitive nature of the world economic environment, every business function, process, team, manager and associate must answer two simple questions: 'What value do you add?' and 'How can you add more value?' If HR is to be acknowledged as generating significant value, we must connect with our businesses in radically new ways. In many companies this will involve re-inventing HR thinking and practices. The supportive – and largely administrative – 'habits' of HR are far from adequate. That's the bad news!

What's the good news? Led by new technology companies, the workplace is changing dramatically. For an increasing number of executives, the critical assets of a business are seen to reside less in physical and financial capital and more in individual and collective human intelligence. Intelligence is a potent mix of imagination, knowledge and expertise which, when amplified by excellent communications, can generate significant performance advantages for a business. We are participants in the 'talent wars', in which the rewards go to those companies who can attract, develop, use and retain talent globally. Given the critical nature of a company's talent asset base, the role of HR must become more proactive and strategic. In this era of world-wide turbo-capitalism, HR must become a fully integrated global business partner.

If talent is one side of the global competitiveness equation, information systems/information technology (IS/IT) is the other. Göran Lindahl, chief executive of ABB, puts it plainly: '[The two areas] which will have the highest impact on our operations for the next five years are human resources (HR) and information technology (IT).'[3] I propose we think seriously about blending these areas into a new organisational change entity that is focused exclusively on the 'mobilisation of every ounce of intelligence'[4] in the global network. One of its key objectives would be to create the collaborative advantage highlighted by Rosabeth Moss Kanter in the quotation opening this chapter.

Why is collaboration so important? Research by A. T. Kearney, Inc. indicates that a company's ability to transfer its distinctive critical capabilities across the organisation is vital to global success. Those companies with a 20 per cent greater capacity to transfer critical capabilities achieved a 7 per cent improvement in global performance. The best performers rated themselves on average 22 per cent higher at transfer capacity than the low performers.[5] The transfer of critical capabilities cannot happen without a high level of collaboration across the enterprise. Let me call the new organisational area I am proposing the *performance advantage group* (PAG). Although my thoughts are speculative, there are immediate practical implications for all HR departments.

The HR–PAG manager must affect the *total* global business agenda in the organisation. Every part of the enterprise has a people component – and increasingly, a technological component as well. Enabling and mobilising intelligence will come from highly productive interactions at work between, for example:

- ⊕ people and people (eg customers, suppliers, colleagues, team members)
- ⊕ people and cultures (eg national, organisational, professional, functional)
- ⊕ people and organisations (eg their own and those of their alliance partners, subsidiaries, suppliers)
- ⊕ people and strategies (eg business unit and corporate)
- ⊕ people and assignments (eg individual and team, short term and long term, domestic and international)
- ⊕ people and ideas (eg best practice, education and training)
- ⊕ people and resources (eg information, capital, equipment)
- ⊕ people and policies (eg rewards and recognition, global ethical standards)
- ⊕ people and processes (eg product development, marketing, delivery).

The role of technology in enabling and fulfilling the promise of such interactions is increasing exponentially. Although the interface between the people and technological sides of business has not always been harmonious, we have now reached a point in history where the human and technological are so intertwined as to provide us with a dramatically new matrix of performance possibilities. Don Tapscott captures this thought well when he says:

> The Age of Networked Intelligence is an age of promise. It is not simply about the networking of technology but about the networking of humans through technology. It is not an age of smart machines but of humans who through networks can combine their intelligence,

knowledge, and creativity for breakthroughs in the creation of wealth
and social development. It is not just an age of linking computers but
of internetworking human ingenuity.[6]

Once HR is positioned as a major change leader and partner in
enabling and mobilising human intelligence for increased global
performance, we begin to see its roles and responsibilities in a more
holistic, value-added and embedded way. Partners in the PAG
would be aligned around the critical mission of identifying and
creating opportunities for global performance advantage (GPA)
through the people–technology interface.

It will always be true that a technological approach is not always
necessary or desirable. You cannot create what Edward M. Hallowell
calls the 'human moment' out of bits and bytes.[7] It is however
equally true that a traditional HR approach is not always necessary
or desirable, eg classroom training. Technologists must understand
more about enabling people to learn, innovate, communicate and
collaborate, and HR managers must increase their ability to recognise and use technological capabilities to create a peak-performance
environment. With imagination, knowledge and expertise the key
sources of global competitiveness, HR has a huge opportunity and
obligation to establish its leadership presence. This, of course, cannot
be done without deep and wide partnering.

Mapping the way forward

The descriptor *Global Business Partner* encapsulates the evolving role
of the HR–PAG manager. If we are to succeed in this role, we must
understand what each one of the terms in the descriptor means –
Global/Business/Partner. The key to success is *business credibility*. In
discussing each term in the descriptor, I shall also identify the business credibility factor for the PAG manager.

Global

*Business credibility factor: Speaking the language of global business with
authority and passion.*

To engage in the global strategic dialogue, the HR manager must be
able to articulate the *why, what* and *how* of globalisation.

Why does a company seek to globalise its business? Two major types of driver exist: risk drivers and opportunity drivers. Risk drivers are those that are pushing the business into the global theatre because they pose a potential threat. For example, your customers are going global; if you cannot deliver your products and services on a global basis, you are likely to lose those customers' business. Telecommunications companies have found it necessary to increase their transnational reach because global customers do not want to be dealing with 50 vendors around the world. So ask yourself this question: to what extent are your competitors building a global presence, achieving greater economies of scale and tempting away some of your key customers?

On the opportunity side, many companies extend their reach to participate in higher rates of growth in developing markets, or to leverage existing world-class capabilities in their organisation. Others look to capitalise on similar customer needs and wants across geographic and cultural borders, eg Nike and Reebok. With unfavourable demographics in the West – and the perception among many senior executives of saturated domestic markets – other companies are also looking to take advantage of falling trade and investment barriers and reduced global co-ordination costs. What risk and opportunity factors are pushing or pulling your company into the global market-place?

''Does geographic presence define what it means to be 'global'?''

What is a 'global company'? Many companies describe themselves as 'global', but the reality is often different from the rhetoric. In one sense, we are all global now. As former Citicorp chairman Walter Wriston is reported to have said, 'There is no place to hide.' But does exposure to global competition make us global? Companies that have built a presence around the world often describe themselves as 'global', but does geographic presence define what it means to be 'global'? Certainly, it is necessary to be able to do business in all strategic markets worldwide, but to understand the essence of being 'global' it is necessary to move beyond geography and grasp the operating principles by which such a company seeks to conduct business. There are four main principles:

- *Integration.* The company seeks to act as a co-ordinated network – 'one company' worldwide – in order to present a consistent face to the customer, build purchasing power and exploit potential synergies. As David Whitwam, chairman and CEO of Whirlpool Corporation, has said, 'We are not planting flags. We are building a global enterprise.'[8]
- *Flow.* To maximise speed and responsiveness, resources (eg information, innovations, capital, expertise) must be able to flow through the organisation to where they can add the most value at any point in time. Flow enables organisational flexibility in a dynamic market-place.
- *Leverage.* To create world-class efficiencies and cost advantages, the company must drive towards standardisation and the reduction of unnecessary duplication. This is why Ford has moved aggressively to build 'world cars' based on a small number of technological platforms.
- *Optimisation.* In order to produce the best results for the *total* organisation, company managers must balance local responsiveness with global responsibility.

These principles generate paradoxes that need to be managed creatively. For example, the drives to integration and leverage can be at odds with flow. Integration and leverage would tend to move the business towards centralisation, whereas flow would move it towards decentralisation. There is no formula for managing this tension. What should be globally co-ordinated and what nationally differentiated must be determined by the nature of each business, function and task, as well as by other variables.[9] One of the major challenges for a global manager is to balance – rather than eliminate – tensions in the business. The HR–PAG manager must engage in this dialogue and seek creative solutions to questions, such as:

- 'How will we maintain control over the global network while also unlocking entrepreneurial drive and innovation?'
- 'How will we derive the benefits of competitiveness in the organisation while also reaping the rewards of global collaboration and partnering?'

⊕ 'How will we derive the benefits from human diversity while also gaining the benefits of commonality?'

This set of global principles is different from those that have traditionally operated in multinationals. Rather than on the basis of integration, multinationals have operated on the basis of the relative autonomy of business units. This has promoted responsiveness to local markets, but often at the cost of overall fragmentation. Each multinational unit has also sought to capture and protect resources, even at the expense of other business units in the same company. This has disabled the flow of resources and organisational flexibility. There has also been a tendency in multinationals to reproduce the 'home country' structure. Each business, therefore, tends to develop its own purchasing processes, product development methodologies, marketing capabilities etc. Finally, multinational business units have looked to maximise their own results rather than optimise results for the total organisation. What operating principles are currently at work in your organisation?

How do companies globalise? There is no one path. Many companies have evolved, or are evolving, along the following trajectory:

⊕ *domestic*: a focus on selling exclusively to the home market. Given the size and wealth of the domestic US market, many American companies moved abroad slowly.

⊕ *international*: the setting up of a cross-border business through licensing, exporting, joint ventures and strategic alliances. In many cases, the establishment of an international division within the domestic business has been the preferred option.

⊕ *multinational*: through direct investment, mergers, acquisitions and strategic alliances, the establishment of relatively independent business subsidiaries and partnerships in multiple locations around the world.

⊕ *global*: the configuration of cross-border business activities to achieve an optimal formation of global co-ordination and local responsiveness.

Where is your company in this process? Many large companies are in the difficult transition between multinational and global. One reason this transition is so difficult is that evolved power structures – country kingdoms, in particular – need to be integrated into more of a network (less hierarchical) structure.

As well as increased integration within firms, we are also seeing the growth of new units of competition, ie constellations of allied firms working together to compete collectively, eg Sprint, Deutsche Telekom and France Telecom. As Benjamin Gomes-Casseres points out, 'Collaboration is woven into the very fabric of competition.'[10]

Although alliances are changing the face of competition, favourable economic factors alone will not guarantee performance. The *Economist*[11] states:

> Fewer than half of all mergers and acquisitions add value ... Most difficult are the 'soft' issues ... the same word keeps popping up: culture ... people never fit together as easily as flow charts ... culture permeates a company ... any differences can poison any collaboration ... Two new things have made culture clashes harder to manage in mergers. The first is the growing importance of intangible assets ... most of the value can walk out the door. The second new thing is the number of cross-border mergers ... the attention seems to be on the deal rather than the integration.

This situation should be a prime target for the PAG. It must partner with business and functional teams to enable the alliance, merger or acquisition to be operating at peak performance as quickly as possible. PAG would help determine intended outcomes, methodologies, behavioural expectations, processes, decision-making, problem-solving approaches and cultural fit. PAG would also be responsible for capturing and sharing learning gained during the collaborative process.

In short, being global is less about *where* you do business and more about *how* you do it. How many HR managers can articulate the *how* of global business?

Are HR professionals prepared for global leadership? In my book *The Global Leader*,[12] I proposed three competency clusters needed by global business leaders:

- business acumen
- relationship management
- personal effectiveness.

Business acumen is defined as the ability to gain and leverage professional knowledge and skills to achieve optimal results for the company's global stakeholders. This cluster consists of the following competencies:

- *depth of field*: being willing and able to switch perspectives between local and global, functional and cross-functional arenas
- *entrepreneurial spirit*: taking initiative and demonstrating courage; pursuing calculated risks based on an identification and analysis of high-potential local and global business opportunities
- *professional expertise*: being committed to the ongoing development of one's own business knowledge and skills to world-class levels
- *stakeholder orientation*: showing a willingness and ability to balance the sometimes conflicting needs of global stakeholders (eg customers, shareholders, employees, communities) in order to achieve optimal results for the whole organisation
- *organisational resourcefulness*: demonstrating insight into 'how the business works' above and beyond one's own immediate area, and seeking to use this knowledge to get things done within and between organisational units.

Relationship management is the ability to build and influence co-operative relationships in a complex and diverse global network in order to direct energy towards the achievement of business strategies. The relevant competencies are:

- *change leadership*: creating new and value-added ways of doing things, and mobilising others to take ownership of and to drive the desired changes
- *community-building*: showing a willingness and ability to partner with others in developing interdependent relationships
- *conflict management and negotiation*: balancing assertiveness and sensitivity in using conflict to generate constructive outcomes
- *cross-cultural communication*: identifying and working with cultural differences to facilitate the achievement of shared understandings
- *influencing*: demonstrating an ability to move others to action without a reliance on positional authority or proximity.

Personal effectiveness is the ability to attain increasing levels of maturity in order to perform at peak levels under the difficult conditions of working in a complex global enterprise. Required competencies include:

- *accountability*: being committed to 'owning' problems, and taking responsibility within one's sphere of influence for the achievement of business objectives
- *curiosity and learning:* demonstrating a desire to undertake challenging new experiences and an openness to learn from them
- *improvisation*: generating creative and value-added responses, often under conditions of high uncertainty
- *maturity*: possessing a strong and stable sense of self with a capacity for resilience when faced with crises and setbacks
- *thinking agility*: demonstrating a willingness and ability to attack global and local problems from multiple angles while maintaining a bias towards action.

In October 1998, before giving a presentation to HR managers in a leading US computer company, I asked them to complete a self-rating on each of these 15 global leadership competencies. Their self-ratings, from lowest to highest, are listed below (1 = low, 7 = high). What is striking about these results is that the five lowest-rated competencies are those under the business acumen cluster. One HR manager looked up from the results and said, 'But those are our ticket to sitting at the global strategy table!'

Organisational resourcefulness	4.4
Entrepreneurial spirit	4.5
Depth of field	4.7
Professional expertise	4.8
Stakeholder orientation	4.9
Maturity	5.0
Thinking agility	5.0
Cross-cultural communication	5.1
Conflict management and negotiation	5.2
Change leadership	5.3
Influencing	5.5
Community building	5.7
Accountability	5.7
Curiosity and learning	5.7
Improvisation	5.7

I also asked HR managers from a US-based office equipment multi-national company to rate themselves on the same questionnaire. In this case, three of the five lowest ratings were again from the business acumen cluster: entrepreneurial spirit, professional expertise and depth of field.

ᴉe right things, as well as doing things right? HR
co Corporation were found to spend 65 per cent of
ɹinistrative tasks, 25 per cent on consulting and
…ᴄnt activities, and only 10 per cent on HR planning. To
ɹefocus HR on adding value, Amoco has formulated a new HR
mission, which is to:

> Provide leadership and support to management by developing, inte-
> grating and implementing HR strategies that maximise employee
> and organisational effectiveness in concert with Amoco's goals.

To accomplish this mission, the intended allocation of a HR manager's time is 25 per cent on strategic HR planning, 50 per cent on
consultative and developmental projects, and 25 per cent on administrative HR tasks.[13] HR managers at Amoco are being challenged
to diagnose performance problems, develop solutions and mobilise
resources. Yet I would suggest that even this bold move is not bold
enough. Rather than simply react to performance problems, we need
to identify – proactively – opportunities for dramatic global performance breakthroughs through people and technology.

Business

*Business credibility factor: Obsessively focusing on creating value throughout
the enterprise.*

In identifying opportunities for building and sustaining global competitiveness, the HR–PAG manager needs to think and act system−
ically. The first step is to visualise the global business as a whole and
explore every element and interaction for performance breakthrough
opportunities and synergies.

The model shown in Figure 1 is divided into three dimensions: the
business cycle, execution capability and system dynamics. Above
these dimensions are the operating principles discussed earlier (integration, flow, leverage and optimisation). Decisions made within the
other components of the model need to be 'measured' against these
principles. Although principles such as 'integration' should not be
iron rules, they should act as decision challenge-points, ie we had
better have a very good reason for managing payroll at each international location rather than globally.

Figure 1
THE GLOBAL ENTERPRISE SYSTEM

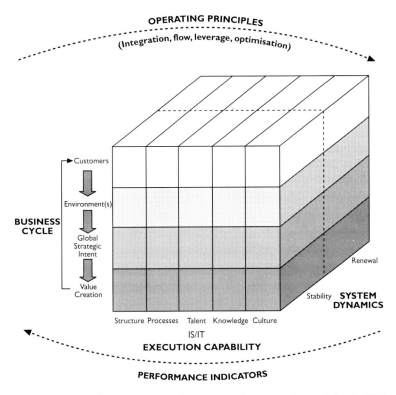

© Transnational Management Associates Limited (tma), 1999

Below the dimensions are critical performance indicators. How are we going to measure our global performance in the enterprise? For example, how fast do we move from local product concept to global product delivery? How fast can we form global teams with the right mix of capabilities to manage cross-border projects? The IS/IT line below the elements of execution capability – structure, processes, talent, knowledge and culture – refers to information systems (IS) and information technology (IT) platforms.

I shall briefly describe each element in the model and highlight what I consider to be a critical success factor for the global business. I shall also present a commitment that needs to be made by company associates (including HR professionals) to achieve the success factor.

Business cycle

Customers

- ⊕ Success factor: attracting, servicing and retaining key customers worldwide.
- ⊕ Commitment: we continuously find ways to delight customers worldwide by having the right innovative products and services, with the right features and benefits, delivered with the right quality and support levels, to the right place, at the right price, at the right time.

The cycle begins and ends with customers. These customers may be global, regional or local. Within each one of these populations may be multiple customer segments. We must have a deep understanding of the actual and anticipated needs of these customer segments, and of the importance of each one to the business over the next 5–10 years.

''What is the customer base of your business and how is it changing?''

One of the businesses that has recently seen a transformation of its status from a backroom operation to a core global strategic force is logistics. The key to this transformation has been the growth and predominance of demanding global customers like Ford, Hewlett Packard, GE, Sony and ABB. The significance of these global customers has been forcing logistics companies to align their services worldwide and to act globally. What is the customer base of your business and how is it changing? What new demands will these changes make on your business? The primary challenge is to connect with each customer segment. How can PAG contribute to anticipating and meeting these demands and facilitate connections to customers, both face-to-face and electronically? The traditional HR answer may be to create a training programme. But we must reach beyond this limited vision of adding value and connecting associates to customers.

Environment

- ⊕ Success factor: focusing organisational attention on global business opportunities and risks.

⊕ Commitment: we continuously scan our external environment in order to identify and prioritise actual and anticipated changes in or around the market-place.

Your company services its customers within a complex global business environment. What are the key characteristics of this environment, and how are you shaping and responding to them? We can think about the overall business environment from several dimensions: industry, competitive, economic, political and legal, technological, physical, social and cultural. Each dimension can be analysed at local, regional and global levels. Associates must be able to swim in a rich sea of environmental data, as well as access mission-critical information.

An important challenge for PAG will be developing tools and techniques for gathering, sorting and sharing information on the business environment. Most companies seem to do this in an *ad hoc* fashion, or the information is trapped in an isolated and protective strategic planning department. What are the major trends in your industry? What are competitors doing? What new technologies are on the horizon? What major cultural changes are predicted? Our challenge is not to gather information for its own sake, but to radically improve problem-solving, creativity, decision-making and empowerment.

Global strategic intent
⊕ Success factor: positioning the company to compete with the best in the world.
⊕ Commitment: we use our best thinking in the organisation to understand what businesses we should be in, where we should compete, and towards what performance goals and objectives.

From an understanding of customers and the actual and anticipated environment, a strategy for global action must be formulated. This strategy should allow for short-term opportunism and long-term positioning. Every business requires a balanced thinking mix between operational and strategic levels. Both need to inform an ongoing strategic conversation about product and service scope, geographic scope and how the business needs to differentiate itself from competitors. All too often, managers are disengaged from thinking strategically. Too much time is spent on narrow and short-term operational issues. According to one study, senior managers spend only 2.4 per cent of their time developing a corporate perspective on the future.[14] One important challenge for PAG would be the development of systems and processes that enable the strategic conversation to take place between all levels and locations.

Value creation

- ⊕ Success factor: generating value for all stakeholders in the global business.
- ⊕ Commitment: we drive hard to create value and enable growth by continuously improving our core capabilities and by developing innovative sources of global competitive advantage.

Our strategy must create value for customers, shareholders, employees etc. But how is value generated? There are at least three primary sources: technical, operational and relational excellence. Technical excellence resides in research and development, patents, copyrights, quality standards and processes. Operational excellence is an outcome of world-class functional capabilities, operating processes and logistics. Relational excellence needs to be both internal to the organisation (eg collaborative global teamwork) and external (eg connectivity to customers, suppliers, retailers etc). With the rapid expansion of customer choice, and the ease with which technical and operational competitive advantages can be replicated, relational excellence is fast becoming the key to market success. This accounts for the rise of the marketing function in many leading organisations. Relationships are hard to replicate.

Execution capability

Structure

- ⊕ Success factor: balancing global and local drivers to generate optimal results.
- ⊕ Commitment: we seek an appropriate blend of centralised and decentralised business activities to achieve both global economies of scale and responsiveness to local needs.

Creating an appropriate balance between globally integrated and locally dispersed business activities is not easy. Each business must analyse and locate the key components of its value chain to derive optimal efficiency *and* effectiveness. These components will include

R&D, finance, marketing, sales, manufacturing, purchasing, distribution and human resources. At one extreme, all of these activities are centralised and, at the other, decentralised.

Another option is to create global centres of excellence. For example, R&D might be located in Japan to take advantage of longer cultural time-horizons. Finance might be located in London or Zurich to tap into local expertise. Alternatively, the company might establish regional centres of excellence to balance global and local perspectives. Sales is likely to be a local activity (although consider Dell's internet strategy), whereas customer service might be handled in regional call centres. It is not unusual to allocate worldwide responsibility to a functional unit that previously had only national responsibilities. Within Avon, the US marketing area was given global responsibilities. This promoted a geocentric viewpoint in an important part of the business.

Whatever structure is adopted, it will be complex and asymmetrical. The demands on human and technological performance in such complex organisations are enormous. What could the PAG manager do to alleviate the strains? He or she could, for example, use both technological and non-technological tools to help associates to understand and to work within the structure. Intranets can be a valuable means of communicating clarity about the company structure, individual unit goals and objectives, capabilities, and roles and responsibilities. It is important that individual associates be able to 'work the structure'. If a global customer, for example, has a problem to be solved, the associate needs to be able to draw upon capabilities across the global organisation.

Processes
- ⊕ Success factor: co-ordinating core business activities to support global interdependence.
- ⊕ Commitment: we keep pushing towards working as an integrated global network to pursue consistency, synergies and scope.

Although it is important to make each unit of the business structure as strong as possible, it is equally important that the integration processes between units be both robust and flexible, ie we need co-ordinating processes that are *plastic* in their consistency. Processes transform a structure into a network. These processes need to facilitate communication and exchange between dispersed units and people. Many global organisations operate with some form of matrix management structure. Business line management and functional areas tend to have a partial view of the organisation (unless they are deliberately given multi-hatted responsibilities that are both narrowband and broadband, eg responsibility for a specific product area and responsibility for a company-wide process such as management of a global brand).

PAG would be responsible for developing tools and techniques to enable rich communication flows between individuals and between units. For example, think of a system that collects critical information both vertically and horizontally, and provides processing guidelines for global and local decision-making and problem-solving.

Talent

- ⊕ Success factor: accelerating the development of global mind-sets and skills throughout the organisation.
- ⊕ Commitment: we hire, develop, motivate and retain talented people who have the capacity to operate and lead in a complex and demanding global business environment.

What people capabilities do you need in the organisation if you are to realise your global strategy? Where do you need these capabilities, and when? My global leadership competency framework (see above) is a step towards understanding the attributes needed to lead and to perform well in a global enterprise. But we must also recognise the need for different global mind-sets and skills within subgroups. John A. Quelch and Helen Bloom distinguish between the following types of international manager:[15]

- ⊕ *Glopats*: managers who are highly mobile and focus on business-building or trouble-shooting; their assignments tend to be short- or medium-term
- ⊕ *Globals*: managers who move around the world on medium-term assignments
- ⊕ *Regionals*: managers who undertake short-, medium- and long-term assignments within a geographic region
- ⊕ *Mobile local nationals*: managers who are functional experts or

generalists and prepared to function well on transnational teams, short-term projects and overseas training assignments
- *Rooted local nationals*: managers who are functional experts or generalists tied to their home base.

Do you know where your global talent is? Do you know what capabilities it has? How mobile can it be? What skill gaps need to be filled, and where? What moves can you make to partner with business and functional executives to recruit, select, assign, develop and retain local and global talent? How can you leverage technology to track, train and network your talent to generate collaborative advantage?

Knowledge
- Success factor: leveraging intellectual capital throughout the global network.
- Commitment: we are creative in seeking ways to generate, capture, validate, transfer, apply and integrate knowledge throughout the network.

Talent generates intellectual capital, the most potent resource in business today. This knowledge can be thought of as *codified* in written documents and graphical representations, or *tacit* in informal routines and implicit know-how. Knowledge may refer to what we know (facts), how and why we know it (research and analytical methods, mental models and paradigms), and whom we know (relationship networks).

The challenge for the globally competitive organisation is to overcome what G. Szulanski calls 'internal stickiness', ie barriers to knowledge transfer.[16] Some of the barriers include:

- the level of tacit knowledge contained in the best practice and, therefore, the degree of ambiguity that must often be overcome
- the unique features of the context in which the best practice works
- lack of motivation and incentive
- an inability on the part of the receiver to value and absorb the knowledge
- lack of persistence in applying new knowledge; lack of fluid and intimate relationships between units.

Szulanski's study points to much work needing to be done in both the motivational and relational aspects of organisational learning, and in the development of practical tools. This is potentially fertile ground for the performance-driven PAG manager.

Culture

⊕ Success factor: establishing an inclusive set of values and norms that promote high achievement and global partnering

⊕ Commitment: we continually re-inforce the development of a global corporate culture that promotes collaboration across the organisation and leadership at all levels and locations.

Culture refers to the dominant values, attitudes, beliefs and behaviours in the organisation and in the wider environment(s). The talent in the organisation must be able to navigate through cultural differences encountered in dealings with customers, suppliers, distributors, partners, governments and international agencies. The company needs to derive benefits from diversity in the organisation through cross-cultural dialogue and the exploration of different world-views. Beyond diversity, it is equally important that the global organisation build common working ground through the integration of shared values and accepted and expected collaborative behaviours throughout the network. Although diversity can be challenging, lack of diversity can also be detrimental. Durk I. Jager, CEO of Procter & Gamble, describes the corporate culture at P&G as 'cult-like'. After completing a three-month tour of P&G sites in nearly two dozen cities around the world, he complained that the company had a tendency to 'Procterise' people: once people get inside the company they tend to sound – and even look – alike.[17] Motorola asks itself the following question:

> As a learning organisation, how can we learn from the various host cultures with which we engage, and weave the best of what we learn into our corporation's culture to make it more robust and socially useful in the new global context?[18]

What values and behaviours contribute to global success? *Fortune* magazine's analysis of the most globally admired companies in 1998 included a review of their common cultural attributes.[19] They found that the most admired companies valued teamwork, customer focus, fair treatment of employees, initiative and innovation. The average companies (not the worst) tended to stress the values of minimising risk, respecting the chain of command, supporting the boss and making budget.

"The culture must reward behaviours that promote openness and learning"

What are the primary cultural values of your organisation? Do they enable you to connect with your stakeholders, and do they demolish the 'Not invented here' syndrome? The culture must reward behaviours that promote openness and learning. What can you do as a PAG manager to align your business culture to the demands of the global business environment? Can you, for example, conduct an organisational culture audit, or offer collaborative techniques and technologies for transnational teamwork?

System dynamics
Stability

⊕ Success factor: anchoring the business in a common identity.
⊕ Commitment: we work hard to align all parts of the global business to a common purpose and direction and create cohesion.

A classic report produced by the Royal Dutch-Shell Group said that 'Successful companies appear to maintain a cohesion at all levels.'[20] Any healthy organisation needs a sense of cohesion and identity. Stability, however, must not be allowed to degenerate into rigidity.

Where does cohesion come from? An organisation's vision and values (if they are lived realities and not just words) create a sense of 'who we are and how we do business'. The culture of the organisation provides familiarity and belonging. Mission, strategy and corporate ethics statements, newsletters and brands provide a sense of continuity. These are all important in a world of rapid and continuous change and fuzzy borders. Having been a manager myself, I know that contradictory messages abound in organisations. The most prevalent today is when the words say 'People are our most valuable asset' but actions say 'People are expendable.'

If we are to provide a stable foundation on which performance break-throughs can be built, we need to align the culture with our performance management systems, eg performance appraisals, rewards and recognition. These, in turn, need to be aligned with appropriate management practices, organisational structures and processes, the global strategy and the guiding vision. One initiative for PAG would be an alignment audit to gauge the impact of contradictory messages and practices on global performance, and the development of strategies for aligning and communicating key messages.

Renewal
- Success factor: challenging existing assumptions, beliefs and strategies to maintain a global competitive edge.
- Commitment: we identify and quickly implement organisational initiatives needed to keep the global business system agile and innovative.

Globally competitive organisations must continually innovate and improve. Someone, somewhere, is at this very moment looking to create something that will threaten your business survival. It could be a teenager with a computer and too little homework! Innovation and continuous improvement requires what Chris Argyris refers to as double-loop learning, ie the continuous process of questioning the effectiveness of underlying operating norms, beliefs and assumptions.[21]

Renewal has been very evident in Jaguar (North America). Since Michael Dale took over the business in late 1990, sales have more than doubled (from 8,681 in 1992 to 20,503 in 1998). J. D. Power ranked the company 25th in customer satisfaction in 1991 and 4th in 1998. What Michael Dale did was to oversee a revolution in the company's culture, quality, processes, management and overall productivity. He focused his revolution on one central objective – customer loyalty. He also learned two lessons from studying highly successful companies such as Disney, Harley-Davidson, 3M and GE – employee empowerment and teamwork. Employees at Jaguar were asked to become the agents of change in 'employee involvement groups' and 'process improvement teams'. When asked what he would like his legacy to be, Dale said, '[for leaving behind] a culture that absolutely embraces change – loves it – that educates itself and understands that it's the way to make the future work.'[22]

What performance challenges and opportunities should *you* attack first? Imagine you were the CEO of your globalising business. What would you want PAG to do for your global enterprise?

Shifting your perspective by putting yourself in the managing director's chair can be a very productive exercise. What factors are most critical to the success of your business? What do you need to start, stop or strengthen over the short-, medium- and long-term to achieve success? Remember also that you are operating in a system of complex interconnections; a change in one part will have intended and unintended effects in others. 'We can never do merely one thing.'[23]

Partner

Business credibility factor: Demonstrating 'no excuses' business leadership.

Steve Baird, head of HR for Warburg Dillon Read (a division of UBS A.G.), says:

> Effective staff management is our responsibility [HR] and calls for an intensive partnership between business/service managers and human resources professionals. While this requires that line management extend their planning and decision making processes to include HR professionals as appropriate, it also implies that HR will have the knowledge and the understanding of business issues to be able to add value.[24]

"As leaders, we must imagine the future"

'Partnering' implies higher levels of commitment to shared goals and objectives than do the terms 'team member', 'colleague' or 'associate'. Commitment is, however, not enough for a partnership to work. Partners must be able to move beyond words and intentions to actions, and these actions must produce results. Partners must continually demonstrate that they add value to the relationship, otherwise the partnership will not survive. Every HR activity must be challenged with such questions as: 'What value does this add?' 'How does this increase our global viability?' 'What is the link between this activity and our global business strategies?' Meeting these challenges is vital if HR is to be seen as more than just an expense item on the balance sheet. As leaders, we must imagine the future and challenge any limiting beliefs or excuses suggesting that it is unattainable.

Many routine HR activities can be outsourced or automated. The HR focus should be on individual and collaborative performance breakthroughs and enhancing organisational capabilities, nothing more or less. Routine administrative tasks add little, if any, economic value to the business.

What does this mean to us? Let me go back to the Global Enterprise System model and look at it from another angle – see Figure 2.

From the viewpoint illustrated in Figure 2, there are four large constituencies in the business: the global executive partnership, business

Figure 2
PARTNERING IN THE GLOBAL ENTERPRISE SYSTEM

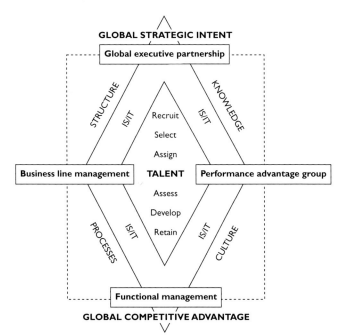

© Transnational Management Associates Limited (tma), 1999

line management, the performance advantage group and functional management. Executives from the three latter constituencies must join with the most senior leaders in the business to form what I shall call a global executive partnership. The primary task of this partnership would be to formulate, monitor and adapt the global strategic intent of the company. To implement the global strategic intent, business line, PAG and functional managers would need to be in very close liaison.

The liaison would be built on a deep understanding of shared business goals and objectives. The focus of all constituencies would be on developing, releasing and using the imagination, knowledge and expertise of talent to generate global competitive advantage.

PAG would need to operate at several levels. First, PAG would partner with individual businesses and functions to develop and implement business-specific performance initiatives. Second, it would seek to identify and exploit performance synergies between related and unrelated businesses and functions. Third, it would look to design, develop and deliver performance breakthrough initiatives at the enterprise level, eg a company-wide global talent tracking system.

How can the HR manager begin?

⊕ Start by building *business credibility*. Be able to articulate the *why, what* and *how* of globalisation. Identify the strengths, weaknesses, opportunities and threats for your business in the global marketplace. Allocate more time for strategic thinking. Demonstrate a clear understanding of global business goals and strategies, and the industry/competitive environment in which targets are to be met. Understand the customer base and how it is changing globally, regionally and locally. Be highly sensitive to what different stakeholders – particularly key customers – perceive as value, and focus all efforts on collaborating with others to deliver those value propositions.

⊕ Study the *execution capabilities* of your company and how they facilitate or inhibit such business objectives as speed, quality, low cost, consistency, innovation and responsiveness. Identify performance opportunities and threats throughout the enterprise.

⊕ Be *proactive* and demonstrate *leadership*. Explore setting up partnerships with businesses and functions – particularly IS/IT – to produce the most value for the company in the shortest amount of time. Look for performance breakthrough partnerships outside of the business with customers, suppliers and joint venture partners.

- Review the time spent on *non-value adding activities*. Outsource what you can as quickly as possible and focus on adding economic value.
- Be *visible*. Measure and communicate results.

‘‘The people–technology interface will drive progress’’

The global business arena is rapidly becoming a battleground for talent. As economies shift from being industrial to knowledge-based, many senior managers are beginning to recognise that profits are generated from the hearts and minds of people. Increasingly, these hearts and minds are being stimulated and connected by powerful new technologies, but technology alone cannot create and sustain performance that stretches the bounds of what is thought possible. As in other human performance revolutions throughout history, the people–technology interface will drive progress. HR will take a giant step forward if it positions itself at this critical interface.

For many HR practitioners, these changes will require a radical shift in mind-set and skills – towards multidisciplinary, high-tech and high-touch expertise. In terms of establishing our global leadership role, we must also learn that 'Impossible!' and 'None of your business!' are just other ways of saying 'Opportunity!'

End-notes

[1] KANTER R. M. *World Class: Thriving locally in the global economy*. New York, Simon & Schuster, 1995.

[2] FRIEDMAN T. L. *The Lexus and the Olive Tree*. New York, Farrar, Straus and Giroux, 1999.

[3] BARHAM K. *and* HEIMER C. *ABB, The Dancing Giant: Managing the globally connected corporation*. London, Financial Times Management, 1998.

4 Phrase used by Mr Konosuke Matsushita, executive advisor to Matsushita Electrical Industrial Co. Ltd Japan, to a group of visiting US and European managers.

5 KEARNEY A. T., INC. *Globalising the Corporation*. Management Report 46. Chicago, A. T. Kearney, 1996.

6 TAPSCOTT D. *The Digital Economy: Promise and peril in the age of networked intelligence*. New York, McGraw-Hill, 1995.

7 HALLOWELL E. H. 'The human moment at work'. *Harvard Business Review*. January–February 1999. pp58–66.

8 TAYLOR W. C. *and* WEBBER A. M. *Going Global: Four entrepreneurs map the new world market-place*. New York, Viking Penguin, 1996.

9 BARTLETT C. A. *and* GHOSHAL S. *Managing across Borders: The transnational solution*. 2nd edn. Cambridge, MA, Harvard Business School Press, 1998.

10 GOMES-CASSERES B. *The Alliance Revolution: The new shape of business rivalry*. Cambridge, MA, Harvard University Press, 1997.

11 THE ECONOMIST. 'After the deal'. *The Economist*. 9 January 1999.

12 BRAKE T. *The Global Leader: Critical factors for creating the world-class organisation*. Chicago, Irwin Professional Publishing, 1997.

13 LAABS J. J. 'Stay a step ahead with 5 key skills'. *Workforce*. October 1997. pp56–65.

14 HAMEL G. *and* PRAHALAD C. K. *Competing for the Future: Breakthrough strategies for seizing control of your industry and creating the markets of tomorrow*. Cambridge, MA, Harvard Business School Press, 1994.

15 QUELCH J. A. *and* BLOOM H. 'Ten Steps to a Global Human Resources Strategy'. *Strategy & Business*. Issue 14, First Quarter, 1999. pp18–29.

16 SZULANSKI G. 'Exploring internal stickiness: Impediments to the transfer of best practice within the firm'. *Strategic Management Journal*. Vol. 17, winter 1996. pp27–44.

17 PARKER-POPE T. 'New CEO Preaches Rebellion for P&G's "Cult"'. *The Wall Street Street Journal*. 11 December 1998.

18 MOORTHY R. S. *et al*. *Uncompromising Integrity: Motorola's global challenge*. Schaumburg, IL, Motorola University Press, 1998.

19 KAHN J. 'The world's most admired companies'. *Fortune*. 26 October 1998.

[20] ROYAL DUTCH-SHELL GROUP PLANNING PL/1. *Corporate Change: A look at how long-established companies change*. Internal study, 1983.

[21] ARGYRIS C. 'Teaching smart people how to learn'. *Harvard Business Review*. May–June 1991.

[22] FREEMAN COHEN S. 'In the driver's seat'. *Continental*. May 1999. pp51–53.

[23] JERVIS R. *System Effects: Complexity in political and social life*. Princeton, NJ, Princeton University Press, 1997.

[24] BAIRD S. Statement made at an internal leadership development programme. Global Corporate Finance, Warburg Dillon Read, UBS A.G., February 1999.

International Recruitment, Selection and Assessment

Paul Sparrow

The extent to which actual selection practice matches the academic specification of appropriate systems has long been questioned.[1] The level of sophistication in international recruitment and selection is still relatively low. The latest IPD Recruitment Survey shows that 23 per cent of UK firms recruit internationally. Of these, 71 per cent look for awareness of international issues, 81 per cent look for the ability to manage in culturally diverse teams, and 85 per cent look for a positive attitude to cultural diversity. The overall situation remains one in which the trend is towards shorter expatriation assignments, more recruitment of foreign nationals, and recruitment mainly of technical and managerial professionals. There is some attention to preparation, but this is still focused on briefing materials, business etiquette courses and basic cultural awareness courses, ie preparation focused on the job and country, not on the family.

Empirical investigation of UK practice also suggests that international selection is rarely a rational and objective process. Organisations operate a range of systems, formal or informal, open or closed. When personnel managers are asked to identify the constructs that they feel differentiate effective from ineffective international managers, little consistency is seen between them, and the criteria tend to reflect broad judgements based on confidence in previous international assignments, managing the interface between the centre and the operational unit, and having an international outlook and a degree of cultural empathy.[2]

The cynical view is that most individuals are informally targeted by managers during discussions by the coffee machine, and that formal systems are then used to legitimise the already made decision. However, it need not be like this, and evidence can be found of more systematic approaches.

This chapter analyses a range of key tools and techniques under four themes:

1 competing selection philosophies
2 attracting and engaging international managers
3 sourcing international managers
4 selecting international managers.

Attention is given to the engagement of international managers through the use of head-hunters and advertising. The sourcing of international managers is looked at through the use of the Internet and international graduate programmes. Two selection technologies are also considered: the use of assessment centres, and the relevance of psychological testing in multicultural settings.

The chapter distils the findings from a study commissioned by the IPD, which gathered in-depth data about corporate international recruitment, selection and assessment.[3] A number of multinational and internationalising companies were selected in order to represent firms of different size and sector, including financial services, retail, manufacturing, consumer products and utilities. Interviews were held with 13 organisations: British Airways, British Petroleum, British Telecom, Cable and Wireless, Cadbury Schweppes, Courtaulds Textiles, Diageo, EMI Music, Hong Kong and Shanghai Bank, S.W.I.F.T., Kellogg's, Unilever and Zeneca. Expert opinion was also sought from a series of service-providers, including Employment Conditions Abroad, Kaisen Consulting, PA Consulting, Saville and Holdsworth, the Quo Group, Bernard Hodes Advertising and Yahoo. The intention was to gain insight into the international resourcing process by tracking developments within the organisations and within their suppliers of services.

‘‘Do we need an international manager at all?’’

It should be made clear from the outset that within the international management arena there is no simple recipe that can be followed – no prescriptions to be foisted on the organisation. Rather, there are choices to be argued out and opportunities to be pursued. Complex technical arguments and evidence have to be considered and the distinctive market positions of consulting organisations and service-providers fathomed. Indeed, HR managers need to start with the basic question, 'Do we need an international manager at all?'

This is because they are solving a business problem in which the decision to resource an international manager may be only one solution among many. The answer to resourcing problems does not just entail selection systems. The link between recruitment and selection processes and other issues such as training can be complex. In many US organisations, the reluctance of candidates to come forward for foreign assignments to underdeveloped countries results in a contracted selection process. There is little time between candidate short-listing and actual assignment. This creates a climate in which the candidate has to rush to close current job obligations and personal matters in order to prepare for the move which, not surprisingly, creates an overload of work upon arrival in the new country and leaves little time for training.[4]

Moreover, for many organisations there is confusion about what is meant by the term 'international manager'. Roles may require people to engage in a truly mobile and transient lifestyle – the international commuter – or simply liaise with people from other countries.

Several different role specifications exist:

- ⊕ home-based manager but with a central focus on international markets and players
- ⊕ multicultural team members who work on a series of international projects
- ⊕ internationally mobile managers who undertake frequent but short visits to numerous overseas locations while remaining loyal to the parent culture
- ⊕ employees in specialist non-management roles which involve international activity or transfer of knowledge, eg sales, training, buying, engineering

⊕ expatriates who carry the parent organisational culture but spend lengthy assignments representing the parent in a limited number of host countries

⊕ transitional managers who move across borders on behalf of the organisation but who are relatively detached from any single organisational HQ.

The question is, 'Does a different set of competencies come to the fore in each of these roles?' There is a re-assessment taking place in terms of what we know about the skills and competencies associated with international job changes. Our early research presented a rather simplistic picture, arguing that expatriates and repatriates experienced high levels of assignment failure, evidenced by aggregated levels of turnover due to a lack of pre-departure training and spouse-adjustment problems. Now that we begin to understand the psychological processes that lie behind such an observation, the situation becomes more complex.

It is important to note that academics are frequently amused by the literature on international management characteristics. One cross-cultural management textbook noted 68 dimensions, of which 21 are deemed to be the most desirable. The practitioner literature is also replete with several lists of apparently predictive factors, many of questionable validity. This problem has occurred because different interest groups have defined our knowledge about effective performance in an international setting.

Expatriation research looks at the causes of international assignment failure and the selection criteria that lead to time being served on assignment. Clearly, several alternative performance criteria could be used to assess the validity of the competencies identified. International joint venture research examines the role of managers in what is often a low-power situation, in which the international manager has to work through partnerships and collaborations. This requires a different skill-set from that of the traditional expatriate role. Cross-cultural management research examines the ability of managers to adapt to unfamiliar environments and new cultures. Finally, research on socialisation considers the skills that managers need to learn about and cope with in new jobs. Socialisation into a new job is all the more difficult for international managers because they have to cross what is called the 'inclusion boundary', ie become trusted by other cultural groups. They must also seek information proactively without being stereotyped as an expensive international manager who doesn't appear to know the answer to anything!

Competing selection philosophies

Not surprisingly, then, there are still some important gaps in our knowledge and some fundamental questions that divide the field:

- ⊕ Can all international management competencies be developed?
- ⊕ Are some competencies so complex, so rare on the ground and so time-consuming to build that the real issue is to select a rarefied élite of managers?
- ⊕ Can we identify a clear hierarchy of international management skills, from the most basic to high levels of performance and sophistication, or must we be left with endless lists of desirable characteristics with assumed relevance?
- ⊕ Do internal resourcing systems realistically make such graded and calibrated decisions about managers?
- ⊕ Are line managers so happy to find anyone who is half competent but also mobile that they will dismiss as impractical calls for more sophisticated recruitment and assessment?

The consensus from HR practitioners is that it *is* possible to specify a set of competencies for the international manager, and that these can be used to assist the selection of some people in some jobs. However, most practitioners know that it is equally, if not more, important to have a detailed and intimate knowledge of all poten-tially mobile managers.

> We're not necessarily convinced or concerned that perfecting the selection process is key to creating the internationally mobile man-ager. It is more important to give them the exposure, the experience. It is then our ability to observe them on the job in a variety of inter-national management events after their entry into the business, and measuring and tracking this. The best strategy is to identify the managers who have to be kept, and then directing them at the right kind of opportunities.
>
> HR manager

The purpose of international assignments is shifting. Although tech-nology transfer or the imposition of organisational control is still a major drive of international work, in many cases managers now work in a loose networking role or come from such functions as marketing and HRM. Here managers have to seek information, liaise, persuade and sell their ideas far more than is the case in a technology-transfer assignment. Several other roles and functional groups are also now being internationalised.

Selection criteria are therefore shifting slowly from ones based on technical and intelligence criteria to a wider range of skills and personality felt appropriate for the flexible manager. The premise is that people who seek certainty, completeness, tidiness and rational logicality are not suited to modern business cultures or an environment that demands international mobility.[5] The ability to deal with the ambiguity of 'what happens next' is seen as central for internationally mobile managers. The characteristics identified are derived from models of high-performance competency and flexibility.

International role specifications now stress that managers must be:

- actively analytical rather than take events at face value
- willing to take risks
- action-oriented, with strong personal goals
- able to look at situations constructively and not defensively
- capable of multidimensional vision rather than unitary thought
- able to deal with information from many sources
- sensitive to the needs of others
- able to delegate and trust subordinates
- able to live with ambiguity and complexity.

Can you develop these capabilities in managers? Many doubt the feasibility of this:

> We have this quaint idea that cultural skills are 'developable' by putting people through half-day courses and briefings full of obvious points about cultural sensitivity ... Because managers think these things are all developable, the view is put forward that as long as you put the right people into these positions, then international competencies will follow ... Some of the competencies are developable, depending on the basic learning competencies of the individual and their motivation to do so, but I do think that going to the next level of international management is not developable.
>
> HR manager

Given that there are different views about the feasibility of developing the full spectrum of international management competencies in a sufficiently large pool of managers, competing resourcing philosophies can be found:

⊕ the traditional psychometric approach to predicting international management competencies
⊕ a clinical risk assessment approach, which investigates the psychological transitions and adaptations that international managers have to undergo
⊕ designing the assignment around the manager.

There is a tension between the skills and competencies that organisations think they should be looking for when they recruit and the skills that are actually needed to make a success of working abroad. The traditional psychometric approach argues that there are identifiable competencies associated with success and that these can be used to predict effective performers in international roles.

Few practitioners doubt that selecting someone for an international assignment draws attention to quite stringent criteria. Openness to experience, tolerance of ambiguity, introversion, the ability to generate and inspire trust in others and proactive information-seeking can be understated in domestic selection systems, which may be geared more to emphasising a task-oriented, aggressive problem-solving and 'time-is-money' management style. Many of the large consulting groups, such as SHL and Hay McBer, have researched and marketed their own set of international competencies, drawing attention to the unique ones. Some organisations, such as S.W.I.F.T. (see below), have actually applied behavioural competency approaches to international recruitment and selection.

The international mind-set critical success factor at S.W.I.F.T.

S.W.I.F.T. (the Society for Worldwide Interbank Financial Telecommunication) provides a technology-based financial processing and communication service across financial markets through member banks. It supplies 24-hour global support to 6,460 financial institutions in 177 different countries, processing over 4 million traffic messages valued at over $2 trillion a day. It employs 1,500 people globally in numerous locations, including the Belgian HQ, the USA, Asia Pacific (Hong Kong, Japan and Singapore), Europe (the Netherlands, UK, France, Germany, Italy and Spain) and Latin America. Staff come from a wide range of nationalities, covering 35 languages.

S.W.I.F.T has recently introduced a focus on an 'international mind-set' as part of a broader change in its organisational culture. As an organisation, it was moving away from a relatively protected and technology-driven institution towards being a more client- and business-driven outfit. New management, deregulation in the sector and a growing client base of financial institutions (that were themselves internationalising) made it possible for S.W.I.F.T. to change its resourcing approach. Teams might include employees from all parts of the world. S.W.I.F.T. decided to build a 'global' culture, not an Anglo-Saxon or Belgian one.

The biggest factor of failure was when people did not see where their value system was different from others', and when it did not map onto another culture easily. Although managers were united by the business language of English, it was clear that Portuguese English or Japanese English, or the many other variants that exist, are quite different one from the other. Without knowing why, communications could become blocked because of simple misunderstandings or even insults read into the language, and because of a lack of understanding of the basic values of the other person's culture.

S.W.I.F.T. generated 30 corporate-wide critical success factors (CSFs) – or competencies – which can be 'permed' against any role. One CSF deemed unique to international roles is called 'international mind-set'. This is used selectively in key roles but felt to be essential among team leaders, global account managers, and sales, consulting and executive roles.

All CSFs were tested against a cross-section of roles. Expert panels judged their importance for each role. A 'language ladder' was created for each CSF, including international mind-set, breaking it down into a series of logically graded levels.

At the simplest level, the focus of the competency is on the ability of staff to be aware of their own style and to be open to different values and styles. This is required for administrative and support functions. The second level becomes relevant for many specialist and project roles, and requires managers to be able to adapt their own behavioural style, have tolerance for the views of others and not allow their own management style and values to override the approach of others. At the third level, managers have to be able to anticipate and reconcile their own differences in style.

The competency is used in the recruitment process, all 'end-to-end' development work that requires people to collaborate internationally, and for any manager on the executive. On an annual basis there will be typically 120 external recruits; they are all assessed against the competency. It is first applied to job communication, starting with the adverts: explicit mention of the competency is made in adverts and all basic communication. It is tested for as part of a criterion-based or situational interview. S.W.I.F.T. does not feel that psychometric testing is appropriate to select for the competency.

A second philosophy can be called the clinical risk assessment approach. Many practitioners argue that there are limits to using personal competencies as a selection criterion for the international manager. The reasons for failure of international management assignments often go beyond problems of the managers' cultural adaptability, maturity and stability. Adaptability of the partner, dual-career difficulties, national attitudes to mobility and pay arrangements clearly all play a role in the success of the assignment. Similarly, the supporting structure that surrounds the international manager plays a part (in terms of localisation policies, management structures, reporting relationships, accountabilities and responsibilities, and the technical difficulty of the assignment). Developments associated with the business need for greater cost-control over international managers and changes in the position power of international managers (related to the growth of joint ventures and strategic alliances) mean that the supply (or lack of supply) of willing managers limits the selection context.

Finally, although international assignments require significant psychological adaptation, the use of competencies may be:

- too cumbersome in an international recruitment and selection-setting
- not actually predictive of success
- difficult to measure reliably based on the quality of data made available to HR managers in a field setting.

This line of argument is followed by Kaisen Consulting, which forwards the use of cultural adaptability assessments. Their thinking has been applied in the area of international resourcing by Cadbury Schweppes, which has a growing population of international managers and is moving an increasing number of managers to strategically important international locations.

Cadbury Schweppes: Making clinical assessments of inter-cultural adaptability and risk factors

Cadbury Schweppes has been running its accelerated development programme (ADP) for eight years. It is designed to identify and proactively accelerate the development of management talent internationally to meet the future resourcing needs of the group. Each year, 16 managers go through the process. The nomination and selection process is managed separately by each business, and selection can take place through an assessment centre or in line with the businesses' performance or succession management process. The programme involves management development through one-year-long international assignments.

Eighteen months ago **Cadbury Schweppes** made a suitability assessment of its managers undertaking overseas assignments. The number of people on international assignments is likely to more than double over the next four years, from 120 to 300. This is a significant investment, and so it made business sense to introduce a cultural adaptability assessment alongside the normal selection process.

International management is seen to revolve around the risks associated with intercultural adaptability. The recruitment process therefore attempts to assess objectively an employee's capability to perform a specific role as well as his or her suitability for an international assignment. The process, designed with **Kaisen Consulting**, helps employees understand the personal qualities required to work overseas and the implications of an international assignment for themselves and their families. It highlights the coping mechanisms that assist them in adapting to their new environment, and focuses on identifying the psychological 'adaptations' that take place on an international assignment.

Not all managers can adapt to living and working in a different country. The answer does not lie in managers' possessing competencies that enable organisations to make yes/no decisions about their adaptability. Rather, a series of contingencies has to be managed – an individual might be able to adapt to one situation, but not to another. The approach highlights four adaptations:

- behaviour towards others and the different norms that exist
- expectations about people, situations and the way things work
- interpretation of the situation and people's behaviour
- feelings about the situation, the emotional side of culture and the display of behaviours.

Rather than attempt to predict excellent performance and possession of competencies, this approach argues that it is better to pursue a selection strategy of risk reduction, ie identify 'risk analysis' factors – the things that, if absent, will affect performance – and contra-indicators – the things that, if present, may suggest a higher level of risk associated with the assignment. It assesses such factors as a 'polycentric mind-set', 'locus of control' and 'tolerance of ambiguity'. A questionnaire is followed by a one-to-one health-screen interview which reviews each factor in the model and considers motivational and lifestyle issues.

Cadbury Schweppes then considers how to structure the international assignment to reduce the risks involved. Judgements are made about three levels of intercultural adaptability:

⊕ suitable for 'nowhere'
⊕ suitable for 'somewhere' (on a contingency basis)
⊕ suitable for 'everywhere'.

This assessment is *not* used as a selection instrument. The results are considered to be valid for only one year, but assessors can have a dialogue with candidates about sensitive issues that might not otherwise be raised.

The role of some important individual attributes, such as locus of control or a polycentric mind-set, is acknowledged in this philosophy, but the assessment of an individual against such criteria is seen only as part of the solution and not predictive of performance. International selection under this philosophy is all about the management of *risk*.

Most HR practitioners believe that whether they adopt a psychometric or a clinical risk assessment philosophy, the whole process must be balanced by other considerations. The solution might be to design the assignment around the individual manager.

Pragmatic pressures are shaping current thinking about international resourcing. Most organisations operate in an environment of tight resources in an era of downsizing. This reduces the range of potential candidates and the subsequent selection choice. Given a smaller candidate pool, and reflecting the higher level of risk associated with international selection decisions, the roles that have to be filled are becoming increasingly individual affairs. The most practical solution is for HR managers to design the assignment to match the skills of the manager, rather than the other way around. The clinical risk assessment approach has an element of this in it – design the assignment so that it reduces the exposure of the manager to their weaknesses.

A similar perspective is taken implicitly by EMI Music.

Using skills database tracking systems at EMI Music

EMI Music has over 9,000 employees worldwide. It is not a labour-intensive or HR-intensive organisation. The role of the international HR function is more to do with negotiation of individual contracts and retention of key staff. HR resources are therefore strategically located around the business. The market for international managers operates in a similar fashion to that at the top end of investment banking. The business skills and knowledge of the managers and the strength of their relationship with local artists and consumers is as important as the possession of a set of international skills. Very specific and individual skills are required to build up relationships, markets and promotions, and to develop an individual artist. Artists, international managers responsible for developing local repertoire, and managers in marketing roles are invariably seen as one of a handful of people in the industry who have that particular skill. Being sensitive to the needs of managers, their strengths and weaknesses, is critical.

The role of assignment planning, tracking systems and skills databases have become critical. An internal database and tracking process helps ensure that EMI is constantly in tune with the issues that restrict the motivation and enthusiasm of managers to be internationally mobile and assist subsequent internal assessment decisions and planned moves. Three hundred managers are tracked worldwide, of which around 50 are expatriates and 90 high-potential managers; the majority

> **are classified as internationally mobile managers. Data is gathered by line managers annually as part of local appraisal processes. Information generated in the organ- isation and management review (OMR) is traded out from this into a common format, which is 'calibrated' by HQ to ensure consistency of assessments. The OMR database contains much qualitative information, such as an employee's expressed wishes and concerns and per- sonal issues that have been discussed, such as dual-career concerns and cost issues.**
>
> **Systematic customisation of the fields means that the database plays a critical role, because the freeform data can be searched to look at 'soft issues' associated with resourcing.**

Armed with such customised databases and skills-tracking systems, it makes far more sense for the international HR manager to devote time and energy to visiting the receiving location and ensuring that the necessary support systems are in place in order to ensure the pro- ject's success than to attempt to create a cadre of like-minded and like-skilled international managers.

Attracting and engaging international managers

Having outlined the broad selection strategies that can be followed, how is the process begun? How do organisations begin to engage international managers? Two processes are discussed: the use of head-hunting and advertising.

Using head-hunters

Executive search is defined as the recruitment of senior executives and specialists with an average compensation level of over $100,000 p.a. The top 15 global search firms had a net revenue of almost $2 billion in 1997, 19 per cent up on the previous year. Worldwide revenues in the search industry are expected to reach $10 billion by the year 2000.

Most large head-hunting firms have been established on the repu- tation of outstanding consultants and charismatic business leaders.

Although the personal chemistry between the head-hunter and international personnel manager is still important, the ability of head-hunters to offer an integrated service with no international obstacles to cross-border co-operation has become the most important criterion.

Nancy Garrison-Jenn[6] argues that the industry is entering a very dynamic phase. In 1998 there were a significant number of mergers, acquisitions, consolidations and new alliances in the industry, as firms tried to provide appropriate geographical coverage.

A trend in the use of head-hunters and executive search firms has been the development of partnerships. Some head-hunting firms, however, are moving beyond partnerships and are going through public offerings, becoming very large players. A number of firms now use preferred supplier relationships, including Andersen Consulting, Apple Computer, American Express, British Telecom, Coca Cola, Ford, IBM, Motorola, Pepsi Cola, Philips, Smithkline Beecham, Sanofi and Viacom. Such partnerships allow much wider geographical sourcing of candidates. The highest growth areas have been Greater China, Malaysia, Taiwan, South Korea and India. Emerging markets such as Russia, the Middle East, Eastern Europe and South Africa may be put on hold, given the fragile business climate. However, there are always areas of ready talent. For example, Turkey is now providing an attractive source of highly talented and educated young graduates. There are also many pragmatic reasons international personnel managers use head-hunters:

> Not every piece of market intelligence that you are gathering is about recruiting now. It is about testing the market: if we went through this kind of change and we have a gap, would there be someone out there? It is about understanding the prices in the market and what is happening out there.
>
> HR manager

Some of the key service-provider selection criteria and considerations to be made by international personnel managers concern the following issues:

⊕ Service providers naturally wish to convince users that their brand of executive search transcends the skills of the individual consultants, but many personnel managers feel that the quality of

the individual consultants working for executive search firms is a
critical factor.

⊕ Key-account management is an important part of the service provided by search firms. For users, the real test is whether the
account manager really has clout within the search firm.

⊕ Anecdotal evidence indicates that up to 50 per cent of executive
searches are now cross-border. Therefore the cross-border capability and geographical spread of individual search firms have
become critical.

⊕ As partnerships between service-providers and organisations
grow, what are the off-limit constraints of the search firm?

Cross-national advertising

Organisations are looking to Europe and beyond to attract professionals to work in the UK or to work in locations around the
globe. If the cost of getting a recruitment campaign wrong is high in
the domestic market, then the potential cost of errors in global campaigns is very high. Trends in advertising vary across sector. There is
a shift away from press advertising into creative alternatives, such as
targeted outdoor poster sites, airport lounges, airline magazines and
journey-to-work routes. Many recruitment advertising service-
providers now operate as part of global networks in order to deliver
targeted pan-European or global campaigns. These may be developed
and managed from the UK or developed for local on-ground support.

Advertising agencies gather a broad spectrum of international intelligence which focuses on:

⊕ the location of the target audience
⊕ the kind of market they operate in
⊕ sample salaries
⊕ recruitment competitors
⊕ whether the job-seeking audience is passive or active.

Knowledge about the best recruitment media for target audiences is
important, as is awareness of national custom and practice, in order to
ensure the 'cultural appropriacy' of a campaign. From an advertising
perspective, the most important cross-cultural differences concern:

⊕ the role qualities associated with jobs
⊕ the desired company qualities

⊕ softer cultural issues, such as what ideal brochures should look like and the wording of adverts.

Advertising consultancies conduct their own research into these issues. For example, in looking at 'role qualities' for European graduates (the qualities that the applicants are looking for when considering their careers), Bernard Hodes Advertising found that important aspects included interesting work, making an impact, job security, the starting salary, challenge, being part of a team, opportunities overseas, and working with like-minded people.

From the research they conducted, they found that UK graduates' role quality priorities were in the above order. For French graduates the order was similar, although opportunities overseas and being with like-minded people were more important than for UK graduates. The most important role quality was that the role must be interesting. What was notable was the consistently low ranking of starting salary – fourth out of eight in the UK, fifth in France, and bottom of the list in Germany and Spain. No single factor stood out in terms of the 'company qualities' that the applicants sought. Good career prospects, structured training, and encouraging and valuing new ideas were consistently in the top three items across countries, whereas leading-edge technology was consistently near the bottom of the list. A good international reputation was the least important factor everywhere, other than in France.

There are also many soft cultural issues associated with the use of advertising, such as the phrasing and design of adverts. In the Czech Republic the language is gender-specific and it is easy to inadvertently place adverts with requests for a *reditel* (a *male* director). When advertising in Germany, the gender associated with certain words in the language can imply the sex of the preferred candidate. This is permissible under the law but requires additional caveats to be placed in the advert clarifying equal opportunities. The text of adverts is traditional, and usually stresses a handwritten application.

Sourcing international managers

Once the attention of international managers has been engaged, attention shifts to the different sourcing routes open to the organisation. Several routes are open, but attention will be given to two of the most popular: Internet recruitment and international graduate programmes.

Internet recruitment

The Internet offers considerable potential as a source of recruitment for internationally mobile managers, small firms seeking specialist skills or larger firms wishing to demonstrate their presence. It is proving most useful for international graduate recruitment, attracting MBAs and PhD-level candidates, and for specific roles such as marketing and IT staff. A series of electronic recruiting products and services are re-shaping the job-finding process. E-recruitment (electronic recruitment) has the *potential* to *reduce the barriers to employment on a global scale.*

Using the Internet allows firms to:

- widen recruitment sourcing at relatively low cost
- attract applicants on a more specialised skills match (by encouraging applicants to use personal search-agent facilities)
- target sources of graduates, such as MBA career centres
- improve on traditional advertising approaches by targeting particular lifestyle or culture-fit groups (such as expatriates or people who make use of services similar to those provided by the host firm).

Job-posting and CV management services are accessible, and electronic sifting services are now being offered. For the applicant, access may be gained to employers, CV-posting facilities, online job fairs and international opportunities. For organisations beginning to manage expatriates as a cadre of professional international managers recruited only for single, short-term and specific assignments, the Internet may become a more formalised source of labour. Expatriates are perhaps the best-networked type of manager, and are often skilled at marketing themselves. Internet-based information or services allow potential expatriates to conduct more realistic job previews as they consider offers of appointment.

The problem for international personnel managers in using the web as a source of realistic job preview is that some of the data may be of questionable accuracy. Many people see expatriates as a source of money, and those who engage in dialogue may get unwanted calls. However, HR departments can make considerable use of the information accessed from the web. Detailed regional guides, resource packs for new employees, cultural guides and stories, acculturation training providers, HR advice for business start-ups and acquisitions, tax and financial service advice centres, employee protection services, relocation service providers, accommodation guides, cost of living data sites and databases of available expatriates can all be found. This can reduce the administrative burden and increases the realistic job preview in the period before a job offer is accepted.

A number of firms have started to use the Internet for international recruitment. It has received a mixed reaction but is slowly emerging as a useful tool. Some firms consciously choose to advertise internationally on the Internet – and so prepare their systems and procedures accordingly – whereas others find that without knowing it they are being exposed to international sourcing because publishers have 'tagged' their magazines onto the net.

When firms develop their own websites for international recruitment, statistics can be analysed to assess the success of the initiative. A difficult choice has to be made. If the website allows people to log on, more precise evaluation is possible, and one can track applicants through the process and see who was successful at what stage. However, applicants may feel they are being watched and be put off by the prospect of receiving unwanted contact.

Firms have faced a number of problems with web recruitment. The main effect is to increase the volume of applicants but, in a time of tight resources within HR, this is not always good news. Here are some of the problems that organisations can come up against:

- Targeting particular populations becomes difficult. For example, in running web pages in Singapore, applications are received from unexpected sources, such as Malaysia.
- Finding out that the company image or brand is not well known in untried markets.
- Quality becomes more variable and needs managing.
- It can move firms away from relying on targeted universities.
- Equal-opportunities issues might exist, in that most Internet-

sourced applicants still tend to be male and from a small range of countries.

⊕ People browsing the web pages may be mid-career surfers outside the target applicant group, or competitors, or people motivated more by curiosity than by a genuine intention to apply.

Many existing service providers do not yet have truly global coverage, and the web is currently not appropriate for all countries. However, looking to the next five years a lot more use will be made of web-based recruitment. International personnel managers should expect to see the following developments:

⊕ providers and competitors catering for different levels of vacancies
⊕ head-hunters allowing clients to search data more intelligently, with greater focus on skills-matching
⊕ services offering electronic sifting of applications
⊕ the technology to conduct interviews over the web using video calls
⊕ live-chat forums, with companies online at set times to answer questions
⊕ the possibility for candidates to offer presentations on the web.

International graduate programmes

Another form of international sourcing is the external recruitment of graduates into international roles. Organisations that have initiated international graduate recruitment programmes tend not to replicate the competencies that they use for experienced managers in these programmes. Instead, they have attempted to understand and manage graduates through the process of developing an international management career.

Several organisations have experienced significant problems with international graduate programmes, and these must be planned for:

⊕ This form of internationalisation acts as a slow-burning fuse, with only a gradual influence on the level of internationalisation.
⊕ Retention rates may prove to be embarrassingly low.
⊕ It may be difficult to encourage the receiving units to prepare themselves to be able to manage the new international recruits accordingly.

- Visa issues mean that the cadres have to be managed for a significant length of time. If graduates are international they may have to do their first two assignments in the UK, work abroad and then return to the UK. It may take up to 10 years to satisfy the visa requirements.
- Many organisations note that graduates are becoming more reluctant to move (as is also the case for established managers). For many graduates, quality-of-life issues and the home–work interface are becoming important considerations. Many are reportedly less willing to exchange as much of their own life in return for international experience as has previously been the case. To use the terminology of research work conducted on 'psychological contracts', they want the 'autonomy' and 'lifestyle' options. They are less willing to abdicate control over the timing of key life-events, and tend to be marrying earlier.
- This reluctance to be mobile is also changing attitudes to compensation, forcing organisations to be more responsive to individual circumstances. Compensation and benefits for graduates are becoming a major issue.

Selecting international managers

The final section of this chapter considers the ways in which two standard selection techniques – assessment centres and psychological testing – may be adapted for use in cross-cultural settings.

Assessment centres for international managers

Research into problems experienced using traditional selection techniques in different cultural settings suggests that where organisations rely on advanced techniques, or indeed even in the arena of the simple face-to-face interviews, the assessors may encounter significant problems. For example, one US multinational, when recruiting managers in Korea, found that interviewers had to be trained in cross-cultural awareness. It is the cultural norm in Korea, when asked a 'good' question, to keep silent as a sign of respect. The better the question, the longer the period of silence the candidate maintains. In US culture, if you ask a good question and receive silence, you do not attribute the behaviour to respect but to ignorance. Face-to-face interviews can therefore create quite distorted judgements. Similarly, when British Petroleum rolled out its cor-porate-wide OPEN competencies internationally in the early 1990s, they found that management competencies were transferable in terms of expressed purpose and key outputs, but the specific behav-ioural indicators used to evidence each competency needed adjust-ment to reflect cultural norms.[7]

''Assumptions made about candidate behaviour in the UK do not translate well abroad''

Given that assessment centres are generally seen to be one of the most robust and valid selection techniques, it should be expected that they would be used to assess competence for international man-agers. The key to cross-cultural assessment centres is to design the assessment process so that it is very adaptable to the local environ-ment in which it will be operated. Differences in the HR market-place often mean that the assumptions made about candidate behaviour in the UK do not translate well abroad. The need for adaptability argues against having overly structured exercises, and most structured tools (such as situational interviews and work simu-lations) have to be modified. Interviews are easy to adapt, but asses-sors also have to build as many anchors into the local market-place as possible in order to give the assessment process meaning. This involves a series of steps, from simple renaming of case-studies and scenarios through to adoption of local norms for psychometric instruments – and beyond.

British Airways has dealt with such issues in its General Manager Programme. This programme recruits internationally. Forty per cent of the graduates are non-UK, and countries such as Germany, France, the USA and Japan have sourced many graduates. The pro-gramme, which began in 1995, assesses a considerable number of graduates. In the latest round, 175 graduates attended the prelimi-nary centre, which involves group discussion and psychometric test-ing. Seventy-five graduates were selected for the final centre, which involves a fact-finding exercise and situational interview, and the final intake is around 25 graduates.

Modifying the Graduate General Manager Programme assessment centre process at British Airways

British Airways has now worked with a series of approaches to international graduate assessment: putting all graduates through the same process run in the UK, and conducting separate processes in major operating countries. Recently a customised process was run in Japan. The recruiters adopted the approach favoured in the UK, including situational interviews and group exercises.

Problems were however experienced in, for example, asking Japanese candidates to offer critical incidents in the interviews, to take the lead in group exercises, or to use the word 'I'. But experience soon showed that, with some modification to interviewer cues, exercise design and prompting, candidates were able to demonstrate the behaviours on which an assessment could be made: 'We were able to assess the indicators, and the process just unfolded in a different way.'

One problem is that assessors may use the positive and negative behavioural indicators as a check-list rather than as a set of indicators across which a judgement may be made. To address this, the local Japanese HR manager looked at the behavioural indicators and modified them so that they fitted the Japanese cultural context.

On the basis of this learning, BA is continuing to redesign the graduate selection process – for instance, the use of local language tests is being considered. Retention rates to date are very good. Attention is also being given to the problem of fitting candidates into the new culture or country of operation. Graduates are assigned a mentor (people who are local or who have worked in the country) to act as an 'interpreter' and provide support. Because all graduates are also selected according to the same specification, they are already internationally minded.

Psychological testing

The internationalisation of education and the movement of larger numbers of international managers have led to an increase in cross-cultural assessment. This may be conducted by organisations either within a single country or as a comparison of characteristics of managers across countries.[8]

❝Can 'culture-free', 'culture-fair' or 'culture-reduced' tests be developed?❞

The increase in assessment raises important questions. Can organisations use psychological tests fairly in multicultural settings? Do the psychometric properties of tests translate to different cultural groups? Can 'culture-free', 'culture-fair' or 'culture-reduced' tests be developed? Or, if tests do not translate from one culture to another, can new instruments be developed? The use of psychological tests has become an increasing problem in the international selection field.

In the pursuit of the global manager, organisations have to look outside their normal recruitment territory in order to benchmark interview candidates. Because they are aware that interviews or behaviourally based work simulations are subject to culturally different behaviours, on the part both of the candidates and the assessor, international HR managers may be tempted to use more testing and, at first sight, psychological tests may be seen as a way of avoiding the subjective bias of other options. Greater international mobility of candidates has indeed increased the demand for tests to be used on job applicants from a number of different countries, and most test producers now sell their products internationally.

The costs of cultural bias in psychological tests does not lie in reduced performance of the candidates.[9] They lie in the perceived stupidity of the assessment process and the effect on motivation. There is also the problem of fairness. Candidates whose poor English in the work situation hampers their test performance can find that they do not progress as well through internal selection systems. Such discrimination is inappropriate.

Countries also differ greatly in terms of the practices related to user qualification, legal and statutory constraints on test use and the consequences for those tested, and controls exercised over the use of tests. A number of well-known instruments have also appeared on the Internet in violation of copyright, creating obvious problems for test publishers but also giving cause for concern to international personnel managers in terms of breaches of test security and validity.

Many assumptions about the objectivity of psychological tests are false. Reasoning tests are, however, generally assumed to have cross-cultural equivalence because they tap traits and skills established across societies.[10] They are based on problem-solving tasks that can be translated in near-equivalent form.[11] There are some concerns about the effect of different national educational traditions, and there is some evidence of different performance among children in such specific abilities as spatial awareness due to perceptual cues in the environment, which may differ depending on the environment in which the children grew up. However, these are minor effects that do not generally affect cross-national performance at the managerial level. Nonetheless, managers from some societies may be insulted by the use of intelligence tests in a selection or assessment decision for an international assignment, given what they perceive to be their educational pedigree.

Cultural adaptation problems are particularly acute in the use of personality tests. The subtle interaction between language and culture means that neither English nor simple translation is effective as an international assessment medium when the goal is to establish core individual differences, as opposed to national norms. It is hard to distinguish whether there are real national differences in personality or whether differences in interpretation explain the observed differences. An example can be given by describing how one instrument – the Perception and Preference Inventory (PAPI) – has been examined for its cross-cultural relevance.

"Profiles from many personality instruments may simply reflect national differences in self-perception and interpretation"

Raw scores for national samples on the original PAPI instrument produced norms that suggested that the Scandinavians were very emotional, the French lazy, Norwegians unambitious and most European managers oblivious to detail. Finnish managers appeared to have a very low need to be noticed, whereas Danish managers were the opposite; Swedish managers came out as remarkably creative and conceptual, whereas British managers did not; and German managers were credited with a very low need for rules and supervision, as opposed to Norwegians, who had a high need. Without international trialing of these items, it is impossible to know whether such results reflect true differences in work style or reflect different levels of self-awareness, cultural biases towards self-assessment and scale use, or linguistic misinterpretation. Profiles from many personality instruments may simply reflect national differences in self-perception and interpretation.

In personality tests, short sentences or single words have to be translated to convey meaning. For example, the questionnaire item 'I work hard', although meaningful to British managers, is associated with the concept of toil for French managers.[12] It is therefore seen as a negative attribute. Once the notion of 'effort' was substituted for 'work', the efficiency of the item was re-established. Similarly, Finnish managers reject such words as 'rules', 'instructions' and 'directions' as authoritarian, preferring instead 'guidelines' and 'framework'.

International HR managers also face several practical dilemmas. If a French manager is coming to work in the UK, is it appropriate to test the manager against the French or the UK norm group? If you test the manager in English, is he or she immediately at a disadvantage?

There are no simple answers to the issues posed by the use of testing cross-national samples, and indeed many of the issues are ultimately irresolvable. If international HR managers insist on using such standardised tools as psychological tests, the degree of confidence in their accuracy has to be tempered, and other aspects of the recruitment and selection process should come into focus. HR managers must give more emphasis on the feedback process.

Conclusions

What lessons can be drawn about international recruitment and selection? This chapter and the research it outlines leads to 10 conclusions:

1   There is a tension between on the one hand the skills and competencies that organisations think they should be looking for when they recruit and on the other the skills that are actually needed to make a success of working abroad.

2   Downsizing and the impact of globalisation have meant that there are few resources available for international recruitment managers to play with in looking for the ideal candidate.

3   Longer-term, the solution has to be to internationalise the resourcing systems of the whole organisation.

4   Organisations tend to adopt one of three competing resourcing philosophies in internationalising their recruitment and selection: the psychometric; clinical risk assessment; and design of the assignment around the individual.

5   Organisations that choose to adapt their existing competency profiles to an international context can adopt one of two strategies: additive or enrichment strategies.

6   International graduate programmes are no 'quick fix' for organisations that need to increase their supply of international recruits.

7   In order to be successful, cross-national advertising requires an awareness of the cultural appropriateness of the techniques and media used.

8   New recruitment techniques, such as Internet recruitment, are altering the economics of the international selection process.

9   Assessment centres can prove a effective tool for international resourcing, but they require careful modification for an international setting.

10   There has been an increase in cross-cultural assessment based on psychological testing.

End-notes

[1]   BREWSTER C. (1991) *The Management of Expatriates*. London, Kogan Page.

[2]   BREWSTER C. *and* HARRIS H. (1999) 'The coffee machine system:

how international selection really works'. *International Journal of Human Resource Management*, in press.

3   SPARROW P. R. (1999) *The IPD Guide on International Recruitment, Selection and Assessment*. London, Institute of Personnel and Development.

4   CHAO G. T. (1997) 'Complexities in international organisation socialisation'. *International Journal of Selection and Assessment*. 5 (1). pp9–13.

5   SPARROW P. R. (1999) 'Abroad minded'. *People Management*. Vol. 5, No. 10. pp40–44.

6   GARRISON-JENN N. (1998) *The Global 200 Executive Recruiters*. San Francisco, CA, Jossey-Bass.

7   BOGNANNO M. *and* SPARROW P. R. (1995) 'Integrating HRM strategy using culturally-defined competencies at British Petroleum: cross-cultural implementation issues', in J. M. Hiltrop and P. R. Sparrow (eds), *European Casebook on Human Resource and Change Management*. London, Prentice-Hall.

8   VAN DE VIJVER F. J. R. *and* LEUNG K. (1997) *Methods and Data Collection for Cross-Cultural Research*. Sage, Newbury Park.

9   VAN DE VIJVER F. J. R. (1998) 'Cross-cultural assessment: value for money?' International Association of Applied Psychology, San Francisco, 10 August 1998.

10   VAN DE VIJVER F. J. R. (1997) 'Meta-analysis of cross-cultural comparisons of cognitive test performance'. *Journal of Cross-Cultural Psychology*. 28. pp678–709.

11   FELTHAM R., LEWIS C., ANDERSON P. *and* HUGHES D. (1998) 'Psychometrics: cultural impediments to global recruitment and people development'. British Psychological Society Test User Conference.

12   Feltham *et al* (1998). See note 11.

Chapter 6

International Compensation

Stephen J. Perkins and
Chris Hendry

> The world's largest companies are in flux. New pressures have transformed the global competitive game, forcing these companies to rethink their traditional worldwide strategic approaches. The new strategies, in turn, have raised questions about the adequacy of organizational structures and processes used to manage worldwide operations.
>
> Sumantra Ghoshal and Christopher A. Bartlett, 1998:3[1]

As pointed out by such commentators as Bartlett and Ghoshal, the strategic environment in which international companies must compete for sustained competitive advantage in the future is one where the emphasis is on organisational capability. Building, consolidating and releasing the potential of such capability is the primary challenge for those seeking to lead their enterprises into the twenty-first century. And at the core of such capability – the means by which it may be operationalised – are the organisation's people. In the global business, by definition, covering multiple territorial and cultural domains, diversity of interest and expectation need to be accommodated. As the symbolic and practical nexus between employer and employee – the point at which organisational and individual aspirations interface – reward is a key aspect that managers are charged with handling, as a contributory investment towards shareholder value creation.

In developing commentaries on employee reward, its role and purpose in the conduct of international business, we believe it is pertinent to ask whether one should focus on those things that trainee human resource managers need to learn, such as job evaluation techniques or interpreting market pay and benefits surveys, or should it be approached by drawing on analytical frameworks and theory from the social sciences, essentially putting managers and employees, their behaviour and interactions, under the microscope?

''The problem is that human beings frequently defy prescription''

Perhaps, in contributing to a management text, the answer is that the two are necessarily interdependent. Reward 'management' constructs, in isolation from their organisational and cultural setting, are purely static and impersonal. They tell us nothing about the employing company's relations with the world it inhabits. HRM literature is packed with prescriptions on the 'latest' mechanisms for structuring contractual considerations that may disappoint managers who try to inject them into the organisations they aspire to lead. The problem is that human beings frequently defy prescription, a situation that is magnified when the manager attempts to move outside the cultural norms of his or her domestic situation. And reward mechanisms, as Professor John Hunt of the London Business School[2] recently reminded us, 'At best ... are clumsy, invariably outdated and insensitive to individual differences.'

Our resolution is to attempt to situate reward mechanisms in the dynamic socio-economic context in which contemporary international firms must compete for investors, customers, partners and suppliers, as well as complying with multiple regulatory requirements in different territories. And, in particular, to explore the impact on these diverse interest groups of the relationships and interaction between firms, their managers and employees.

The story of international compensation is a story of change. This is driven by the same motor that is propelling business generally to exploit opportunities of widespread deregulation, technological innovation and increasingly competitive global markets. The practical implication of this environment is a requirement for businesses simultaneously to match their capabilities to customers' distinctive demands, and continuously to reduce operating costs. The other imperative is the fact that most foreign direct investment capital is derived from the English-speaking world (Monks, 1998[3]). The

Anglo-American corporate governance requirements accompanying this phenomenon, despite more pluralistic traditions in other economic systems, have meant more demanding requirements of investment institutions.

Considerations surrounding the development and enactment of reward management policy now concern identifying and integrating workforce skills and competencies up to the most senior levels, sourced from wherever they can add greatest value to strategy implementation, at the most economic cost. The emphasis is now on what international reward strategies deliver for corporate performance (Bradley, Hendry and Perkins, 1999[4]). As with reward policy in a domestic context, international compensation is increasingly contingent on organisational performance aligned to the returns to investors. It was not always thus. As Employment Conditions Abroad director, Alan Chesters,[5] has observed, historically there was a dichotomy between domestic and international reward approaches. He offers two reasons for this:

> First, unlike domestic appointments, international assignments have traditionally been perceived as temporary. As a result, reward considerations have concentrated on employee needs in coping with this temporary situation. Additionally, corporations have usually considered the corporate benefit from an international assignment to outweigh employee benefit resulting in an unbalanced negotiating scenario leading to a stronger focus on employee needs.

> At a broader level, there is often an absence of a strong market reference point and an unclear societal context with which to develop corporate driven strategies. As a result tactical considerations such as tax planning often overwhelm strategic considerations such as contribution and value.

The transnational solution

In their prescription of the emerging form of organisation and managerial style applicable to businesses trading outside domestic markets, Ghoshal and Bartlett (1998 – see end-note 1) suggest that, when managing across geographic borders, leading firms are increasingly being forced to adopt what they describe as a 'transnational' solution to the competitive challenge. The transnational corporation develops multidimensional strategic capabilities, which are a prerequisite if reward investment and operationalisation are to be fully integrated with, and aligned to, the pursuit of sustained competitive advantage in global markets. The transnational relates efficiency to global competitiveness, and rewards and recognises appropriate behavioural inputs and performance outcomes accordingly. Simultaneously, the transnational solution demands local responsiveness to diverse market conditions and continuous innovation, underpinned with suitable incentive and recognition programmes.

However, such apparent 'best practice' needs to be considered in the light of the existing human resource management superstructure, including why and how the transnational rewards and recognises its people individually and collectively in the different sectors of the corporation. Vested interest, conditioned expectations and managerial traditions in structuring and practising performance and reward management will be embedded in the organisation's culture. Such culture, research suggests, is likely to reflect a uni-directional organisational form, rather than the integrated settings configured as the transnational.

Classic multinational model

The evolution of the 'decentralised federation' (the classic multinational organisation, currently the most widespread model) was based in particular on the traditions of family-centred ownership among European businesses. The multinational offshoots of such businesses tended to be run by trusted appointees sent to manage overseas operations, with a remit to respond to the differences in the various territories invested in, with a tendency among those in charge locally to 'go native', integrating themselves with the national commercial and cultural scene.

Corporate financial systems were designed simply to facilitate accounting consolidation and to manage capital outflows and returns. The imperative was for each national unit, managed as a separate entity, to optimise its situation in the local environment. In such circumstances the focus for reward policy was naturally fragmented, in line with the commercial and organisational characteristics of the businesses concerned. Local market rates set the structure of compensation, and performance recognition and incentive plans were linked to the outcomes achieved by the quasi-independent business units. Taking a lead from most federal institutions, the operating principle was one of subsidiarity – a presumption that it is in the best interests of the constituent parts to address issues independently, with central initiatives only in instances where the local entities believe it will be to their advantage to permit them, or where the capability simply does not exist in an efficient or effective form.

Co-ordinated federations

> **“Unlike the European traditions, business in the USA has enjoyed a predominantly professionalised managerial population”**

An alternative version of this model – placing a greater degree of influence at the centre – is the co-ordinated federation. This model came into widespread operation in the years following the Second World War, with the spread of US influence around the globe. Unlike the European traditions, business in the USA has enjoyed a predominantly professionalised managerial population (as opposed to family owner-managers), and a governance structure favouring sophisticated management systems (in particular, financial), enabling significant delegation while maintaining overall corporate control within the 'home' market institution. The driving force for this 'internationalisation' approach was the identification of growth potential in the developing nations, where technical and managerial know-how was less advanced than in the 'developed' Western nations, and so the primary objective was the efficient transfer of capability, in return for income generation.

The culture of dependency meant that, in reward and recognition, there were clear distinctions between the value placed on parent company managers and staff, deployed on short- to medium-term expatriate assignments to transfer the requisite know-how (with a clear intention that 'localisation' would rarely apply), and to ensure compliance with corporate norms. Encouragement for capability development and alignment of interests, supported by appropriate reward systems, was limited. The emphasis tended to be on preserving expatriates' home standards, with company-provided (or at least company-funded) residential and attendant family facilities, security and clubs, to enable the expatriate community to maintain a 'home-abroad' community lifestyle (creating obvious divisions, especially where superior expatriate living was funded beyond that available to individuals on local-national incomes).

Such support was frequently supplemented with generous 'hardship' and incentive premia to induce the expatriate temporarily to interrupt his (it was generally men) career and personal life to 'help the natives abroad'. This sort of generosity was capable of being funded by internationalising corporations during the time when demand for their products and services was strong, and competition was limited.

The increasingly challenging commercial environment that emerged in the 1980s and early 1990s forced many of these firms – where US influence was particularly strong – significantly to re-think their business model, and with it the reward framework. Not only was there an increasing focus in corporate headquarters on cost control; it was also beginning to be recognised that long-term success in international markets would require executives and professionals, situated around the world, willing to align their talents and energies – in particular the valuable local intelligence networks – in the interests of corporate-value creation. Less divisive reward and recognition signals were slowly perceived to be essential if the re-engineering and rationalisation (of expatriate numbers, for example) were to be achieved while sustaining effective local operations.

Despite such signals, there is recent evidence that, for many US organisations operating internationally, divisive reward arrangements continue to dominate. Two-thirds of US subsidiaries have US-style executive compensation plans that are different from pay practices at their foreign parents', indicated by a survey of 109 large multinational corporations published in 1999 by consultants, Watson Wyatt.[6] The most common differences are that:

⊕ some types of incentive plans are available only in the USA
⊕ a broader base of employees is eligible for annual and long-term incentives in the USA

- ⊕ different performance measures apply to US executives
- ⊕ and incentive opportunities are higher in the USA.

Centralised hubs

The third organisational and management model for developing business in worldwide markets that has been identified is that which may be labelled the centralised hub. Ghoshal and Bartlett (1998 – see end-note 1) argue that this configuration is particularly suited the managerial norms and practices of Japanese companies. In such 'globalised' organisations, managers focused more on world markets than did their counterparts in either of the 'federated' organisations. However, the 'hub' model depended on centralised decision-making, suiting top managers and owners from cultures where group-oriented behaviour was the cornerstone of management systems. Such characteristics, depending on a complex system of personalised commitments and interdependencies, were notoriously difficult to transfer abroad. With headquarters management keeping a tight control on subsidiary operations, the flow of materials, knowledge and support was one-way, resulting in overseas-based international managers forming only a limited appreciation of local environmental differences against which commercial opportunities could be evaluated and exploited.

In such circumstances, careers and associated reward structures remained firmly embedded within the parent company, making almost clinical distinctions in some cases between 'corporate' and other staff. With access to development and recognition at the highest levels effectively closed off to non-country-of-origin employees, building a sense of reciprocal commitment and cohesion at levels throughout the global firm was problematic, to say the least. In contrast, the transnational business and organisational model is one attempt, acknowledging the increasing requirements to blend corporate efficiencies with a need for nimbleness in the face of increasingly discriminating customers in markets around the regions of the world, to follow the managerial exhortation often attributed to a prominent architect of the transnational form at Asea Brown Boveri, Percy Barnevik, simultaneously to 'think global – act local'.

HRM and strategic reward in the transnational

In implementing the transnational form of organisation and its accompanying managerial practices, companies recognise the particular contribution that HRM can make. In particular, HRM can facilitate resolution of the conflicting pressure that will continue to appear in balancing centralisation and decentralisation. Practical assistance may be given through policies that create an overarching corporate culture that encourages voluntary interdependency between devolved strategic business units, some of which increasingly comprise joint ventures and strategic alliances (so that ownership agendas are pluralised). A second key source of practical support for transnational functionality is policies to guide international executive development. As part of an integrated approach to HRM, reward and recognition processes have a useful role in each of these imperatives.

"It was even not uncommon for an unscrupulous manager to subvert the system by using it to dump a subordinate"

One example of simultaneously tackling these challenges, reported in research published by a team from INSEAD,[7] comes from international electronics firm Philips. In the past 'Expatriate assignments spelt career doom, distancing the exile from the headquarter politics of a successful career.' These perceptions enabled corporate managers to cream off their most talented individuals, and it was even 'not uncommon for an unscrupulous manager to subvert the system by using it to dump a subordinate'. In performance appraisals, managers 'can rate a poor performer as superior and appraise his potential unrealistically high, thereby making it easier to transfer the subordinate to another unit'. This kind of behaviour and exploitation of corporate HRM systems can act to create an 'us and them' culture between the centre and subsidiaries – in the way the centralised hub and co-ordinated federation models of international management did, where headquarters executives either failed to trust locally dispersed colleagues, or treated them as parochial. In return, local management culture tends towards retaining the best people and intelligence for 'proprietary' use locally, denying the corporate whole the vital competitive resources it needs to survive globally.

A fundamental success requirement is thus the capacity to mobilise corporate capability and associated resources, engaging all parties in voluntary co-operation in this endeavour. The INSEAD team concluded, 'Getting managers to understand the importance of mobility and the strategic reasons behind it is part of the solution. But the distinguishing characteristic of the leading companies is that they put their money where their mouth is . . . the corporate measurement and reward systems are behind it.'

At Philips, the measurement and reward system works in this way in relation to transnational career management:

> What we did is to officially announce to all managers responsible for larger units that they have an obligation to make available for corporate purposes a certain number of people. So the boss of the audio division gets a letter from the president telling him six months in advance that 'You will make ten people available this year'. Now if they don't, the remuneration of this boss is affected. Instead of getting a 100 per cent bonus on the basis of his results, he may only get 80 per cent, and the argument will be given to him that the 20 per cent is missing because he didn't supply the people.
>
> It is not so long ago that local managers said that they were responsible for their own operations, not for the rest of the corporation. Today it's a different story. When you can feel it in your bank account, your reaction is different.
>
> Paul Evans, Elizabeth Lank and Alison Farquar, 1989

The message is that compensation is a source of mobility facilitation. But the challenge for policy advisers in the transnational corporation is to find a balance between national and expatriate equities, between simplicity and complexity, while minimising the *ad hoc* incentives that are sometimes needed in circumstances where an internationally mobile posting is not an individual's first choice – and experienced executives frequently have a choice, if not with their existing company then with a competitor for scarce skills – and the organisation requires a special blend of experience and expertise, perhaps for a limited trouble-shooting role, before handing on to a successor where the motivation is more mutual. Integrating appropriate reward frameworks with clear norms and expectations around mobility requirements and then supporting individuals in managing their lifestyle preferences have been found to reduce resistance. This calls for novel thinking by employers about the definition of reward and its flexible application in respect of internationally mobile employees.

In March 1999, the American Compensation Association (ACA) reported a study by Organization Resources Counselors Inc (ORC) which found that 29 per cent of companies are currently localising reward arrangements for their expatriate employees, and 18 per cent have plans to do so. The explicit driver is cost reduction, but this is not the whole story.

The ACA report[8] quotes Geoffrey W. Latta, ORC executive vice-president, as stating:

> Although cost has traditionally been a driving factor in localization two other important reasons underlie a company's decision: the expatriate's own desire to remain abroad and corporate concern over pay equity between expatriates and local nationals.

There have been territories – China is an obvious example – where, in the past, pioneers such as truck manufacturer, Iveco, and Unilever, the Anglo-Dutch consumer goods group – who arrived in the 1980s – were willing to waive their usual investment criteria in order to stake out a position in the world's most populous nation and most promising economy. The second wave of companies – such as General Motors and many of the world's biggest banks – brought record flows of foreign investment, which fuelled China's rapid growth in the 1990s. Patience seems to have encountered an ebbing tide, however.

In the past year, what has been described as 'the China goldrush' (Harding, 1999[9]) has come to an end. Figures published in March 1999 show a 9.5 per cent decline in foreign direct investment in January and February, raising the likelihood that inward investment will fall in 1999 for the first time this decade. After nearly two decades in which companies have made allowances for China's idiosyncrasies, corporate attitudes towards the People's Republic are perceived to be changing: 'business has begun to treat China more like any other country', Harding concludes.

Making more businesslike decisions, of course, is not to say that foreign investors are deserting China. There are many companies still making money, for whom 'the China dream is still alive'. It seems that 'retrenchment is more common than retreat'. As part of this, attention has been turned to areas like employment costs, and international assignee rewards are put under the spotlight. Harding's research indicates that companies such as Unilever and Motorola have been cutting costs by 'replacing expensive expatriate employees with local staff'. This strategy has been implemented alongside moves to place new projects on hold. 'Last year, the value of foreign investment deals fell by 7 per cent, while the number of contracts signed was down to nearly half of what it was in 1995.' Despite the growing interest in 'localisation', however, only a quarter of those that Harding surveyed have a formal policy to deal with the transition. This suggests that a majority of organisations have yet to take action to ensure they implement changes in a fair and equitable manner.

‘‘The traditional overriding focus on 'expatriates' is being questioned’’

In some instances, though, we are aware that organisations are currently quite radically rethinking their approach to international employees and the way in which terms and conditions are defined. In particular, although there are increasing numbers of internationally mobile employees in major businesses and smaller organisations alike, reflecting a general business imperative to expand operations beyond the domestic market, the traditional overriding focus on 'expatriates' is being questioned.

Increasingly, on a regional basis there are issues as to whether special terms are required for expatriation or simply employment and reward arrangements that reflect flexibility and mobility. In particular, among the younger generation – among whom culture and language barriers, in Europe for example, are being overcome (especially with English as the language of business, and Anglo-Saxon corporate governance requirements following foreign direct investment) – moves between, say, Birmingham and Paris are increasingly regarded as little different to more conventional transfers between Glasgow and London.

''The mobile lifestyle reflects the new 'manager-as-coach' profile required of executives''

According to a senior HR practitioner in one major hi-tech business with pan-European business operations, 'movers and shakers' now tend to retain a family base in their country of origin, a *pied-à-terre* in Geneva, where the firm has its European headquarters, and spend most of their time travelling within the region. People find they are able to achieve work–life balance and 'quality' family time in this manner, without the traditional disruptions to spouses and offspring arising from expatriate relocation. The nature of telecommuting is changing too, so that the term does not simply reflect the quaint 'cottage industry' stereotype (although home-centred international working may apply in certain circumstances), but more the fact that individuals operate wherever they can connect, electronically, to the network. Corporate technology and support services are being wrapped around them to make this a reality. The mobile lifestyle also reflects the new 'manager-as-coach' profile required of executives, enabling 'high-touch' continuous interaction in support of members of their teams, the technology facilitating more efficient administration and co-ordination of activities throughout the boundary-less, de-layered structures.

Recognising international mobility aligned to core business model

Reward strategies in companies operating beyond their country of origin have been described as following an evolutionary path, relating to the purpose of the assignment and the expected corporate and employee benefit (Chesters, 1998 – see end-note 5). Rather than taking a linear trajectory, however, on the basis of individual firms' 'internationalisation', it may be argued that the driving force will be the organisational and managerial form prompted by the manoeuvres required of organisations as they seek to adapt to the realities of global market competition while continuing to be shaped by their cultural and governance heritage.

As businesses seek to move into the international arena, limited assignment of executives from the domestic business will be used for the purpose of business development opening up new markets. Once sales have developed beyond the optimal use of agents, however, international assignments provide an integrating force – albeit dependent more on personalised senior-level relationships than sophisticated management control systems – in further business development within the decentralised federation. Performance recognition will tend to be contingent on local rather than corporate interests.

As a local business becomes established, particularly in developing economies, shortages of particular skills may require the further use of international assignments. Under the co-ordinated federation business model, such initiatives may also be characterised by the use of international assignments to provide a more systematic monitoring and co-ordinating role for the corporate entity. Reward contingencies, at senior levels at least, will tend to include some recognition of corporate contribution. Under the centralised hub format, the bias of contingency reward is likely to be further in the direction of continuous corporate contribution, ensuring maximum utility of, and investment returns on, 'parent' capability. In each of the cases described – in particular at the top echelons of the business unit – there is likely to be a significant disparity between the philosophy underpinning reward management applicable to expatriates and local-national employees.

"Organisations that are serious about competing along transnational lines put their money where their mouths are"

The attempted initiation of transnational behaviour is exemplified by the use of international assignments when corporate learning is developed through skills transfer, not only from the centre but from and between substantial subsidiary operations. The emergence of a truly international business generates the need for an international management development process. As in the Philips example, organisations that are serious about competing along transnational lines 'put their money where their mouths are'. Both the awareness that managing an international business requires international experience and also that, in a situation of domestic skills shortage, talent is available internationally suggests the use of international assignments with the subsidiary purpose of 'growing' the necessary human resources. The development of a transnational organisation dictates, among other things, the development of a global perspective exemplified by the decentralising of key business activities away from a unitary geographic centre or headquarters; greater interdependence among the various nodes in the network; and the encouragement and reward additionally of international mobility and performance contribution to the whole, with the aim of enhancing organisational development in regional commercial blocs as well as in 'centres of excellence'.

Comparative corporate governance and the trickle-down effect on reward practice across international boundaries

A crucial factor influencing the approach that organisations adopt in setting reward philosophy around the world is the governance standard relevant to the dominant source of investment capital. Research by Colin Mayer, a corporate finance specialist, highlights the material differences between the models of corporate financing and consequent control that prevail in the contemporary Anglo-American economies on the one hand and the continental European and Asian capitalist systems on the other. Mayer points out that remarkable differences exist in respect of the ownership of companies across countries. There are, in particular, striking differences in the degree of *concentration* of corporate ownership. Mayer notes that in 80 per cent of the top 170 firms quoted on the French and German stock exchanges there is a single shareholder who owns more than 25 per cent of shares. In the UK, in only 16 per cent of the top 170 quoted companies does a single shareholder own more than 25 per cent of shares. In the USA, the figure is similar to that in the UK.

＂Who owns and controls corporate Europe?＂

Based on several studies that have looked at patterns of ownership in different countries, Mayer asserts that concentration of ownership is 'strikingly higher' in continental Europe and in the Far East than it is in the UK and USA. The reason given is primarily associated with ownership by families and other companies in the former regions. Banks are not particularly prominent in the ownership of firms in most countries and the degree of ownership by the state varies quite considerably across countries, Mayer says. His results draw heavily on an international comparison of corporate governance in nine European countries presently being undertaken by a team of economists operating as the 'European Corporate Governance Network'. The question that the network has been asking is 'Who owns and controls corporate Europe?'

The results of the Network's analysis demonstrate that a large proportion of the largest Continental European corporations are owned by a small number of individuals who exert an immense amount of power but derive little direct financial benefit. By contrast, UK and US corporations are owned by a large number of predominantly institutional investors, which typically have shareholdings of less than 5 per cent. Between them, they receive all corporate earnings but individually they have little direct control. The reason those with a concentration of ownership appear to place only a modest claim on their firms' earnings is that, at each point in a complex hierarchy of ownership (through off-shore enterprises and holding companies and the like), they share profits with outside investors. The rationale for this action is that in this way outside capital is brought in, thereby reducing the cost of the principal investor's investment.

The obvious question is why not make greater use of the public stock exchanges? The situation appears to come down to questions of the classic principal-agent relationship. The problem of aligning interests of owners and managers has, it seems, been resolved in diametrically opposite ways in the continental European and Anglo-American systems.

> The principal-agent problem is concerned with how one should trade off the incentive benefits of giving managers large shareholdings in their companies as against the risk sharing benefits of spreading shareholdings amongst a large number of investors. The answer in the UK and US has been to spread shareholdings amongst a large number of outside shareholders. Berle and Means pointed in the 1930s to the separation of ownership and control to which these dis-

persed shareholdings gave rise in the US. On the Continent, there is a similar separation of ownership and control but in exactly the opposite direction: control is highly concentrated in the hands of a small number of investors who have few financial claims on their firms. The principal-agent problem of companies operating in the same industries has therefore given rise to precisely opposite outcomes in different countries: in Continental Europe there is control without ownership of earnings, and in the UK and the US there is ownership of earnings without control.

Mayer, 1999[10]

The rationale for this situation is that concentration of control in the hands of a few investors who have little direct financial interest can be justified if they derive other benefits – what economists term 'private benefits'. In developed economies, private benefits evoke images of empire building, expense accounts and extravagance. The reality, in the situation outlined here, may be more prosaic. Mayer asserts that 'Private benefits are extensive and explain differences in control-ownership relations across countries.' In some cases – in developed economies – these may well be of the kind that the term 'corporate extravagance' implies – use of corporate jets, privileged lifestyles for capitalist bosses and their families. In the less developed nations they may degenerate into 'cronyism, corruption and crime'. For example, Mayer notes that 'The income of organized protection rackets in Russia – the Mafia – is estimated to be somewhere in the range of 25 to 40 per cent of Russian GNP. But even within the developed country context, there may be significant variations in the scale of private benefits.' In the developed economic systems of continental Europe too, high rates of corporation tax in Germany may encourage dissipation of earnings through expenses and extravagance.

At a less scandalous level, however, Mayer suggests the impetus towards private benefits may be a force for social good, promoting the brand name associated with a particular firm, hence enhancing its long-term commercial success and survival in a competitive environment. As he puts it:

> In particular, non-pecuniary benefits in the form of honour, prestige and family names provide cheap ways of overcoming capital market constraints. The dominance of family control in many countries may reflect the powerful incentives to invest that this form of corporate organization provides. I have suggested that the prevalence of private

benefits is a reflection of structural characteristics of corporate sectors as well as cultural differences between countries and that different systems may be best suited to different types of activities.

Mayer, 1999[10]

What are the implications for reward expectations across different geo-cultural boundaries? One may conclude that, whereas clear separation of the transactional and social contracts is the prevalent governance model in Anglo-Saxon economies, the evidence suggests a greater blurring – with social consequences that are deemed beneficial in the countries concerned – in many other parts of the capitalist world. Trickling down from this position at the top of corporate life, conditioning the aspirations and expectations of all those seeking their livelihoods from working in commercial organisations, it may be argued, are notions that the non-cash, 'social' (power, status, prestige) benefits associated with occupational position rank highly in people's portfolio of actual and psychological demands.

For this reason, reward policy makers should not be surprised to find a differential emphasis among people whom they inherit with a foreign acquisition or recruit on local labour markets. They should not simply dismiss such claims and expectations as anachronistic because they fall outside the accepted Anglo-American reward paradigm. Such reasoning and ideology are deeply ingrained in people's psyche, and carefully designed and executed strategies will be required if corporate standardisation in reward management, linked transparently to shareholder-aligned performance outcomes, is the aim.

The globalisation phenomenon and convergence theory

We have argued that methods of practising reward management, as part of an integrated approach to human resource management (HRM), need to be considered in the context of the corporate governance framework and associated organisation structure. The former depends on the various interests associated with ownership and control of the business in which they have invested financial capital. The latter is likely to be a product, at least in part, of strategic choices resulting from governance principles and the stage of development of the business in its commercial market place. However, this is a book about practising HRM in a setting that takes the organisation and its people beyond the country of origin. Therefore, another factor needs to be taken into account at the macro level – one that is currently the subject of intensive and controversial debate: 'globalisation'. In his 1999 Reith Lecture series for the BBC, the director of the London School of Economics, Professor Anthony Giddens, addresses this controversy head-on:

> The term may not be – it isn't – a particularly attractive or elegant one. But absolutely no one who wants to understand our prospects and possibilities at century's end can ignore it. I travel a lot to speak abroad. I haven't been to a single country recently where globalisation isn't being intensively discussed. In France, the word is *mondialisation*. In Spain and Latin America, it is *globalizacion*. The Germans say *Globalisierung*.
>
> Giddens, 1999[11]

The global spread of the term, Giddens says, is evidence of the very developments to which it refers. As little as 10 years ago the term was rarely seen, either in the academic literature or in everyday language. In his words, 'It has come from nowhere to be almost everywhere.' In view of the term's sudden popularity, it is not really surprising that its meaning is not always clear, or that people are reacting to it in ways that are not always positive. Giddens summarises that globalisation has something to do with the thesis that we now all live in one world. But he invites us to ask in what ways exactly, and is the idea really valid? Such a challenge certainly needs to be addressed by those purporting to influence their organisation's attitude and decision-making in respect of business-aligned rewards, prosecuting convergence over diversification, or vice versa.

❝International mergers and acquisitions in 1998 increased 60 per cent over 1997❞

The acceleration in cross-border investments from mergers and acquisitions is another driving force behind the arguments of those who see convergence as the ultimate outcome of global business evolution. International mergers and acquisitions in 1998 increased 60 per cent over 1997 – the value reached an all-time high of $544.31 billion, according to the KPMG Corporate Finance Survey of global take-over activity.[12] The survey draws on data from more than 5,000 cross-border M&As and investments during 1998, worldwide. Despite the recent economic and political turbulence in Asia Pacific, Central and Eastern Europe and Latin America, 1998 remained 'a record year'. But it appears the average size of cross-border transactions has increased sharply, based on the decrease in the number of deals in 1998 (from 5,775 in 1997 to 5,153).

Remaining with the discussion framework offered by Giddens, we may examine the potential for globalisation of reward policies and practice, and associated attempts by managers to secure the commitment and motivation of employees in the various territories in which they wish to transact business, aligned with short- and longer-term objectives. It tends to follow that, in responding to the highly competitive conditions in which organisations must trade in the contemporary world economy, managers, in addition to the aims for their workforce outlined above, will wish to achieve this with a level of flexibility of employment relations such that the organisation may be free to adapt its employee resource in a relatively unconstrained manner. Moreover, the organisation's beneficial owners will be likely to expect that its management will seek to minimise the degree of financial risk to which their asset is exposed. Hence a prevailing popularity of making rewards for everyone employed by the firm contingent on results, to minimise fixed costs.

As we have observed, much of the investment capital for business development around the world tends to emanate from the English-speaking countries, and hence is accompanied by Anglo-American corporate governance expectations among owners, conditioning the approaches adopted by their managerial agents. This suggests that, in setting reward policy and practice, the driving force will be experience of the Anglo-Saxon business enterprise. To many living outside Europe and North America, the globalisation of business (and with it HRM and reward policy) looks uncomfortably like Westernisation – or, perhaps, Americanisation, since the USA is now the sole superpower. Many of the most visible cultural expressions of globalisation are American – Coca-Cola and McDonald's exemplifying this phenomenon. Most giant multinational companies are based in the USA, and those that are not all come from the rich countries. In Giddens' analysis:

A pessimistic view of globalisation would consider it largely an affair of the 'industrial north', in which the developing societies of the south play little or no active part. It would see it as destroying local cultures, widening world inequalities and worsening the lot of the impoverished.

Giddens, 1999[11]

A superficial conclusion is that the practice of reward management will tend towards convergence, irrespective of where it is to be located. This is part of the globalisation thesis. But, as Giddens demonstrates, there are what he terms the radicals and the sceptics engaging in the controversy.

According to the sceptics, all the talk about globalisation is only that – just talk. Whatever its benefits, its trials and tribulations, the global economy isn't especially different from that which existed at previous periods. The world carries on much the same as it has done for many years ... The notion of globalisation, according to the sceptics, is an ideology put about by free-marketeers who wish to dismantle welfare systems and cut back on state expenditures. ... The radicals argue that not only is globalisation very real, but that its consequences can be felt everywhere. The global marketplace, they say, is much more developed than even two or three decades ago, and is indifferent to national borders.

Giddens concludes that both the radicals and the sceptics on globalisation have set their lens on the world with a rather narrow focus. Although he has no hesitation in saying that globalisation, as we are experiencing it, is 'in many respects not only new, but revolutionary', he believes that neither the sceptics nor the radicals have properly understood either what it is or its implications for us. Both groups see the phenomenon almost solely in economic terms. This is a mistake, Giddens believes – and we would agree with him. Globalisation is political, technological and cultural, as well as economic. This conclusion is particularly important when considering reward management. While the legal and contractual underpinnings of the relationship between employees and organisations are to the forefront, if managers are to deliver previously rehearsed outcomes from their engagement of people, they cannot neglect to consider the implications of social and personal factors, as conditioned in diverse ways, based on the regional and national contexts from which they are recruited. As Richard Hyman, of the University of Warwick, asserts in a recently published essay exploring the tension between

economic internationalisation and national industrial relations systems:[13] 'The notion of "globalization" identifies real and substantial
developments which challenge established forms of employment
regulation, but these developments are contradictory and create new
possibilities for strategic intervention.'

Disparities in reward at the top

In 1998, journalist Tony Jackson[14] asked about comparisons in
executive earnings in different countries. He found that 'data are to
hand from the international consultants Towers Perrin. Based on its
own experience, the firm offers estimates of CEO compensation versus
factory wages in medium-sized companies across 23 countries.' The
UK is situated in the middle of the range, CEOs earning 18 times the
average wage of a manual employee. The USA, where CEO compensation is vastly bigger in absolute terms, comes only a little higher,
with a multiple of 24. As Jackson observes, 'The real eye-openers are
at the two extremes of the scale. The multiple in Venezuela is 84, and
in Brazil 46. In Japan and Switzerland it is 10, and in South Korea 8.'

The countries at the top of the scale tend to be comparatively poor
and those at the bottom are mostly rich. Those above the UK have
an average gross domestic product (GDP) per capita a quarter lower
than the British: those below – mostly from Europe – have an average GDP slightly higher. However, social insurance and purchasing
power need to be taken into account.

> The figures for CEO pay disguise the true picture across countries,
> being stated before tax. Broadly speaking, the more unequal the
> country, the lower the tax rate on top salaries. The average for coun-
> tries above the UK on the scale is 33 per cent, and for those below,
> 48 per cent. So screamingly high inequality in pay, as in Latin
> America, is associated with poverty and social division. Relative
> equality, as in Sweden or Germany, is associated with wealth but a
> high level of state involvement in the economy.
>
> Jackson, 1998[14]

Again, reward policy makers need to be sensitive to the expectations
and intricacies flowing from this diversity of practice. This sensitivity will need to be reflected in reward policies both for application
in multi-domestic employment contracts and also in managing the
consequences of transnational mobility requirements.

International compensation in context

We have argued that international reward policy and practice must be approached using a wide-angled lens if practitioners are to develop strategies that reflect the dynamics of developments in world markets, including governance, organisation, inter-cultural and globalisation possibilities. The 'contextual' framework (Figure 1) attempts to synthesise the illustration that reward policies and practices are impacted by external factors, for example, by legislation or union involvement through a direct influence channel, as well as by the organisation and its corporate strategy. This prompts the suggestion that, in considering available approaches to investing in

Figure 1
CONTEXTUAL INTERNATIONAL
REWARD MANAGEMENT FRAME

Environment   **Organisation**

Supranational context ——————— **Corporate strategy**
European Union, OECD, etc.

National context ————————— **Performance management
strategy**

Politico-legal
Economic
Cultural
Social
Patterns of corporate
   ownership (active stock
   market?)
	Integration
	Devolution to line
	Involvement policies
	Reward structure(s)
	Pay-performance system(s)

**Reward management
practice**

National reward context

Fiscal regime
Professional/employment
   markets
Trade unions
Employment relations
   (industry/firm focus?)
	Performance appraisal
	Pay level adjustments and
	   bonus awards
	Collective-individual focus
	Communication
	Explicit-implicit total
	   compensation balance

Brewster[15]

people through rewards and incentive payments, international managers need to be aware of, and adapt their actions to, a blend of supranational, national and local environments. They must do so in the context of creating the right cocktail of reward structures and systems to stimulate and support the release of their firm's people potential, in line with its unique corporate characteristics and goals, to achieve sustainable success.

Significant challenges in undertaking compensation analysis internationally

Of course, in order to develop an appropriate reward cocktail relevant to the transnational and supporting a focus on performance interdependence, corporate practitioners need access to sound intelligence. In a recent internal William M. Mercer survey of 30 large US multinationals it emerged that, when it comes to global pay issues, a key priority for corporate HR managers is to obtain quality data that are easily accessible and reasonably priced. Brown (1998[16]) argues that 'the need to be competitive and knowledgeable about local market practices in a given country is often important to global companies and has a direct impact on the company's growth and profitability'. But there are important differences in both the availability and the quality of pay benchmarking data between emerging and developed markets.

> For many organisations, the quest for quality data around the world not only is a challenging experience, but occasionally a frustrating one as well. This is particularly true for compensation professionals who are used to working in the United States, the United Kingdom and a few other developed markets where the availability, depth and quality of data far exceed that in other markets.
>
> Brown, 1998[16]

Brown summarises the challenges, which she argues are generally faced by firms operating transnationally, as follows:

- selecting the right peer group and determining the degree of data specifically needed
- finding the right source of data
- determining what elements need to be analysed and what information is required to complete the task
- interpreting the data.

The advice is to ascertain the cost of data in each market to set reasonable budgets. A 'perfect' solution is rarely possible and the HR professional must accept the need to compromise on the basis of balancing priorities. For example, is it critical to secure an absolute focus on the 'right' comparator group, irrespective of the often escalating price tag, or is it possible to rely on more broadly-based survey data, to facilitate informed managerial judgement? Decisions will be possible only in the context of specific business conditions, guided by market and investment priorities.

The international assignee's perspective

Despite a more cost and performance orientation and greater openness to securing talented employees from a variety of sources around the world, organisations cannot focus exclusively on corporate considerations. Although no longer biased towards creating a 'protected' – even ghetto – experience for internationally mobile executives, firms need to take into account the likely aspirations that employees will bring to the experience. Such expectations may be informed by the availability of guidance from a variety of external sources, beyond a corporate literature extolling the virtues of accepting an 'expatriate' posting and vicarious experience from fellow employees already seasoned on the international mobility circuit. The professional services firm, KPMG, suggests that, in considering an international assignment, employees evaluate the opportunity in terms of three critical success factors:

⊕ What is the financial impact to you and your family?
⊕ What personal adjustments must be made by you and your family?
⊕ What lasting impact will the assignment have on your career?

The KPMG consultants set out an explanation of the way in which internationally mobile employees are likely to see their compensation and benefits structured. They say that internationally mobile employees should approach each assignment by evaluating both the current and long-term financial impact of the assignment.

> On a current basis, the major items to review are your expenditures for goods and services, housing, taxes, transportation, education, etc. How will the assignment and your employer's compensation package maintain your spending levels? Will you be required to incur

duplicative costs at your home location as well as the assignment site?
From a long-term perspective, you should review the impact, if any,
on your ultimate retirement benefits, and the potential for increased
compensation once you have international experience

KPMG, 1998[16]

So compensation issues are firmly positioned first in terms of the
ability of individual employees to maintain their lifestyle – not only
during a period outside their country of origin, but also longer-term
(particularly important in this era of self-managed careers and self-
financed retirement support), and second in terms of the career
enhancement gains, with a particular reference to the likelihood that
proven international competence will lead to enhanced earning
potential.

In firms still in the early stages of internationalising their activities,
there may be a number of myths circulating about the likely implications for those employees accepting postings outside their country
of origin. These tend to be (mis)informed by practices that may have
applied in the past, where international postings were unusual for
members of the mainstream professional workforce. The most prevalent of these is the notion that employees working abroad will be
able to save a significant proportion of their income from employment. As KPMG (1998) point out, 'although this may have been
typical several years ago, the tide appears to have turned towards
more fiscal responsibility by multinational employers'. KPMG
observe that:

> In the initial years of global expansion and development, many
> companies over-compensated assignees when entering foreign mar-
> kets. Over time, these programs have been fine-tuned to more
> accurately reflect global living costs and the employers' overall com-
> pensation philosophy. Those employers that have adopted the balance
> sheet approach in its purest form of cost equalization do not intend
> to provide incentives through the assignment allowances. Although
> some assignees do save a significant portion of their income while
> overseas, this usually occurs only if the assignee decides to live below
> the standard his or her employer is trying to help him or her
> maintain.

KPMG, 1998[16]

Despite increasing prudence in setting international assignment
compensation, there is evidence that a number of employers still

continue to pay incentives such as foreign service or mobility premiums and location-specific 'hardship' premiums to induce employees to accept overseas assignments. It seems that 'federated' and 'hub' managerial philosophies are still being widely reflected in international compensation practice

Conclusions

Approaches to employee motivation, reward and recognition, to be effective, need to be developed so that they are aligned to the dynamic business and organisational priorities of international firms. In some analyses they may in fact inform the refinement of such priorities around core business competencies. This will reflect the fact that companies operating within international markets are at varying stages of development, from simple export operations and the use of local agents through to comprehensively globalised firms operating a complex web of substantive businesses, joint ventures and alliances across a majority of the world's economies.

Such analysis may be operationalised to set a context for developing employee motivation, reward and recognition strategies at the leading edge. Paralleling marketing strategies, to secure global-scale benefits combined with local sensitivity, the description may be refined to suggest that, when operating internationally, firms may be best advised to adopt a multi-local or transnational orientation. This comprises a global perspective on the drivers of reward and recognition policy, including an overall philosophy, but with the flexibility to anticipate the commercial and organisational setting in which it will be applied, whether on a regional or country basis. The emphasis is on leveraging competence wherever it may be mined and applied, focusing performance goals around reciprocity and interdependency of people and business units irrespective of their physical or organisational circumstances.

"It is important not to lose sight of the continuities that exist between domestic and international business""

Such an approach does not imply simple conformity with legal and regulatory demands. While such compliance is a taken-for-granted requirement, organisations will wish to determine the framework for reward and recognition investment contingent on dynamic business priorities. Moreover, it is important not to lose sight of the continuities that exist between domestic and international business, and which can be used to 'propel a firm into international activity' (Hendry, 1994: 42[17]). There are a number of reward policy contingencies to be taken into account; in particular, as noted already, the organisational form, whether federated, centralised or effectively transnational. This will have affect stakeholder performance expectations currently and for the future, with implications for performance management. Reward and recognition approaches will require qualitative attention, for example, to reflect changing resource priorities between expatriate and localised workforces. Issues for particular consideration in that context will be contingent on the imperatives for knowledge transfer at a corporate and cross-border level.

Competitive business strategies are an important contingency, depending on the organisation's core capabilities to position itself within the competitive market-place; also, to reflect decisions ranged between opting for premium service (with associated investment requirements to deliver medium- to long-term revenue appropriation) on the one hand, to cost minimisation (with early and continuing attention to the bottom line) on the other. An organisation's assessment of market pressures will be an important determinant of strategic direction in this context. The implications of the balance between external *versus* the internal context for business and HRM operation will also be a material consideration.

Organisations are discovering that they must integrate aspirations to standardise reward systems intended to communicate strategic business priorities and to provide a sense of 'corporate glue', with the imperative to accommodate diverse cultures, values and market practice (Perkins, 1997[18]). Fine-tuning and sensitivity will be required to support the firm's competitive interests. Fiscal considerations will also apply, and decisions will be necessary as to whether an emphasis on creative fiscal management has equal or greater priority for the organisation than the scope for creative management to attain its broader HRM goals.

Exemplary international firms are now setting a more appropriate balance between reward and recognition policies designed to encourage sustained performance among both internationally mobile and local employees. While internationally mobile staff, whether global or third-country national (or regional), are set to increase, they will be different in character from traditional expatriates. Also, firms with global aspirations are recognising the political and commercial imperative to demonstrate diversity in organisational character, reflecting this in their HRM policy focus, including areas of reward management. As a key part of the organisation's investment in people, channelled to communicate organisational priorities, reward and recognition must be managed to inform and support appropriate international business strategy intentions.

End-notes

[1] GHOSHAL S. *and* BARTLETT C. A. (1998) *Managing across Borders: The transnational solution*. Revised edn. London, Random House Business Books.

[2] HUNT J. W. (1999) 'Reward systems and disincentives'. *Financial Times*. 21 April.

[3] MONKS R. A. G. (1998) 'The corporate cost of capital: the informing energy of corporate governance'. *Inaugural Lecture – City University Business School*. 9 November.

[4] BRADLEY P., HENDRY C. *and* PERKINS S. J. (1999) 'Global or multi-local? The significance of international values in reward strategy', in C. Brewster and H. Harris (eds), *International HRM: Contemporary issues in Europe*, London, Routledge.

[5] CHESTERS A. (1998) 'Reward in an international context'. *Journal of Professional HRM*. Issue 10, January.

[6] WATSON WYATT (1999) *Adapting to Succeed: Incentive practices at US subsidiaries of foreign parents*. Watson Wyatt Worldwide.

[7] EVANS P., LANK E. *and* FARQUAR A. (1989) 'Managing human resources in the international firm: Lessons from practice', in P. Evans, Y. Doz and A. Laurent, *Human Resource Management in International Firms*. Basingstoke, Macmillan Press.

[8] AMERICAN COMPENSATION ASSOCIATION (1999) 'Employers localize expatriates to reduce costs'. *ACA News*. March.

9 HARDING J. (1999) 'End of the China goldrush'. *Financial Times*. 25 March.

10 MAYER C. (1999) Inaugural Lecture, Said Business School, University of Oxford, February.

11 GIDDENS, A. (1999) *Globalisation* http://bbc.co.uk/hi/english/static/events/reith_99/default/htm

12 AMERICAN COMPENSATION ASSOCIATION (1999) 'Global cross-border deals increased in 1998'. *ACA News*. April.

13 HYMAN R. (1999) 'National industrial relations systems and transnational challenges: an essay in review'. *European Journal of Industrial Relations*. Vol. 5, Issue 1. March.

14 JACKSON T. (1998) 'The fat cats keep getting fatter'. *Financial Times*. 1–2 August.

15 BREWSTER C. (1995) 'Towards a "European" model of human resource management'. *Journal of International Business Studies*. First quarter. pp1–21.

16 KPMG (1998) *Transferring Abroad: The 50 most common concerns*. International Headquarters, KPMG.

17 HENDRY C. (1994) *Human Resource Strategies for International Growth*. London, Routledge.

18 PERKINS S. J. (1997) *Internationalization: The people dimension*. London, Kogan Page.

Chapter 7

International HR: Career Management

Yochanan Altman

An international career – can you do it single-handed?

I'm writing this chapter with my left arm in a sling, temporarily incapacitated. In the olden days, when texts were first handwritten and then typed by a dedicated secretary, that would hardly have posed a problem, because I am right-handed. In the contemporary world of PC technology, however, in which everyone is expected to master the art of typing their own manuscripts, it's no longer so simple. To my surprise, my natural right-handed dominance is much less relevant now than it used to be: you need both hands to manage a PC. One literally can't do it single-handed.

It then occurred to me that there's a lesson here which might be of relevance to the topic of international careers. In the course of our professional development we tend to cultivate our strengths; we are encouraged to capitalise on our natural dominance. One becomes an expert in a field: finance, marketing, human resources or general management. No one (yet) has become an expert in internationalism.

More often than not, we are posted overseas because we proved competent in one area or another. So, we carry with us our well-developed, well-ingrained competence and we try our hand. And, more often than not, it doesn't quite work. The way we do finance, marketing or human resources differs across cultural borders – even more so for general management. We find out (often at considerable cost) that what works at home doesn't apply abroad. Nor is experience gained in one culture easily transferable to another. I have come across many who, say, made a smooth transition from England to Switzerland but, moving on to France, found it extremely difficult.

Dominance equates with hindrance to learning. Being accustomed to using both my hands, which is essential when ordinarily using a PC, I'm now left coping with only one. In order to manage in the new situation, I have first to *unlearn* what I know so well. That's quite difficult – not merely the technical aspects, but also the wider ramifications. It affects my self-confidence, which centres on my competencies: it annoys and frustrates me not to be able to accomplish a 'simple' task. It certainly affects my productivity. And I have to accept that, 35 years after mastering the keyboard, I am back to being a novice.

Yet I understand what is happening to me, and that helps. I can clearly articulate the reasons for my difficulties and can attribute them causally to a precise source. Furthermore, I know that I am in a temporary 'abnormal' set-up, and so does everyone else in my surroundings. I also have a clear idea when things will turn back to 'normal' again.

❝Whether in Penang or Paris, the mix of familiar and new can be bewildering❞

Not so in an international career. Whether in Penang or Paris, the mix of familiar and new can be bewildering. The host of diffused, intricate and complex stimuli that bombard you may be construed, literally, as mind-blowing. Substandard performance, a common malaise of working in a foreign milieu, is not normally attributed to the 'novelty' factor, neither by the person concerned nor by others. And there is no guarantee that a return to 'normal' is possible. We no longer think of expatriation as a stand-alone situation, but increasingly view expatriation and repatriation as one complex issue.

International careers are not merely a variant of the usual career path or another step up the ladder. The issues raised by international careers are specific to the complexities embedded in working across cultures and in the need to operate outside one's natural habitat.

International careers: the state of the art

With globalisation rapidly reaching the status of a cliché and the prevalence of so many executive positions with 'international', 'worldwide' and 'European' tacked onto them, we had better start with a classification exercise.

As a main criterion I would propose to distinguish between levels of intensity (or frequency) in international careers. If we take that as the principal frame of analysis, then five options,[1] plus an additional residual option, seem to encapsulate well the variety of approaches to international management careers. The titles aim to portray, in a metaphorical way, some critical features of each option.

The empire option

Antecedents

Some of the leading world multinational corporations (MNCs) may be readily associated with this model. A key feature is their having a history and tradition of globalisation. International careers are part and parcel of the normal career path of 'corporate wo/men'. Indeed, they constitute the essence of a corporate career. Size matters, too: a small company may not be an empire, by definition. And time is of relevance. In the typical course of development, the period required to reach an empire state will be measured in decades rather than years. Consequently, a career in an empire would comprise of a string of international assignments (even though some may be spent in the person's home country).

Embedded values

Implicit to the management of these giants is the willingness of employees to move regularly from location to location. Unwillingness to do so is as good as kissing goodbye to one's career prospects. Adaptability and cultural openness are the building-blocks of empire-minded careerists.

Organising principles

For an employee of the empire organisation, global trotting becomes a way of life. Expatriation and repatriation are at the core of the organisational process. The notion of a 'home base' is drastically losing its meaning, for headquarters may be geographically located literally 'nowhere', that is, in a small provincial town where few, if any, of the employees have any personal roots. Take the case of Caterpillar in Peoira, Illinois, or Thomas Cook in Peterborough, England. The home base represents only a fraction of the corporation's business activity, as with Nestlé (Switzerland), Ericsson (Sweden), Shell (UK/Netherlands), to name but a handful of well-known examples.

The colonial option

Antecedents

The colonial option is characterised by an organisational culture imbued with an ingrained obligation – a sense of duty to 'God, King and Country' (ie the corporation). Historically, this was the establishment model for the colonial culture of world domination by European nations in the eighteenth and nineteenth centuries. It is now common, among others, in Japanese and Korean MNCs, including most electronics and car manufacturing giants, although Nissan, for one, allows its subsidiaries an unusual degree of autonomy and decision-making powers.

Embedded values

An overseas posting is seen as a mission away from the centre of the civilised world, away from the central power base of the corporation. One would typically undertake this either out of sheer 'patriotism' or lack of choice. The strong bonding with the home base ensures continued loyalty and inoculates people against 'going native'. Some may spend most of their career in overseas missions on behalf of the mother company.

Organising principles

In exchange for the necessary evils of an overseas posting, the company provides a comprehensive back-up package for its people and creates for them, perhaps in collaboration with other companies from the same cultural origin, a 'home from home', a tight community of expatriates, with typical services such as schooling, churches, social clubs, information (journals and radio) and cultural activities – even specialised shopping centres.

The dialectics of home–abroad are the essence of the organisational career path. Dispersed with frequent episodes of service 'abroad',

followed by sojourn 'at home', one's international career is paradoxically anchored in a precise geography. Here is the quintessential
Brit, French or Japanese international careerist, whose personal and
cultural loyalties are unequivocally placed with the home country
and home company.

The colonial option may be more comfortable for the international
careerist who is less adaptable and perhaps not a natural polyglot.
Such values as cultural openness and flexibility, critical for success in
the empire case, may be less stressed in the colonial company.

The professional option

Antecedents

This model fits the company that cannot, or does not wish to, build
on either of the two previous options, and thus chooses to hire international experts to act as its 'Foreign Legion' troopers. Hence this
option suits the international careerist who does not wish to attach
him- or herself to a particular job, geography or company. Employer
and employee alike are driven by a market-oriented culture, which is
fluid and *ad hoc*, and promotes an explicit 'give and take'
relationship.

Embedded values

The core identity of the international careerist is professionally
anchored. Professional challenges punctuate one's career path.
Hence, opting out for another job or changing company should only
be expected. It would not be unusual for the 'professional' international careerist to get into conflict with the corporate. We hear
again and again of clashes between the 'foreign legionaries' of the
International Monetary Fund (IMF) and the World Bank as they take
sides with the local community against their paymaster.

Organising principles

This model is in line with the now famous 'shamrock' organisation[2]
in which there is a core (internals) and a periphery (externals). The
'foreign legionaries' are the perpetual outsiders, although one may
rise to become an honorary internal or indeed transfer to an internal
core career path. Gillette, an advocate of this approach, endures high
levels of personnel turnover, (about 40 per cent). Yet it does fit to a

context where 75 per cent of its employees and more than 70 per cent of its customers live outside the USA.

So these are the three frequent configurations of an international career. We are likely to find the empire, colonial and professional employees working for larger MNCs where spending a long time abroad is only to be expected. Frequent travel overseas, indeed globe-trotting, is a usual feature of work at managerial level. The next two options are less intense variants of international careers, in which the expectations to spend time abroad and otherwise engage in world-wide activities are significantly lower.

The peripheral option

Antecedents

Organisations that operate in special niche markets and are far from the mainstream in either geography or business activity belong to this category. The minor MNCs in smaller countries are a prime case. For example, Israeli corporations such as Teva or Elbit, although fairly large in local terms (some 3,000–5,000 employees), are too small to become global empires; nor do they have a colonial tradition. Physically, these organisations are relatively 'isolated' from the world. Size matters here as well, because larger organisations may overcome the handicap of geography, whereas smaller ones commonly follow this option.

Embedded values

An in-bred propensity to crossing borders is found among companies that operate in niche environments or that provide a highly special-ised product or service. Their positioning may be described as 'peripheral', in that they are on the margins (sectorially, geographi-cally). The necessity to operate globally is strategically of the essence and hence a 'pro-foreign' attitude prevails here. For these companies, the critical success factor lies in their ability to 'export' themselves, to transfer know-how and to expand in foreign markets. Nokia, based in Finland, is a prime example.

Organising principles

International careerists in the peripheral model welcome overseas assignments precisely because they are rather rare and they open up opportunities, as well as providing change and variety (and so help to differentiate oneself in the market-place). International careerists here tend to be open to new experiences, tolerant of unfamiliar environments and forbearing in the face of the hardships of cultural diversity. We would expect them to be responsive to an offer of an overseas posting and perhaps to be less concerned about issues of remuneration and compensation.

The expedient option
Antecedents

‘‘One is either pro-foreign or one ain’t’’

The majority of organisations, however, find themselves in a dilemma. There are not many companies that may boast the cloak of 'empire'. Not every US company is an IBM, a Coca-Cola or McDonalds; nor is every European company as mighty as Shell, Daimler Benz or Rhône-Poulenc. The colonial model suits larger companies with ample resources, because the investment it requires for its activation is considerable. The peripheral model, on the other hand, is something of a 'given': One is either pro-foreign or one ain't. The company that cannot opt for one of the above models is likely to 'try to do its best'; therefore we term this last option the 'expedient' model.

Embedded values

From an international careerist's standpoint, the overseas assignment poses a risk, yet sometimes one well worth taking, particularly when faced with no other option, or if one's career is faltering. Unlike the empire or the colonial models, here an overseas assignment is optional. As an uncommon occurrence, each opportunity will be judged on its merit. Paradoxically perhaps, taking up such an assignment may be real proof of commitment and motivation, because it is not part of the mainstream career, and bearing in mind its associated hazards.

Organising principles

Lacking in basic resources and without adequate infrastructure overseas, the company following this model is likely to be opportunistic in its approach, that is, expedient, although some may opt for an *ad hoc* approach as a matter of strategy! So we would expect minimal investment in preparation, induction and the more mundane aspects of relocation (housing, schooling, information). The international careerist of the expedient model is likely to be expected to tough it out, and may indeed be the adventurous type who can take the occasional hardship in his or her stride.

International careers on the fringe

The last category is the case of the international careerist in the making – or the company that is hesitantly sending out feelers abroad. Overseas exposure is very occasional, and it could not really be referred to as working and operating abroad, but is more likely to be manifested in visits, attending conferences and professional meetings, exchanging information and keeping abreast of developments outside one's homestead.

There is not much that can be said about the fringe phenomenon, except that it seems to describe the international involvement of a large number of companies, many of them small and medium-sized, that have come to recognise the need for exposure to overseas markets and know-how. The international scene thus becomes of interest to workers in such companies, who may until recently have limited their foreign horizons to a three-day city break in Rome or a week's slog on the Costa del Sol. Spending working time abroad has entered the vocabulary of these companies, but it is not yet a critical constituent of their make-up, nor of their executive cadre. Table 1 summarises the values, options and outlines their key features.

The management of international careers

How do companies manage international careers? To answer that, I conducted a survey of IPD members, with the help of the IPD's International Department. From the results the following picture emerges.

A critical determinant of an international career is whether the company in question defines itself as a multinational or not. Sixty-four per cent of non-MNCs in the survey regard an international career as *unimportant*, compared with only 16 per cent of MNCs. On

Table 1
INTERNATIONAL CAREERS: KEY FEATURES

Intensity	Organisational frame	Antecedents	Values	Organising principles
FREQUENT	Empire	Established MNCs. Global enterprises.	International careers are the standard.	Globe-trotting is the lead institutional process, reflected in organisational structures.
	Colonial	Established MNCs. Centralised decision-making.	Loyalty and patriotism; international careers seen as a mission.	Episodes of service abroad and sojourn at home are common throughout.
	Professional	External hire for assignments abroad.	Professional identity.	Overseas posts (periphery) separated from home base (core).
INFREQUENT	Peripheral	Minor MNCs. Niche markets.	Overseas posts highly desirable.	Transparent and equitable HR policies for service abroad.
	Expedient	Little experience of international careers and few resources.	Ambivalence; potentially high failure.	Ad hoc – learning as one goes.
OCCASIONAL	Fringe	Small organisations. First attempts at internationalising.	Necessity-driven; possibly curiosity also.	Marginal activity: visits, trade conferences etc.

the other hand, 68 per cent of MNCs consider an international career *important*, and a further 16 per cent regard it as *essential*. The differences between MNCs and non-MNCs in this aspect are statistically strongly significant. The position of companies is reflected in the attitudes of employees towards their international careers, as reported by HR functionaries. Among non-MNCs, most (60 per cent) regard an overseas assignment as 'a job to be done', and only a few (30 per cent) regard it as 'a prize'; whereas among MNC employees, just 36 per cent view it as 'a job to be done' and 43 per cent as 'a prize'.

From that follows what an international career constitutes. For non-MNCs the stress is on collaborating with other companies outside the UK (60 per cent of respondents), whereas MNCs view an international career as actively spending time overseas (27 per cent) and working abroad for at least six months (31 per cent).

Another major difference between the two camps as regards international careers is whether the company in question currently employs expatriates. Whereas 87 per cent of MNCs do currently employ expatriates, only 45 per cent of non-MNCs do so. The difference is highly significant statistically. Size matters, of course: the average number of employees in the companies in our sample that currently have expatriates is 16,500, compared with only 600 for companies that do not currently employ any.

MNCs are more likely to recruit expatriates at all levels, whereas non-MNCs do so only at middle and senior management level. For rank-and-file positions, non-MNCs prefer to hire locally (60 per cent), whereas MNCs prefer home country 'new blood' (46 per cent), clearly as a way of inducting young, promising individuals into international careers. For top and middle management, MNCs prefer home country individuals possessing a long service record with the company.

Most companies currently employing expatriates have an expatriate policy – but not all. These latter companies are less likely to define an international career as important in the organisational context. There is also some indication from the data that they experience a higher failure rate. As for repatriation policies, none of the non-MNCs has any, compared with 21 per cent of MNCs that do. Yet 68 per cent of MNCs have no repatriation policy!

Companies with developed international careers tend to have an established HR function compared with companies in which international careers are in their infancy. There is a strong association between having HR represented on the board and the following:

⊕ having an expatriate policy
⊕ a stronger overseas presence (ten markets on average, compared with only six)
⊕ the likelihood of having an active policy on international careers
⊕ the likelihood of having dedicated international HR services.

To sum up, the data informs us about the dynamics of internationalisation among companies operating in the UK. The key features that seem to affect attitudes, policies and practice are:

⊕ having or not having expatriates
⊕ having or not having an HR seat on the board
⊕ the importance attributed to international careers as manifested in a company's strategy.

We cannot however generalise, at this stage, about the wider community of UK companies operating internationally, because our sample is not sufficiently large (48 companies).

To sum up...

International careers are clearly in the ascendant. Of our sample, only 29 per cent saw no change in the importance attached to an international career in their organisation. All the rest did, 35 per cent of which being in the past three years. Another indication of the salience of the 'international' in general is in the way companies benchmark their HR activities. We would expect, of course, MNCs to benchmark themselves against other international companies, and we have confirmation of that in the data. However, we also found that non-MNCs do so: 9 per cent benchmark against international companies and 36 per cent against European companies (as opposed to 27 per cent against UK companies).

‘‘International careers are here to stay. OK?!’’

A sea change? Perhaps. If you happen to work for an empire or a colonial company, it is likely that you are already 'enlisted' into an international career. If you follow the professional or peripheral model, you are likely to be internationally oriented anyway. If a member of the expedient or fringe fraternity, you may well be experiencing a conversion. International careers are here to stay. OK?!

This is set against the background of how a company benchmarks itself. MNCs benchmark their HR activity against other international companies (47 per cent), whereas only 9 per cent of non-MNCs do so. (The latter, however, benchmark themselves against European companies (36 per cent) and UK companies (27 per cent).)

End-notes

[1] For further elaboration see Baruch Y. and Altman Y. (1999), 'Expatriation and repatriation in MNCs: a taxonomy', Academy of Management meeting, Chicago.

[2] HANDY C. (1984) *The Future of Work*. London, Penguin.

Chapter 8

Sustaining Constructive Relationships across Cultural Boundaries

Ann Parkinson

Introduction: the wider environment
From industrial to employee relations

The manner in which the organisational dialogue takes place has undergone dramatic changes during the latter part of twentieth century in the developed industrial countries, and those change drivers can also been seen in many of the emerging economies of Central and Eastern Europe. Traditionally the exchange between labour and capital has been characterised by collective bargaining, where the dialogue has been between the trade union and personnel in an industrial relations arena – the trade union representing individuals and, almost exclusively, the personnel function representing the organisation, both sides seeing it as a professional role. The formal agenda for bargaining was usually restricted to pay and conditions, in line with a Taylorist view that the basic employment relationship was no more than the straight exchange of 'a fair day's work for a fair day's pay', with neither side seeking more from a formalised contractual relationship. Certainly in the Anglo-Saxon world, trade unions had emerged to protect workers from exploitative and coercive employers driven by the tenets of scientific management, which in the UK reached their peak of influence in 1970s, with large organisations allowing the trade union effectively to manage their relationship with their employees.

The final 20 years of the twentieth century have seen strong forces for change, which have in turn changed the nature of industrial relations in Europe and beyond. Although many of the drivers are common, there are still substantial disparities across national boundaries to the extent that trade unions are influential in the employment relationship, which Morley *et al* (1996) see as partly a matter of perception affected by the differences in national culture and expectations. However much trade unions are involved in the 'formal' contract relating to pay and conditions, it is with the more informal side of the relationship that this chapter is concerned. Those common forces for change have played a part in the wider category of 'employee relations' being identified in the 1995 Cranfield Network survey (Morley *et al*, 1996) as one of the key HR or personnel priorities across Europe, except for Sweden, Denmark and the Netherlands, which already have cultures that emphasise and value relationships.

The critical forces for change have stemmed from at least four directions, all interlinked and affecting each other:

- *Political* – Increasing focus on the free market in the UK and USA in the Reagan and Thatcher era, combined with global competition, as well as shareholder emphasis on short-term returns, have put organisations under increasing pressure on costs and prices.
- *Technological* – Much of the pressure has been addressed with the advent of new technology and the possibilities of flexible ways of working. In some organisations this has resulted in a straight reduction of their labour force, whereas in others it has been the opportunity to develop new systems of working arrangements and organisation to provide the necessary flexibility to adjust to the competitive conditions by focusing on the individual using 'HRM techniques'.
- *Economic* – Linked to global competition, in the 1980s was the beginning of the excellence movement, coming at a time of examining how the Japanese companies managed to provide high quality at lower costs, and the recognition that there were Western companies that exhibited similar traits. This also coincided with the birth of the Human Resource Management school with its goals of commitment, competence, congruence and cost effectiveness (Beer *et al*, 1984) giving rise to 'techniques such as elaborate communications mechanisms, career development,

employee involvement initiatives and performance related pay'
(Morley *et al*, 1996).

⊕ *Socio-demographic* – Underpinning the focus on excellence could
be seen rising expectations from an increasingly better educated
workforce and customer base. The work values of the 'post-war'
generation and the traditional 'command and control' style of
management that attended them were no longer appropriate; the
values of the 1960s generation onwards would no longer be content with being treated as one of a collective (Cox and Parkinson,
1999). Table 1 illustrates the shift in values in the latter half of
the twentieth century, certainly in the English-speaking world or
Anglo-Saxon culture.

All these forces have combined to provide an increasing focus on the
individual at work in Europe, and the need to connect and communicate directly with employees to enable a mutual understanding of
the needs of both parties to the employment relationship, irrespective of whether there are also established collective bargaining
arrangements.

Table 1
DOMINANT VALUES IN THE WORKFORCE

Category	Entered workforce	Approx. age now	Individual work values	Organisational work values
Protestant work ethic	1945–59	55–65	Hard work, conservative, loyalty to organisation	Command, control, efficiency, compliance, dehumanisation
Existentialism	1960–79	40–54	Quality of life, non-conforming, seeks autonomy, loyalty to self	Teamwork, quality, respect for individual, involvement
Pragmatism	1980–89	30–39	Success, achievement, ambition, hard work, loyalty to career	Efficiency, cost reduction
Generation X	1990s	under 30	Lifestyle, self-development, loyalty to peers	Empowerment, organisational learning, employability

Adapted from Cox and Parkinson, 1999, with acknowledgement to Robbins (1989)

Dimensions of culture

The previous section has demonstrated that global forces are increasingly affecting organisations – and therefore the people who work in them – and the impact of national culture on the employment relationship has to be recognised by those organisations seeking to establish operations outside their traditional culture or to enter into any type of strategic alliance across boundaries. Even for those organisations operating within a single national boundary there is a need to recognise the impact of an increasingly multicultural workforce. This section will focus on those aspects of culture that may influence how people behave in a work setting that are not immediately obvious, described by Hofstede (1984) as 'the collective programming of the mind which distinguishes the members of one category of people from another'. We are often aware of cultural differences and national stereotypes, based on tangible signals such as language and costume, which we adjust for, but it is the less visible, intangible, areas that unconsciously provide the most causes for misunderstanding, as outlined in Figure 1. These factors all contribute to the make-

Figure 1
EXAMPLES OF CULTURAL FACTORS AFFECTING
INDIVIDUAL BEHAVIOUR

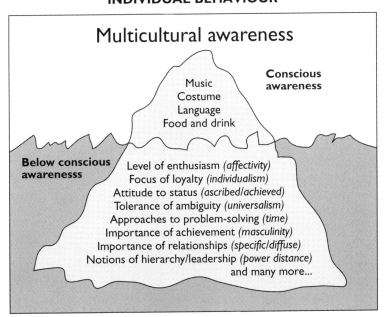

Multicultural awareness

Music
Costume
Language
Food and drink

Conscious awareness

Below conscious awareness

Level of enthusiasm (*affectivity*)
Focus of loyalty (*individualism*)
Attitude to status (*ascribed/achieved*)
Tolerance of ambiguity (*universalism*)
Approaches to problem-solving (*time*)
Importance of achievement (*masculinity*)
Importance of relationships (*specific/diffuse*)
Notions of hierarchy/leadership (*power distance*)
and many more...

up of the individual, in terms of their personality and behaviour, the organisation in terms of the culture and the management style, and the environment in establishing the context in which the other two operate. As Hofstede (1984) reminds us, 'people build organisations according to their values, and societies are composed of institutions and organisations that reflect the dominant values within their culture' (page 82).

There is now a growing body of research into the impact of national culture on work-related values and attitudes, led by the work of Hofstede and Trompenaars, which suggest that these differences explained more than age, gender, profession or position in an organisation. They have defined several dimensions in common, which were also related to other psychological or sociological factors that were found in the research introduced in the next section. Although this research took place in the UK, within a multinational company, it is not difficult to suggest how the dimensions identified below need to be taken into account when applying the findings more widely, or how they would explain any differences in approach needed.

Hofstede's original work in IBM in the 1980s across 64 countries confirmed that national culture had a major impact on work-related attitudes. He identified four main dimensions, which are now well known and used, later adding a fifth, the dimension of long term versus short term, which is omitted here, as it has yet to be fully described. The four main dimensions are:

- *power-distance* – the extent to which less powerful members of organisations and institutions (including the family), accept and expect that power is distributed unequally. Scores tend to be higher for Latin, Asian and African countries and smaller for Germanic.
- *individualism opposed to collectivism* – the degree to which individuals are integrated into groups, and the level of freedom that society allows individuals. Individualism prevails in Western and developed countries, with collectivism in Eastern and less developed countries, and with Japan occupying the middle position.
- *masculinity and femininity* – the distribution of roles between the sexes: societies displaying feminist characteristics, such as the

Nordic countries, allow both men and women to take many different roles, whereas the opposite, masculine societies, such as Japan, Germanic and Anglo countries, make a sharp division between male and female activities.

⊕ *uncertainty avoidance* – a society's tolerance for ambiguity and the extent to which its members feel comfortable in unstructured situations. These scores are higher in Latin and Germanic countries and lower in the Anglo and Nordic cultures.

All these terms are further explored in the context of developing management teams by Malcolm Higgs in Chapter 10.

Trompenaars has developed a similar framework with additional dimensions, which can be seen to have parallels with Hofstede's. To the notion of power-distance he has added the extent to which people feel controlled by, or in control of, their environment, which he calls *outer- or inner-directed*, as well as the role of status in peoples' lives, whether it is *ascribed* – deriving from position and motivating them to succeed – or whether it comes from success and *achievement* derived from what they do. Hofstede's masculinity has parallels with Trompenaars' *specificity* and *neutrality* dimensions, with their suggestion of superficial relationships, emphasis on facts and concealing emotions, whereas he adds *diffuse* and *affectivity* to femininity, with their emphasis on developing relationships, concepts and appearing 'engaged'. His *individual/communitarian* dimension is almost identical to Hofstede's individual/collectivist, and the *universalism/particularism* dimension parallels uncertainty avoidance (Trompenaars and Woolliams, 1999).

These dimensions all relate to the work situation and affect what either side wants out of the employment relationship, and they also suggest that management skills and attitudes in managing that relationship are also culturally specific. For example, in an individualist culture one would expect the employment relationship to be more calculative, based on the exchange of labour for money to mutual advantage, and in more collectivist cultures there is often a moral element, with the protection of the employee exchanged for loyalty and commitment. In a weak uncertainty-avoidance culture, where developing relationships are valued, the manager from the opposite culture, which values rules and contracts, would find their previous skills unhelpful and would need to learn to develop their interpersonal skills. The difference in the extremes of the power-distance dimension would lead to potential clashes when the manager expecting obedience and deference from their subordinates takes over managing a team used to a supportive democratic management style. The objectives sought differ; a feminine culture is more likely to be quality-of-life-oriented, with masculine cultures more competitive and achievement-oriented.

There is no evidence that any particular dimension is more successful, but often experts and consultants who have been successful in one culture, when moving into another, are unable to recognise that they need to change and adapt to a culture that has developed over time to fit the values of the people within it. It is those who are 'culturally sensitive' who are likely to be most successful in adapting to a different environment.

The employment relationship from an individual's viewpoint

Recent research undertaken to discover how a particular group of people viewed the employment relationship in the 1990s in a multinational hi-tech company revealed a number of different perspectives or 'psychological contracts' (Parkinson, 1999). The typology (see Figure 2) that emerged from this research provides a useful framework to illustrate the multiplicity of differing perspectives from which the employment relationship can be viewed within any single organisation.

From the formal contract aspect, everyone had similar terms in their tangible contract, but there were at least four different types of perspective on the more intangible elements, or informal/psychological contract. The research suggests that the key dimensions that influence people's view of the employment relationship are related to what they are looking for from that relationship, whether the focus is on the purely 'formal' aspects or on looking for a wider involvement in the organisation – as gained from the 'informal' or 'psychological contract'. The second factor that seemed to influence their view of relationship was that of how active they were in pursuing their career, which has its roots in the psychological concept of 'locus

Figure 2
VIEWS OF THE EMPLOYMENT RELATIONSHIP

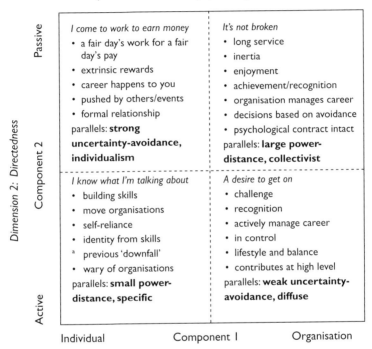

Source: Parkinson, 1999; © Ann Parkinson

of control'. The factors that influence the view taken can also be seen to have a number of parallels with Hofstede and Trompenaars' cultural dimensions, which have been added to Figure 2.

The first dimension encompasses the extent to which people identify themselves with the more abstract, informal aspects of their employment or the more formal, tangible pole, focusing on their own needs and being able to separate work from the other aspects of life. It is bound up with issues such as sense of identity, self-image, commitment, job, family; focus on themselves or on the wider world;

separation of different life aspects; and the extent to which they want involvement with the organisation or their manager. This has echoes in Hofstede and Trompenaars' dimensions, suggesting that there would be differences in expectations of the relationship in different cultures.

''Some people may never have had the need to take control of their careers''

The second dimension helps clarify whether the formal relationship pole is about self-reliance, independence with self-image and identity, tied up with being the expert in the field, and deriving security from that expertise. Alternatively, the other extreme could be about letting someone else take control or abdicating responsibility, either through circumstances, not feeling in an appropriate position, or not knowing how. As knowledge workers with scarce skills in this study, some people may never have had the need to take control of their careers and change. This dimension also has parallels with Trompenaars' inner- and outer-directed dimension and Hofstede's power-distance.

The views of the employment relationship that emerged from this research could be broadly categorised into four main types and, interestingly, a fifth type emerged which represented the managers' views of people's goals, although these seldom reflected their own expectations.

It's not broken

This first view seems to come from those who have relatively long service in the organisation. While everything is going well there is a feeling of inertia with the 'psychological contract' intact, the job is enjoyable, and the career seems to manage itself. Although people with this view have some sense of career direction, they consciously or unconsciously expect the organisation or their line manager to take responsibility for their career. This group is looking for achievement, recognition and enjoyment from their work, and any career decision happens only to avoid being in situations where they are unable to obtain these states. It is not until something goes wrong, or they are offered an alternative, that they assess the extent to which their psychological contract is being fulfilled.

I know what I am talking about

Those in this group are focused on building their skills, prepared to change organisations to pursue their career, or to set up on their own. They have a sense of self-reliance through constantly developing and practising their skill base, which enables them to move easily between companies. The sense of identity that comes from their skills has given many of them the confidence to set up on their own at various stages of their careers. The managers saw management as an alternative to using their technical skills: almost 'something to do when I am not using my core skills'. Another factor in common was having had a 'bad' experience previously, with the subsequent impact of wariness in future relationships with organisations.

A desire to get on

Members of this group positively look for challenges and are concerned about being recognised for their efforts. Expecting both to contribute and receive in the employment relationship, they feel that by contributing and being loyal to the organisation at a higher level, they will receive back the means to manage their career actively and be more in control of their lives. They do not want to compromise on lifestyle issues and are highly aware of the problem of balancing family life with a career. These people have had a clearer idea of what they wanted to do from early on and have recognised the need to plan their careers, moving to take up the next challenge rather than waiting until something goes wrong; but when it does, they suffer a personal sense of failure and sadness.

I come to work to earn money

This group views the relationship as the traditional basic exchange of 'a fair day's work for a fair day's pay', where motivation is the extrinsic rewards of pay and benefits and the security of a large organisation. They would see their career as something that happens to them, particularly early on, having often 'drifted' into their first job, allowing themselves to be pushed along by circumstances and other people, often ending up in situations they would not otherwise have sought. With no specific career goals to pursue, their main drivers are extrinsic rewards and security; and outside the formal terms of their employment contract they prefer to keep their relationship with the organisation at a minimum.

The managers' view of the relationship reinforced their role in the informal relationship. Everyone had the same formal, legal contract with the organisation, managed via personnel, but their informal 'psychological contract' was personal, however, and was managed by themselves and their manager as an agent of the organisation. The quality of the relationship between the manager and employee was an important factor in how the overall employment relationship was viewed. With the delegating of key people management tasks to line managers, they come to represent the organisation in the eyes of the employee, 'to me the organisation is my manager and my manager's manager', but that manager is also subject to the same factors that colour how they view their relationship with the organisation, leading to a large number of different 'psychological contracts' operating at any one time. Structural changes have meant that the HR function, in many organisations, manages only the formal contract, while the line manager manages the psychological or informal contract, as illustrated in Figure 3.

These same structural changes have also introduced more flexibility into organisations, leaving managers no longer in a position to work closely with their people, either through working in different locations, often in different countries, often from home, or through

Figure 3
WHO DETERMINES THE EMPLOYMENT RELATIONSHIP?

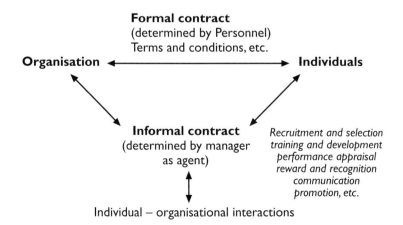

Source: Parkinson (1999); © Ann Parkinson

working at different times especially as the 9 to 5, five-day week working pattern becomes less prevalent. Overlaid with a more global workforce, the pressure is on managers to find different ways of developing a relationship with their workforce than they had when they sat in the same work area at the same time of day, with the same people. In the same way that the culturally sensitive manager has been demonstrated to be the high performer by Trompenaars and Woolliams (1999), Golzen has also highlighted that successful leaders manage relationships through 'emotional intelligence', which is also indicative of the importance of interpersonal skills; as he suggests: 'Social skills at a personal level translate into the ability of companies to handle diversity, both within their own workforce, and in their global activities' (Golzen,1999).

How culture affects the employment relationship dialogue

In applying the lessons from research into the employment relationship there are three key roles for HR professionals:

⊕ The first involves their role in employee relations, in terms of clarifying the expectations and the obligations that make up the organisational part of the employment relationship at the macro level, through the 'formal' process of delivering corporate communications to employees and enabling feedback on how it has been received through instruments such as attitude surveys or focus groups. In order to deliver a consistent organisational message, each aspect of the communication process must be reviewed to ensure that the various filters, whether they be cultural, organisational or individual, have been understood and adjusted for. There is much that can be gleaned from the marketing function in managing internal communications, especially where organisations have to re-establish themselves in a role that had previously been delegated to their trade unions to manage.

⊕ The second is related to the first; in HR's role in ensuring that line managers, who represent the organisation as far as employees are concerned, have both the ability and the motivation to deliver those consistent corporate messages. There is a necessity to ensure that messages and communication from managers and various management practices to employees, are consistent with those that the organisation wants to send to an increasingly diverse workforce.

⊕ The third role for HR professionals is in supporting and advising line managers to develop the skills they need to manage the 'informal' relationship with their staff, particularly in terms of the design of performance management processes, in management development to undertake those HR practices that have been delegated to them over the last few years, and in the area of developing an awareness of the need to improve those interpersonal and 'soft' skills that have traditionally been seen as outside the domain of operational management.

The rest of this section brings together theory, research and practice to provide some thoughts, frameworks and examples aimed at providing a resource and ideas for those faced with the practical management of these issues. The work of Hofstede and Trompenaars, as outlined above, has been drawn on as their research has found resonance with both the employment relationship research and experience working with other cultures. To a certain extent it is unnecessary to understand the precise details of each dimension and which framework is more appropriate; the key message is the need to understand the impact of differences and similarities between people when creating a constructive dialogue. The following broad analysis of the impact of cultural dimensions on aspects of managing the employment relationship may provide insights into particular situations, underpinned by a mapping of representative national cultures on to Hofstede's dimensions in Figure 4.

Within clusters, two countries sharing similar dimensions may differ in degree and it is in these subtleties that major misunderstandings can occur, especially as these are usually factors beneath conscious awareness. Wilde's reference to the British having everything in common with America except language is well made. It is in the dimension of uncertainty avoidance or Trompenaars' dimension of universalism/particularism, and to a lesser extent power-distance (see Figure 5), that the differences become apparent, suggesting that the USA tends to be focused on facts and structure with a preference for legal contracts, rather than valuing relationships. In the same way, links between cultures shown below may also be explained by history, for instance the British influence on Hong Kong and India may

Figure 4

COUNTRY FIT TO NATIONAL CULTURE DIFFERENCE DIMENSIONS (HOFSTEDE, 1995) WITH COUNTRY CLUSTERS (RONEN AND SHENKAR, 1985)

	Femininity			**Masculinity**	
strong	*Far Eastern* Thailand [Brazil]	Singapore	*Far Eastern* Hong Kong [India]	*Latin American* Venezuela [Japan]	**Collectivism**
Power-distance	*Latin European* France			*Latin European* Italy	
weak	*Germanic* Netherlands	*Nordic* Sweden	*Anglo* UK USA	*Germanic* Germany	**Individualism**

Uncertainty-avoidance

strong ⟷ weak   weak ⟷ strong

Note: countries in [ ] are seen as independent of cultural clusters

explain their weak uncertainty avoidance, and the proximity of the Nordic, Germanic and Anglo clusters may reflect their common early histories.

Uncertainty-avoidance

Those people who come from cultures with weak uncertainty-avoidance are likely to feel more comfortable with ambiguity, uncertainty, unstructured situations, and change. They are likely to be more involved, preferring an more 'informal' relationship with their manager, and would probably value a degree of autonomy. They would be happy to be managed by objectives relating to broad assignments, in a looser timeframe. These people are likely to come from the Anglo, Nordic, and the Far East cultures with higher masculinity.

However for those cultures that prefer strong uncertainty, performance management systems need to be more structured with precise objectives and detailed tasks, and people are more likely to be

Figure 5

CULTURES PLOT – UNCERTAINTY-AVOIDANCE BY POWER-DISTANCE DIMENSIONS

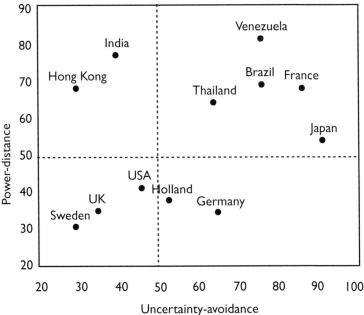

focused on the formal contract they have with organisation. This can be seen with the Germanic preference for structure and their ability to separate work and personal life, rarely working after the formal working day and the subsequent preference for flexible working hours as a demonstration of the humanisation of work.

Power-distance

Those who come from cultures with a large power-distance have a respect for authority and want to be told what to do, and be given targets rather than being involved in determining them. They are more likely to expect a traditional hierarchical career path, and may have assumed that the organisation will develop them without much input from them. So far, their career moves are more likely to have been as a result of circumstances or being pushed by other people. This is a likely reaction from the Latin and Far Eastern culture clusters. Those who fall along the smaller power-distance dimension, which tend to be the Northern European and Anglo groups, would expect to be consulted and managed more as equals, expecting their manager to be supportive. They feel more able to control their own destiny and expect be in control of their career, making their own choices and decisions.

Individualism

The key factor that seems to determine whether a culture is individualist is that of economic development, which gives its people the opportunity to pursue development, fulfilment and individual reward and not need the community support outside the immediate family group. As with small power-distance, which the individualist cultures also espouse, people would also have the expectation of being treated equally. People coming from the Nordic, Anglo and Western European cultures are comfortable with the expectation of the performance management systems inherent in Western management thinking, that direct feedback will motivate them.

To give direct feedback in collectivist cultures, however, can lead to losing face and therefore people's loyalty to the organisation, as it destroys the harmonious relationships that are the foundation of maintaining group loyalty. In these cultures Hofstede (1995) suggests it would be more appropriate to give feedback via a trusted third party. Most of the collective cultures also fall on the large power-distance dimension where respect for the manager as an authority figure reinforces the negative impact of losing face. People accept that there would be different standards for treating different groups, and they would also expect to be rewarded as part of the team effort rather than as an individual.

Masculinity

''Feminine cultures are characterised by caring and modesty''

Feminine cultures are characterised by caring and modesty, and those values would lead to expectations that it would be possible to achieve an effective balance between work and family life, as shown by the extensive provision of childcare in countries such as France and Sweden. People from these cultures are likely to undersell them-selves and prefer working co-operatively with others. They will be more open to working in a more intuitive environment, involving concepts and ideas and probably looking for the more intangible, intrinsic aspects of work that come from the diffuse dimension, and more likely to want to continue their career in an organisation with which they have developed an 'informal' relationship.

> **The difference between the poles of the diffuse dimen-sion can be illustrated by the example of the US busi-nessman meeting potential Italian partners for the first time and being taken out to lunch. During the lunch he repeatedly tried to discuss business issues, wanting to make a 'professional' impression; the lunch became increasingly frustrating for him, because he had failed to recognise that their concern was more to understand him and determine whether they could build a relation-ship, therefore deciding whether to do business with him before discussing such issues.**

At the opposite end, those from more masculine societies are likely to be seeking to make a career for themselves, seen as assertive and often overselling their capabilities. In considering the dimension of specificity alongside masculinity, employees from these cultures will be more likely to focus on the facts and bottom-line aspects of their jobs, making decisions in order to move on to the next task, rather than consider the wider possibilities and the people implications of their decisions. In giving and receiving feedback they are likely to be results oriented, often with specific examples, rather than looking at the impact of behaviours on those around them. When combined with achieved status or inner direction, as in the Anglo and Germanic clusters, people from these cultures are more likely to change companies for money, than to want to develop a relationship with a particular organisation.

Positive dialogue

The underpinning concept in the dialogue between the individual and their manager is the importance of understanding the underly-ing assumptions, and recognition that people have different perspectives on the same situation based on such aspects as their values, nationality, experience, personality and socialisation. As illustrated by the research introduced above, managers often manage people as a collective with the same career goals, which can lead to misunderstanding what motivates them. Trompenaars and Woolliams (1999) have demonstrated from their recent research that managers who appreciate and reconcile differences in cultural values demonstrate high performance in the job, which they refer to as 'trans-cultural competence' which often reflects the extent of their experience with international assignments or managing diversity. The effect of experience also strikes a chord with Goleman's view that emotional intelligence reflects experience, and he cites self-awareness, both through knowing yourself and the impact you have on others, along with empathy, motivation and social skills as key abilities in high performers (Goleman, 1998).

Experience has shown that giving managers and employees an appropriate framework and opportunities to build their relationship can have a positive impact. This is both in terms of day-to-day performance, as each party is clear about their expectations of each other, but also for the future, where by understanding both the individual's and the organisation's needs early on, there are more opportunities for ensuring an appropriate match of skills to requirements when the time is right, especially when dealing with knowledge workers with scarce skills, thus avoiding misunderstandings leading to losing those skills.

Some frameworks are already in place in many organisations through appraisal and development processes. What is often missing is understanding the key role that such processes play in the development of the informal employment relationship or psychological contract between the manager and employee. They are often the only opportunities in the year that the two parties are able to take time out to get to know each other and to understand how to get the best out of their relationship. For some this may need to remain on a formal basis, but for others a less formal atmosphere may be more motivating. Such meetings have become even more important in a flexible or global environment. Often, these are processes that are either suspended at times of operational pressure, or paid lip service to in order to meet a perceived obligation to go through the motions, with neither side feeling a benefit.

"All too often, people make assumptions that everyone else wants the same things"

What is often also missing is the interpersonal skills and training for managers in undertaking these processes, many of whom have taken on what they would deem a 'personnel' role for which they have not been trained or, indeed, which they are not interested in. In the same way that personality profiling can help people not only understand themselves but also how they may be different from others, and the impact that they have on them, getting managers to think about how their career has developed, the influences, and what they want out of it, can help them appreciate and be able to work with their own team on their mutual expectations of each other. All too often, people make assumptions that everyone else wants the same things out of their psychological contract or their career as themselves, thus leading to misunderstanding, forgetting all the factors that are included in developing those requirements, especially in a more pressured workplace or when people are dispersed either by time or location.

Schein (1993) also suggests that building common ground and trust in relationships within an organisation requires time. Within a cross-cultural context there is a need for more time to develop the 'shared mental models' or assumptions about reality to enable people to work together constructively. In recognition of not only the shift from collective bargaining to individual 'contracting', but also that the responsibility has moved from the personnel/HR function to the line manager, both sides of the new contract demand both time and support in establishing the dialogue needed to develop the new relationship.

Schein describes a formal process of dialogue that he has used to bring groups to a common understanding of each other and working together, which has principles that are equally applicable to organisations, their managers and employees. He suggests that discussion and debate can be constructive if one can assume that parties understand each other well enough to be 'talking the same language' but that it would normally need to be preceded by 'dialogue', especially if working in a second language. Taking the principles of the dialogue process in which the players begin to recognise 'what we perceive is often based on our needs, our expectations, our projections and, most of all, our culturally learned assumptions and categories of thought' (Schein, 1993, p46), by listening to and understanding one's own assumptions and expectations, both the line manager and the employee can build their relationship on common ground, minimising breakdown in their informal contract. As Trompenaars and Woolliams (1999) found, some people start from their own orientation and then take account of the opposing values to come to a reconciliation; others start with the opposing view, then return to their own value orientation to ensure it is accommodated. Schein (1993) advocates the effectiveness of dialogue over discussion (see Figure 6), much favoured by the more specific Anglo cultures, as typified by their adversarial legal and political systems and love of debate.

Once people have reached a better understanding of themselves, they find it easier to appreciate the differences in others. Practical examples of applying such a process include working with individuals, and teams using reputable personality instruments such as the Myers Briggs® Type Indicator. Using career development as a tool has also proved effective, through such instruments as Schein's *Career Anchors* (1990).

Figure 6
DIFFERENCES BETWEEN PROCESS OF DIALOGUE AND DISCUSSION

Suspension – internal listening; accepting differences; building mutual trust   v   **Discussion** – advocacy; competing; convincing

Dialogue – confronting own and others' assumptions; revealing feelings; building common ground   v   **Dialectic** – exploring oppositions

Metalogue – building new shared assumptions in psychological safety   v   **Debate** – potential for false consensus – built on differing assumptions

Adapted from Schein, 1993

Conclusions

‘‘The pressures on today's businesses lead them to rely on building relationships’’

This chapter has taken a broad view of the changing environment in employee relations, coupled with the burgeoning need to manage diversity, whether it is within national boundaries or through developing business across national borders. The pressures on today's businesses lead them to rely on building relationships, especially as employees are no longer located immediately outside their manager's office, but work at different times, in different locations whether part-time or in a different time zone, working from home or in a different country. It has also built on recent research to propose a framework for understanding what underpins individuals' views of their employment relationship and how this might be affected by similar dimensions of national culture.

While recognising that individual and collective approaches to managing the formal employment relationship can and do coexist (Storey and Sisson,1993), it is suggested that it is in supporting the dialogue that determines the less recognised, but no less influential, informal employment relationship that HR managers should be targeting resources. At a strategic, organisational level, this relationship centres around communicating shared values or a culture that people can feel committed to through the consistent messages and behaviour of its managers who represent the organisation; at an operational, individual level, that relationship is between line manager and employees. It is this relationship that can play a major part in the development of the psychological contract or informal relationship that the employee feels that they have with the organisation, and a number of other factors including personality, values, nationality and experience contribute to the interaction between the organisation and employee that determines their view of what type of employment relationship that they have and want.

In a specific and masculine culture such as the UK's, it is more difficult to recognise the value of relationships, and increasingly it is the task of the HR professional to enable both the organisation to communicate to all its workforce in a way that they will receive a consistent message, irrespective of culture, and to enable individual relationships to be based on valuing and building on the diversity that is inherent in them. It is, therefore, through the lead and support of the HR function that organisations and their employees can develop a realistic dialogue on the expectations each has of the other.

The author would like to acknowledge and thank Dr Helene Coxhead for her contribution to the inception and discussion of the ideas for this chapter.

References

BEER M., SPECTOR B., LAWRENCE P. R., QUINN MILLS D. *and* WALTON R. F. (1984) *Managing Human Assets.* London, Free Press.

BOYACIGILLER N. A. *and* ADLER N. (1995) 'Methodological considerations in studying cross-cultural management behaviour', in T. Jackson (ed.), *Cross-Cultural Management*, Oxford, Butterworth-Heinemann.

COX P. *and* PARKINSON A. (1999) 'Values and their impact on the changing employment relationship', in G. Hollinshead, P. Nicholls and S. Tailby (eds), *Employee Relations*, London, Financial Times Management.

GOLEMAN D. (1998) *Working with Emotional Intelligence.* London, Bloomsbury Publishing.

GOLZEN G. (1999), 'Executives with EQ (not IQ)'. *Human Resources.* April.

HOFSTEDE G. (1984) 'Cultural dimensions in management and planning'. *Asia Pacific Journal of Management.* January.

HOFSTEDE G. (1995) 'The business of international business is culture', in T. Jackson (ed.), *Cross-Cultural Management*, Oxford, Butterworth-Heinemann.

LARSEN H. H. (1996) 'In search of management development in Europe: from self-fulfilling prophecies to organizational competence'. *International Journal of Human Resource Management.* No. 7. 3 September.

MORLEY M., BREWSTER C., GUNNIGLE P. *and* MAYRHOFER W. (1996) 'Evaluating change in European industrial relations'.

International Journal of Human Resource Management. No. 7. 3 Sep-tember.

PARKINSON A. (1999) *The Changing Nature of the Employment Relationship: Mapping a subjective terrain of the psychological contract.* Unpublished doctoral thesis. Henley Management College.

ROBBINS S. P. (1989) *Organizational Behaviour.* Hemel Hempstead, Prentice-Hall.

RONEN S. *and* SHENKAR O. (1985) 'Clustering countries on attitudinal dimensions: a review and synthesis', *Academy of Management Review,* quoted in S. P. Robbins, *Organizational Behaviour: Concepts, controversies and applications,* 4th edn, Hemel Hempstead, Prentice Hall International, 1989.

ROSENZWEIG P. (1998) 'Managing the new global workforce: fostering diversity, forging consistency'. *European Management Journal.* Vol. 16, No. 6.

SCHEIN E. H. (1990) *Career Anchors: Discovering your real values.* Pfeiffer and Company.

SCHEIN E. H. (1992) *Organizational Culture and Leadership.* 2nd edn. San Francisco, Jossey Bass.

SCHEIN E. H. (1993) 'On dialogue, culture, and organizational learning'. *Organizational Dynamics.* Vol. 22, No. 2.

STOREY J. and SISSON K. (1993), *Managing Human Resources and Industrial Relations.* Milton Keynes, Open University Press.

TROMPENAARS F. *and* WOOLLIAMS P. (1999) 'Trans-cultural competence'. *People Management.* Vol. 5, No. 8. pp30–33.

Chapter 9

Collaboration

International Teamworking

Linda Holbeche

> An essential cornerstone of any corporate strategic plan must be the
> development and maintenance of a highly skilled workforce well able
> to operate within the global marketplace.
>
> Sansom, 1993

As we approach the end of the 1990s, the trend towards globalisation in both the market-place and production has caused many
organisations to push back their operating boundaries and become
'international' players. A recent survey carried out by Roffey Park
Management Institute (1999) found that 39 per cent of respondents'
organisations were trading in Europe, though other parts of the
world were also well represented, with 16 per cent of companies
trading in Asia, for example. The shift to emerging markets such as
the Pacific Rim, Central and Eastern Europe, South America and
India is evident across most sectors. At the beginning of the 1990s,
academics and management gurus were advocating the development
of the Euro-manager. Now that Euroland has finally become a
reality, the centre of attention is international, if not global.

How well organisations are able to succeed in commercial and cultural situations that may be unfamiliar depends to some extent on
the skills and attitudes of employees and their willingness to work
effectively in teams that extend beyond familiar boundaries. How
close are we to the stage predicted by Robert Heller (1994) where

> management teams are likely to include several nationalities, people
> to whom the boundaries between nations mean no more than those
> between departments?

In this chapter we shall explore a number of aspects related to
international teams. We shall start by looking at different forms of
international team operating in organisations of different types. We

shall explore some of the implications of cross-boundary working – particularly the cultural and behavioural challenges to be overcome – and touch on some of the potential contributions to be made by HR functions to effective international teamwork.

Types of international team

International teams take many forms. They may be set up as short-term, *ad hoc* project teams, or as medium-term transnational teams created to help a company achieve greater flexibility to serve a variety of customers in different regions, while maximising the efficiencies of the organisation as a whole. Teams may enjoy a degree of autonomy and be working inside the company's formal structure or alongside it, for instance, as part of a joint venture.

The main obvious difference between international teams and others is that they require people of different nationalities to work together. 'International' team members may share the same nationality as each other but be providing a service to a client (internal or external) whose nationality is different. Teams are often multifunctional and may contain people at a number of management levels. They may be co-located or working remotely from one another. Team members may or may not be required to travel. In some organisations international teams are no longer led by expatriate managers but by 'local' managers who are expected to operate to international norms.

In many organisations, teams are primarily home based, but with international assignments of varying lengths. These may range from a six-month technical assignment to a short business meeting with clients or team members in different locations. The Roffey Park research suggests that this is by far the most popular form of international working from the employee perspective since it avoids disruption of relocating families abroad.

‘‘Virtual teams are a means of tapping into the best brains’’

'Virtual' teams may mean that members of an international team have no need to travel at all. In theory, a virtual team works across national and organisational boundaries, assisted by communication technologies. This form of working appears to be on the increase, since the increasing pace with which new products are brought to market means that projects need to be carried out quickly. Virtual teams are a means of tapping into the best brains for a particular task, wherever they are located, and of ensuring that local customer needs are met.

Truly 'transnational' teams bring together people from different cultures to work on projects or activities which span national boundaries. According to a major study of transnational teams (Snell *et al*, 1998), such teams have to balance three concerns relating to international competition. These are local responsiveness, global efficiency and organisational learning. The challenge for the teams is to be able to 'leverage knowledge continuously around the world'.

What is an international organisation?

What is required of international teams is to some extent determined by the degree of 'internationalism' of the company. Many organisations which claim to be international are in fact predominantly national companies that export overseas. Their main international effort may lie in the sales, marketing and customer service arenas. Management teams are likely to be largely made up of nationals, and opportunities for an international career may be rather limited. The Roffey Park survey (Devine and Hirsh, 1998) found that, while the majority of participating organisations are conducting business internationally, only 56 per cent of respondents agreed that their organisation provides the opportunity for international careers. Other companies, more truly international, may be multinational or multidomestic companies or, as discussed elsewhere in this book, transnational companies.

Joint ventures are increasingly replacing wholly owned subsidiaries as the dominant form of overseas investment. Typically, the main problem areas are likely to lie in relations between the overseas company and the local company, especially on issues concerning communication and decision-making. The nationality of the parent company is likely to have a significant effect on how teams operating joint ventures will interact. Child's study (1990) of joint ventures in China found distinctive differences of approach of parent companies from different countries. In US-owned joint ventures, there was a strong tendency for the procedures and approaches of the parent company to be introduced into the joint venture partner, despite the problems this caused in the fields of informal communication, decision-making and training. By contrast, Japanese companies were found to be less likely to impose home-based Japanese management styles on to their partners, preferring instead to adapt to local circumstances.

Working across boundaries

Cross-boundary working involves working with people whose culture, the 'way they do things', may be different from your own. It also means being able to work outside your own comfort-zones, whether these be based on knowledge, experience, habit or national culture. International teams encounter many aspects of working across boundaries, that extend beyond national differences.

An increasingly common form of cross-boundary working is where employees of different corporate cultures are required to work closely together. Widespread competition from a range of sources is leading to greater corporate amalgamation within the market-place. Joint ventures, partnering arrangements and other forms of strategic alliance are calling on employees to work in teams with former competitors, customers or suppliers whose working practices may be very different. While a formal merger may be publicly celebrated as a 'marriage', as was the 1998 merger of jewellers Asprey and Garrard, employees may see the relationship more in terms of a divorce from all that is familiar. In international mergers, teams have to deal with a cocktail of cultural differences that can add to their challenges

The skills needed in international teams

Clearly, the scope of the organisation's international activities will have a bearing on the skills required of international team members. However, there are certain skills and characteristics that most international teams have in common. According to Peter Smith (1992);

> Working effectively across cultures is not therefore simply a matter of applying skills found to be effective within the culture of one's own country or organisation. It requires also that one can understand and cope with the processes of communication and decision-making in settings where these are achieved in a different manner.

International teams and leaders need to change their frame of reference from a local or national orientation to a truly international perspective. This involves understanding influences, trends, practices, political and cultural influences and international economics. Team leaders in particular need to understand and develop competitive strategies, plans and tactics that operate outside the confines of a domestic market-place orientation. Maury Peiperl of the Centre for Organisational Research at the London Business School has carried out a survey in 15 countries, looking at the skills of international managers. Peiperl's (1998) survey found that British and German managers had the same two gaps in their skills portfolio: being able to motivate cross-border teams and to integrate people from other countries.

Being able to understand and lead multinational teams is critical. Leaders need to be able to deal with issues of collaboration and cross-cultural variances. Merely recognising that cultural differences exist is not enough. International managers need to be able to manage those differences, if the team is to operate successfully. They need to develop processes for coaching, mentoring and assessing performance across a variety of attitudes, beliefs and standards.

‹‹Language skills are an essential gateway to understanding and working effectively››

Language skills, and being willing to continue to learn new languages if, for example, your specialist service centre is in a different location, are also clearly important. Language skills are an essential gateway to understanding and working effectively within the culture of the country in question. Being limited in language ability therefore runs the risk of missing out on the subtleties that can make the difference between business success or failure.

According to a report published by the Economist Intelligence Unit (Krempel 1998), businesses are looking for graduates who are multilingual and able to understand business practice and how it differs between countries. The Peiperl study found that when it comes to language skills British managers compare unfavourably, speaking on average 1.7 languages in contrast to their counterparts in 14 other countries who speak an average of 2.8 languages. In the Roffey Park study, 35 per cent of the sample recognised language skills as being the main skills required, closely followed by cultural awareness and understanding.

Some leading industrialists suggest that even these skills are not enough to ensure that future international leaders are able to lead effectively over time. According to Michel de Zeeuw, General Manager of Unisys, graduate recruits ideally have specific skills such as computing ability, as well as good communication and team-working skills, since they will be required to work with people from different countries. This is in addition to specific technical skills such as accountancy if they are moving, for instance, into a finance function.

The traditional role of making order out of chaos will shift to one of continually managing change and chaos in ways that are responsive to customers and competitive conditions. International leaders will need to be effective well beyond traditional management practices to reflect sensitivity to cultural diversity and perspective. They need to understand different, and sometimes conflicting, social forces without prejudice. They need to speed up business development where possible by exploiting and adapting learning between countries and markets. They also need to be able to manage their personal effectiveness and achieve a satisfactory balance between work and home.

Potential barriers to effective international teamwork

So if working across boundaries is on the increase, what are the challenges for employees? Some of the barriers to effective international teamworking are the cultural differences which are inevitable when people of different professional, organisational or national backgrounds work together. These differences should of course be a source of strength, but the benefits of diversity are sometimes undermined by individual behaviours or organisational systems that are inappropriate to what the team has to achieve. HR can play a significant part in ensuring that HR systems do not undermine international teamworking.

Reward systems

Even where teamworking is well established, relationships within the team can suffer if organisational systems are at odds with cross-boundary teamworking, even though this may be unintentional. Working across boundaries requires people to bring their particular skills and knowledge to the achievement of a joint task for which no individual is likely to take the credit. If the organisation's reward processes reinforce the importance of individual, rather than team performance, employees may consider that doing their 'day job' is what will be taken seriously when performance is being assessed, and may lack commitment to 'cross-boundary' work.

In many global organisations, virtual teamworking is driven by the need to offer worldwide customer service to agreed standards. One software supplier enjoyed a period of considerable business growth during the mid-1990s. The increasingly global nature of the business led to a restructuring of operations. Instead of all country operations being able to sell software and provide customer service independently of one another, the new 'global team' system meant that the UK became the primary 'sales' operation, with all other regions reduced to providing customer service only. This should not have become a problem except for the fact that the unchanged reward system clearly favoured sales. It is hardly surprising that employees outside the UK were unenthusiastic about the new 'team' system, and team training did little to improve morale.

Lack of trust

In a matrix structure, team members often continue to have a clear reporting line back to their functional manager, with only a dotted line to the person responsible for the team. When project teams are seen as a 'bolt on' to the team members' ordinary work, employees can experience mixed loyalties. In practice this can mean that people lack commitment to the team or that they are withdrawn from the project before their work is done. Some employees consider that they have to become guardians of their functional specialism within the multifunctional team, putting their own functional standards and 'turf' issues ahead of the need for collaboration.

For many people, working in this way for the first time requires them to develop a specific mind-set, one in which flexibility and responsiveness to others form the basis for collaboration. Lack of employee trust can lead to a loss of commitment to the team's task. Roffey Park's research into the human aspects of mergers (Devine and Hirsh, 1998) is littered with anecdotes that illustrate the dangers to the organisation of this lack of trust. In a merger between two major pharmaceutical companies, some employees in the acquired company simply hid the outputs of research projects until they felt that their position was secure and that they could work in the new combined organisation. This phenomenon was named 'burying our babies'. Clearly there has to be a shared platform of trust and the opportunity for employees to develop valuable new skills through the team process if people are to see benefits in collaboration.

Knowledge as power

A more fundamental barrier to effective teamworking may have its roots in the ongoing uncertainty of local employment markets. In these days of knowledge management, there is the potential collision of two apparently contradictory edicts. One is 'knowledge is power' and the other is 'knowledge is to be shared'. From the organisational perspective there are clear benefits in the pooling of information – about clients for example – and the generation of shared knowledge, thus preventing the organisation becoming dependent on any single employee's knowledge.

❝Some people believe that sharing their expertise is not in their own interest❞

Many individuals, however, have recognised the importance of building their expertise to the point where they are valued for it and become indispensable. Some people may indeed believe that sharing their expertise beyond their own boundaries is not in their own interest since it can represent a reduction of their own power base, status and job security. Outside the team, knowledge is often a political issue, reflecting power and factional interests. Higgs and Roland (1992) describe the difficulties in imposing an egalitarian culture on traditional hierarchies. Managers and teams are both capable of hanging on to their knowledge as a source of power.

Status

Teamworking can put pressure on hierarchical relationships in organisations, and often accompanies restructuring and de-layering. Teamworking can appear to challenge the traditional management structure, posing a potential threat to the role and status of senior people. Authority from formal position will be challenged by authority from technical knowledge with a new generation of highly qualified specialists seeking decision-making powers to work more effectively. Even where the organisation has assumed a flat and flexible appearance, old hierarchical policies may still be barriers to effective teamwork.

Power-distance, both inside and outside the team, can threaten the development of creativity and mutual responsibility. From within the team it may mean that members with lower power status feel that their contributions are constrained and not valued. In the past, the traditional hierarchy was underpinned by the belief that knowledge is brought to the workplace by technicians and scientists, while managers and engineers solve problems using skilled and semi-skilled workers to carry out the work. In cross-functional international teams there can be a tendency for technical experts to pull rank, with the financial expert always having the last word. The customer-driven approach to running businesses now suggests that the people closest to the customer are likely to be the source of new knowledge, products and development.

In international teams these functional status differences may be only one source of constraint. Different approaches to management, decision-making and communication can lead to team members having very different expectations about how the team should operate.

Cultural differences

Perhaps some of the biggest obstacles to international teamworking lie in cultural differences that become apparent as people work together, whether the cultures in question are national, departmental, functional, age or gender related. Cultural differences of any sort can lead to an 'us and them' approach which is unhelpful in cross-boundary teamworking. The perception of who is 'us' can change almost overnight.

‘‘Winner and loser behaviour is more likely when people feel threatened’’

A few years ago an international merger between two major manufacturing companies, one French, the other British, resulted in managers from each of the two national groups reverting to national stereotypes and perceiving the other as 'them'. However, when the company was later acquired by a US company, the French and British managers realised that they had more in common jointly than with the US management team. British managers found themselves acting as a bridge between the more hierarchical, long-term focus French and the more democratic, 'do-it-now' Americans. From the Roffey Park research into the human aspects of mergers (Devine and Hirsh, 1998), it seems that 'us and them', 'winner and loser' behaviour is more likely when people feel threatened or are acting in unfamiliar settings. This suggests that some forum, whether training, teambuilding or other means of getting people talking with each other, and better understanding each others' needs and strengths, is important.

If international teamworking is to be successful, it is essential for the key differences in culture to be identified and taken into account when people are expected to collaborate. There can be fundamental differences in what two groups believe to be important, and in how they expect staff and customers to be treated. Peter Smith's work has led to a detailed understanding of ways in which people from different national backgrounds seem to experience cross-cultural working, and pinpoints some of the areas where specific help, such as training, may be necessary. In his extensive study of joint ventures in China, Smith (1992) has identified a number of key areas where cultural differences become apparent. To name but a few, these include the ways in which decisions are taken and tasks are allocated, attitudes to time, including the keeping of deadlines and punctuality, the ways in which meetings are conducted, how poor performance is evaluated, and how work is co-ordinated.

There have been many attempts to categorise national cultures, which are always open to the accusation of reducing national characteristics to the level of stereotypes. As with all cultural stereotypes, caution should be used before generalising about individuals; however, these categories can be helpful in developing an appreciation of the potential strengths of different approaches. They can nevertheless help teams to better understand where potential 'hotspots' from their cultural mix are likely to be.

As stated in the previous chapter, Geert Hofstede's cultural dimensions highlight where corporate cultures can unwittingly cut across national cultures and cause difficulties for team members. Taking just two of these dimensions as examples illustrates how employees in international teams may experience corporate messages differently. In countries where there is high uncertainty avoidance, such as Switzerland, people prefer to reduce the stress of uncertainty by having rules and set procedures, for instance over timekeeping. This can lead to relatively bureaucratic approaches and formalised relationships that may seem at odds with corporate demands for flexibility, innovation and customer sensitivity.

Power-distance relates to the degree to which society permits highly centralised decision-making. In societies with high power-distance, the idea of empowerment may seem out of sync with how things are really done. In US companies for instance, employees are likely to be required to adopt corporate approaches rather than having local management autonomy. Similarly, relatively high power-distance is reflected in the way in which different roles are rewarded. Status symbols such as pay highlight some of the mixed messages being sent to employees in international organisations, and some of the ways in which people's expectations of their own and others' roles may differ.

Any combination of cultural dimensions provides an interesting way of diagnosing the likely range of expectations held by team members about how international teams should operate. Take, for example, two parameters such as:

self-focus ⟵————————————⟶ *group-focus*
(whether you look to yourself or the group as a means of justifying action)

high-power ⟵————————————⟶ *low-power*
(whether or not it is acceptable for one individual to order another about)

According to these parameters, some national differences are potentially likely to lead to conflict over power within an international team. So, in cultures that have a high-power and high self-focus, people tend to answer to themselves but will respond to authority and have a strong sense of duty. Countries in this group include France, Germany, Italy and Spain. In contrast, in countries with low-power and high self-focus, people answer to themselves and do not mind breaking rules to get things done. Countries in this group include Australia, Britain and Ireland and the USA. Team members from countries with a high group-focus and high-power are likely to support the group fully, accepting hierarchy within and outside the group. Countries in this group include Latin America, Greece, Portugal, Japan, Saudi Arabia. Employees from countries with light group-focus and low-power approaches tend to endorse what the group thinks is important, and make sacrifices for the group. They are also likely to reject rules and strong leaders. Countries in this group include Sweden, Switzerland, Israel, China, Poland and Russia.

‘‘Members of an international team need to be aware of stereotypes’’

Cultural differences are also apparent in communication styles, especially when there has been a misunderstanding. Using stereotypes again, a typical Italian response might be to increase verbosity whereas a French response might be to appeal to imagination and logic. A German response might be to absorb the counter-argument and make a logical reply. The typical UK response would be to understate and use humour whereas the US response would typically be to restate more firmly, provoke a fight, concede and conciliate. Members of an international team need at least to be aware of stereotypes so that they can avoid seeing differences as problematic and identify how to make the most of the different approaches within the team.

An interesting example of where cultural differences can be reconciled is illustrated by the case of GE Lighting, which acquired a half share in Tungsram, the Hungarian light bulb manufacturer in 1989.

Shortly after GE's arrival, Tungsram lost a record $1.5 million in 1993 due to the collapse of market economies in former Comecon countries, which had accounted for around 30 per cent of Tungsram's sales. It was into this climate that the CEO Jack Welch's vision of a boundary-less organisation was put into place.

Standards were improved using Western-style teamwork and project management, backed by systematic skills training of a kind unheard of in a company whose previous culture was based on rigid demarcation. This required employees to make a very major culture shift. As Tamas Palotai, senior leadership technology director at the time states,

> People who were used to a hierarchical structure where the boss gave the orders had to adjust in a very short time to the idea that decisions were now taken by teams, not individuals.

This was against a cultural backdrop of the post-Communist era, in which exhortations to greater productivity and efficiency were treated as political slogans and ignored. Concepts such as empowerment were initially confused by workers with the old order and GE had to invest considerable time and effort to transform their thinking. An influx of new skills training equipped the Hungarian management team to convert local staff to the new way of thinking throughout the company's expanding operations in central and Eastern Europe.

Another example of the interface between corporate and national culture is at the US semiconductor company, Intel. The preferred approach to team meetings at Intel, wherever they are run, is to ensure that the meetings are structured and run in a particular way. This approach is based on the belief that having a common framework and routine provides a stability which helps to overcome potential difficulties that may arise from cross-cultural differences. Similarly, IKEA requires employees, wherever they are based, to recognise the fact that they are working for a Swedish company. Procedures, approaches to the customer and standards are common internationally. Recruits are made aware of how the company operates and given a thorough induction into the corporate approach.

Enabling international teamworking

In the broadest sense, any team – whether it operates internationally or not – needs to have clarity about what the team is to achieve, and team members need to understand their role within the team. Obviously, if people lack the skill or the motivation to contribute to the team, the team's performance will suffer. Consequently, it is important to select the right people, provide appropriate training, and eliminate where possible the conflicts of loyalty that being a team member can entail. HR can have an important role in getting international teams off to a good start by addressing these issues.

Preparing international team leaders for their role can also be helpful. The role of the international manager seems to be changing. No longer is it sufficient for an international high-flycr merely to have technical skills and to be a trouble-shooting manager who can go from country to country. With barriers coming down and organisations trying new forms of international co-ordination and integration, the international manager is someone who can exercise leadership across a number of countries and cultures simultaneously, perhaps on a global or regional basis. Increasingly, personality factors and the ability to manage local operations are seen to be critical to effectiveness.

Leadership

Leadership can be a crucial issue in negotiating the team's relationship with the organisation and beyond the organisational boundaries. Leadership is often a fluid concept within a team, and particularly so in virtual teams where people are called on to manage people whom they see only infrequently. Charles Handy (1998) points out the difficulties of managing at a distance, suggesting that the managerial tradition believes that efficiency and control are inextricably linked. According to this tradition, employees cannot be trusted or relied upon. In contrast, Lipnack and Stamps (1997) suggest that in virtual teams, multiple leaders are the norm rather than the exception. This is partly aided by the democratising process of equalising communication 'airtime', regardless of status. It may also be explained by the nature of different team members' expertise becoming more evident thanks to the technology. In a sense, in a virtual context, leaders are effectively co-ordinators of the task.

Expectations about the role of the team leader are likely to differ in international teams. A number of international surveys suggest that, in most countries, subordinates find the following characteristics undesirable, where their leader:

⊕ is individualistic and self-interested
⊕ is non-egalitarian, domineering, distant and élitist
⊕ is punitive and vindictive
⊕ is narcissistic, cynical and arrogant
⊕ exercises close supervision and is a non-delegator
⊕ saves face
⊕ is secretive, cunning.

Conversely, almost universally desired characteristics appear to be where the leader:

⊕ is visionary, a team-builder
⊕ is rational, analytic, intelligent
⊕ is team-oriented and collaborative
⊕ has integrity
⊕ is decisive.

In broad stereotypes, UK teams look for 'casual' leadership, whereas French teams may expect more directive, autocratic leadership. Swedish teams may expect their team leader to be the first among equals, whereas Germans may expect a formal hierarchy with consensus. Asian teams may expect a leader to offer consensus, whereas Latin and Arab cultures may expect a more familial approach from their leader. Clearly, in a multinational team, the leader should ideally be at least sensitive to different expectations and flexible in approach.

Selecting and developing international leaders

> **"Few organisations use a specific list of international competencies when selecting people for international roles"**

A key element of a successful international team is leadership development. While there appears to be a reasonably consistent picture about what is seen to be desirable in a leader, the selection and development of international teams and leaders is often *ad hoc*. Interestingly, few organisations appear to use a specific list of international competencies when selecting people for international roles. In many organisations, functional expertise appears to be the most important criterion in selecting and preparing employees for international work is often neglected. International assignments are often used to address a particular business problem or opportunity, and their potential use as an excellent training ground for refining the core skills of future organisational leaders is often missed. Yet arguably, the skills and competencies involved in performing effectively in an international context are of a high order and should not be left to chance. HR can play a useful role in assisting those responsible for setting up teams in the selection of team personnel.

Research (Tung, 1998) has found that the greater the emphasis on adaptability and the ability to communicate during the selection process of leaders, the higher the success rate in the assignment. Other research suggests that several factors that should be included in the selection criteria for international leaders are:

- conflict resolution skills
- leadership style
- effective communication
- social orientation
- flexibility and open-mindedness
- interest in, and willingness to try, new things
- ability to cope with stress.

Given the growing shortage of international managers, a number of companies are seeking to recruit employees, especially graduates, who are willing to manage abroad, rather than trying to persuade reluctant existing employees. They market the international nature of their activities and emphasise the prospects of early international experience to attract graduates who are specifically seeking an international career. The recruitment of foreign students is becoming easier and cheaper through the use of technology. Accessing on-line CVs of overseas university students over the Internet is becoming a common feature of sourcing for graduate entry. Mobility and the willingness to move across borders are seen as prerequisites to future success.

The Volvo Car Corporation operates internationally and has built partnerships with a Japanese and a British company. Most of the management group and 60 per cent of staff are Swedish, although the biggest markets for Volvo cars are the US and UK. Volvo is keen to globalise and internationalise the way it does business. A set of global competences underpins recruitment and a global management development (GMD) programme is a key component of the internationalisation process. The goal of the programme is to prepare for a new generation of world-class leaders with international experience who have the potential to contribute to the future success of the Volvo Car Corporation. Criteria for selection on to the programme are that participants are:

- flexible
- open-minded
- able to speak several languages
- team players and also effective individual performers
- able to demonstrate leadership talents
- able to relocate
- interested in cross-cultural working.

They are also required to have physical stamina, be resilient and able to maintain high standards of behaviour, even when stressed.

Everyone who takes part in the GMD programme works for four months in Sweden, where they learn about themselves and the company, especially the corporate culture demonstrated through the company's core values. Each programme lasts for 14 months. This includes two six-month periods abroad. Every participant has his or her own development plan and mentor at Volvo Cars.

Case-study – cross-boundary teamworking in an international engineering company

An effective team leader

In a Roffey Park research project (Glynn and Holbeche, 1999) into effective cross-boundary working in an international engineering company, two teams were studied to identify factors that contributed to their success. Key factors appeared to be the role of the team leader and the way in which team members interacted. The leader was the person who not only set the direction for the team but also negotiated and obtained resources, including people for the team. This meant that the leader had to be sufficiently competent technically that he or she could appreciate all the functions encompassed within the team, but needed distinct leadership competencies beyond technical ability. The leader was expected to manage the diversity inherent in the team and enhance the performance of the team as a whole by building on individual strengths.

In the teams studied, the leader was a senior manager who effectively acted as sponsor of the team at senior levels. An essential aspect of the role was clarifying the roles and responsibilities of individual team members and managing the conflicts that arise across functional boundaries. As such, having an effective leader becomes perhaps more critical for a cross-boundary team, especially when the team operates internationally, than for a conventional functional team.

Given the diverse backgrounds of team members, and that there was initially not much common ground between them, the role of the leader in providing a tangible focus and direction for the team became all the more important. The leaders needed to be both strategic and operational. It was important that they were seen as someone who 'leads from the front', setting a strong vision and objectives for the team. They performed the important role of providing drive and determination in the face of difficulties.

Team leaders need to be 'sold on teamworking'. In the case-study, it was widely recognised that the team leaders needed to have excellent interpersonal skills not just for communicating with the team, but for helping the team communicate effectively with each other. In terms of style, team members felt that decision-making should be the ultimate responsibility of the leader, to avoid functional experts pulling rank, but that decision-making should be carried out in a participative way. The team leader was also seen as being responsible for communicating the team's successes to the wider organisation and building up a strong profile for the team throughout the business. The team leader, therefore, needs to be visible, both to the team itself and within the organisation as a whole.

Team members

The case-study suggests that individuals must be committed to the team, with a real desire to achieve team goals. This means that team members must be able to balance their focus on team goals alongside functional goals. Individuals must also be willing to share success and failure with the rest of the team. Accepting their share of responsibility for both means that team members must also be prepared to confront others who fail to deliver, or who blame others for things for which they are accountable. In the teams studied, some team members who were good at defusing conflict were helpful in creating a constructive problem-solving climate. Facilitators also proved useful in one team in enabling open communication, mediation, breaking down hostilities within the team and reviewing team processes. Interpersonal relationships were strengthened in one team in a social context.

"Simply relying on one's own functional knowledge is not enough"

Variety in the team is important, as is the team's ability to respond to local issues. Individuals within the team need to learn about the specific concerns of different countries within which the team is operating. Team members must be willing to help each other but they should also be willing to learn from others and explore new areas outside their own area of expertise. Simply relying on one's own functional knowledge is not enough. After all, members of a cross-boundary international team are likely to be people who are experts in their own field, but who may not know much about other areas.

It is important that members understand the broader business context within which the project is being conducted and appreciate the different elements of the project being carried out by others. This does not entail having a detailed understanding of other people's technical specialisms, but enough of a sense of their priorities and requirements to ensure that the project plan can work smoothly, without people making unnecessary demands on others through ignorance. They therefore have to be able to liaise across boundaries within their team, and between the team and the rest of the organisation, including their boss.

Developing international teams through training

A key area in which HR can support international teams is through training. There are many advantages to training a team before it has to begin its task. The training should enable the team to 'gel' as a group of individuals, but also to expand the team's ability to respond to local needs. This can be achieved in a number of ways, but Snell *et al*'s research (1998) suggests that training programmes that emphasise the company's strategies, structures and processes can help team members use their judgement when faced with local situations. Cross-cultural teambuilding can also be helpful, enabling the team to develop work processes that maximise the benefits of diversity. The team can be helped to develop ground rules and team learning processes that will assist the team in spreading the benefits of learning from experience. Interpersonal skills training such as in conflict resolution and negotiation, as well as technical training such as project management skills, may prove useful.

Virtual teams in particular need to focus on teambuilding and inter personal skills. The team needs to be able to understand what working 'virtually' will actually entail. Communications skills may need to be given a special focus so that team members can develop ways of getting their messages across to one another via different media – e-mail, telephone, videoconferencing – in ways that are sensitive and effective. Training in aspects of knowledge management can be helpful in enabling the team to capture and share knowledge as well as data. Some team members may need help with personal organisation skills since they will be working in isolation from the rest of the team. Teambuilding should ideally be a regular event so that teams can focus on how they are working together and develop the common ground which is the basis of effective collaboration.

Team leaders need to be trained in agreeing goals and responsibilities within the team. Unless people understand what they are doing, and why, there is a potential risk of team members focusing exclusively on local issues at the expense of the bigger picture. The team leader may need help in creating a shared focus and direction. This needs to be sufficiently clear that team members have a common framework, but not so rigid or culturally insensitive that the scope for local responsiveness disappears.

Developing effective communications

Clearly, co-location, though ideal, may not be practicable, especially in global organisations in which virtual teams become the norm. However, the engineering company case study highlights the importance of at least an occasional opportunity to 'personalise' the relationship through meetings, visits, videoconferencing, the use of electronic 'team rooms' and other means of helping people to establish a relationship with one another. This is in addition to the need for regular briefings and updates so that people can feel part of the bigger whole. Communication then loses its impersonal aspect and real teamwork becomes more likely. Conversely, communications may need to be formalised in order to facilitate group learning. In some organisations, team members are required, as part of a formal planning process, to learn as much as they can about external bodies, whether these are customers or competitors, and update the rest of the team.

Technology can support the process of people feeling that they know each other, but it cannot replace face-to-face interaction. Of course, electronics firms have long perfected the 'team room' concept whereby team members interact with each other via video links at particular times according to team conventions. One relatively advanced use of an electronic 'team room' was designed and installed by NCR at three of its sites in the USA. Known as the 'Wormhole', the facility consisted of a sophisticated audio, video and data link. Camera angles were arranged so that, by leaving the door open, it was possible to see people walking along a corridor (even though they were several thousand miles away). This sense of contact and immediacy no doubt helps in the maintenance of the 'human factor' of effective teamworking, but the importance of enabling teams to meet each other physically should not be underestimated.

International teamworking at Ericsson

International teamworking is a key part of the success story at Ericsson, the Swedish-based global communications company. This reflects the increasingly international nature of the business. In line with many companies, the continuous drive for growth and increased margins means that Ericsson is consolidating production, out-sourcing more, and moving its operations closer to the main points of sale and where there is a lower cost base. Units exist in the USA and other global centres, and in China alone there are five production centres.

On the other hand, although European countries such as Germany, Italy, Spain, Sweden and the UK are main markets, the relatively high cost of labour means that production costs have to be kept under the spotlight. The global supply chain is closely monitored so that change can be implemented, if need be, within a six-month period. Growth rates are driven by national and global markets. Investors are now more sophisticated than in times gone by; so too are customers.

Sales are carried out by region, with a strong focus on multinational customers. The importance of meeting the differing needs of an internationally diverse customer base means that the composition of sales teams must reflect the cultures of the customers. With widely varying customer perceptions of what constitutes value and quality service, international sales teams need to be competent in the 'soft' issues of customer care and be able to marry perceptions to reality. Sales teams tend to be based in the lead country of their major inter-national clients, whether this is the operating centre or headquarters. The important thing is to be close to where the powerbase of the cus-tomer is so that the team can fruitfully spend time on key issues.

Tony Booth, UK Chairman of Ericsson Ltd, believes that such sales teams need to be empowered to negotiate the sales pitch and any trade-offs within a broad negotiation margin. The desire to give sales teams ownership of the sales process has to be balanced against the need for pricing consistency across Europe. The advent of the Euro, for example, means that customers can compare prices across Europe instantly. The separate teams therefore need to operate as a higher-level corporate team to avoid damaging one another while improv-ing their own local sales figures. Some customers are looking for global trading agreements and do not want to negotiate in each country.

"Team members need to be credible to the customer"

The teams report both to local managers and the corporate centre. They are supported, rather than controlled, by the centre. Tony Booth believes that there is no one model of reporting that works in every circumstance. The key thing is to put people with the appropriate skills and ability close to the customer. Team members need to be credible to the customer. Credibility is often based on what the individual has achieved in their career to date, and, in some countries, their perceived power within the company. The team needs to be made up of self-starting, experienced individuals who have learned from their mistakes elsewhere before becoming responsible for a major account.

In addition, team members have to work together as a real team, supporting each other on issues, where in the past they might have expected help from HQ echelons which no longer exist. They have to work together physically and virtually and to act as their own team catalysts. Increasingly customers want to see that the whole team is credible, not just the individual sales person. The team also has to dovetail resources and skills in tough market-places.

The team leader, a global or international account manager, can be based with the team or operate in a 'virtual' way. The leader is expected to help win the business and help the team deal with the challenges of delivering the business. The influencing skills of the leader therefore need to be of a high order, as there are in effect two types of negotiation taking place. First, the sales negotiation has to reflect the complexities of local requirements and styles. Second, from an internal company perspective, the leader has to win support from production and other parts of the supply chain in order to succeed.

It is often assumed that sales people are primarily individual performers rather than team players. In Ericsson, the team aspect is taken seriously and is reflected in the bonus scheme. There is a potential team bonus of 20 to 30 per cent, which reflects team effort as well as achievement. Teams would have to demonstrate, for instance, how they have taken the whole team's needs into account when bidding for resources. As part of a global supplier, teams also need to be able to negotiate with other teams when bidding for resources. This can result in conflict which has to be dealt with internally and not be evident to the customer; no matter how complex the internal organisation may be, the customer has to be the prime focus.

Naturally, in a global business, international exposure is seen as an essential part of preparation for senior management. Typically, people move on from leading an international team to running a big division with profit and loss responsibility. Sometimes people are given the chance to work for a major subsidiary to gain additional experience. Ericsson has a wealth of experience in international team working, developed over more than 100 years of worldwide operations – Tony Booth says it's in their bloodstream!

Supporting international teams

Hackman (1990) identifies six key areas where teams need organisational support: targets, resources, information, education, feedback and technical/process assistance. To some extent all of these involve the sharing of knowledge, particularly in supplying information and feedback on performance. For team members who are about to go on an international assignment, help in preparing for the experience can make the difference between an effective start to the assignment and a dismal failure. HR can play a significant role in supplying preparatory help such as training in cross-cultural issues, setting up procedures to maintain contact with the home office, and help in finding employment for spouses. Once on assignment, employees look for help in adjusting on a practical level. A mentor can be useful here: not only someone who is familiar with the local customs and who can ease the process of integration, but also someone at the home office who can be a vital link for the assignee on career issues. Support networks involving communication through travel and company newsletters can also be useful.

“Practical help and moral support are often needed to enable families to adapt to the change”

Perhaps the main area where employees look for support from the home office is in preparing for their return on repatriation. While this is not entirely an HR responsibility, relocation research has shown that this is a serious area of shortfall. Many employees are dissatisfied with the quality of the communication, support and advice they receive prior to, and following, repatriation. Practical help and moral support are often needed to enable families to adapt to the change. There is evidence that many returning employees suffer 'reverse culture shock' and other problems of adaptation. This often happens because of a significant mismatch between people's expectations prior to their repatriation and what they actually encounter when they return home. The greater the clarity about possible return roles before the assignment begins, the better.

Benefiting from international employees' experience

One of the biggest challenges for both organisations and members of international teams is making the most of the enhanced skills and knowledge gained by the individual through their international role. If a team member has returned from an international assignment, the commonest problem is making best use of their talents on repatriation. Individuals are often expected to slot into any available role. If the person's knowledge is not used to good effect, the employee typically leaves the organisation within a short time.

The phenomenon is not simply that of a bruised ego and the individual finding him or herself to be a small fish in a big pond. It is more that there are potential business benefits in enabling the individual's enhanced skills and knowledge of the local market, with its challenges and opportunities, to be put to good use. In many cases there is not even a formal debriefing of the individual after the assignment. Frustration at having no outlet for these skills, together with dissatisfaction about career prospects, are the common reasons given by individuals leaving after an international assignment. HR has a key role to play in assisting line managers in making use of the skills and experience developed by individuals as members of international teams.

Conclusion

Creating high-performing international teams is a challenging business. Many teams operate as virtual teams. The temptation is to underestimate the needs of the team as a whole, simply because the whole team rarely comes together. Yet the complex nature of such teams' work, blending as it does the demands of both local and the global business perspectives, calls for a high level of skill and team understanding. The added complexities of cultural difference, including the potentially conflicting functional demands, means that teams who are able to produce good results are extremely able.

HR professionals have a key role to play in ensuring that international teams have the skills and ability to perform effectively. Training can be helpful, and team members can be encouraged both to develop their own team learning and also to add to the organisation's learning about its changing market-place. Better use of technology will help in the management of international teams but will not replace the need for people to meet together face to face. More skilful support of employees and their families who are on assignment may reduce the number of expensive assignment failures. Better use of enhanced skills may retain valued employees for longer. Giving people the chance to develop and apply the high-level skills required of international teams is only one part of the equation. Rewarding and using these enhanced skills to greater effect to the mutual benefit of the organisation and the employee is the surest way to tap into the motivation and commitment of international teams.

References

BARTLETT C. A. *and* GHOSHAL S. (1998) *Managing across Borders; The transnational solution*. Revised edn. London, Random House Business Books.

CHILD J. (1990) *The Management of Equity Joint Ventures in China*. Beijing, China-EC Management Institute.

DEVINE M. *and* HIRSH W. (1998) *Mergers and Acquisitions: Getting the people bit right*. Roffey Park Management Institute.

GLYNN C. *and* HOLBECHE L. (1999) *International Leadership*. Horsham, Roffey Park Management Institute. May.

ETTORE B. (1993) 'A brave new world: managing international careers'. *Management Review*. April.

HACKMAN R. (1990) *Groups That Work and Those That Don't*. San Francisco, Jossey-Bass.

HANDY C. (1998) *Beyond Certainty: The changing worlds of organisations*. Harvard, MA, Harvard Business Press.

HELLER R. (1994) 'The manager's dilemma'. *Management Today*. January, pp 42–7.

HIGGS M. J. *and* ROLAND D. (1992) 'All pigs are equal?' *Management Education and Development*. Vol. 23, No. 4. pp 349–62.

HOFSTEDE G. (1994) *Cultures and Organisations*. London, Fontana.

HOLBECHE L. (1998) *Motivating People in Lean Organisations*. London, Butterworth-Heinemann.

KREMPEL M. (1998) *Shared Services: A new business architecture for Europe*. London, The Economist Intelligence Unit.

LIPNACK J. *and* STAMPS J. (1997). *Virtual Teams: Reaching across space, time and organisations with technology*. New York, John Wiley.

LOOSE A. (1998) 'Jobs sans frontières'. *The Times*. 12 November.

PANTER S. (1995) *Summary Report of a Qualitative International Research Survey*. Ashridge Management College.

PEIPERL M. (1998) in M. Coles, 'Global managers despair at heirs', *The Sunday Times*, 8 November.

SANSOM J. (1993) *Survey of Repatriation Assistance*. London, University of Westminster and CBI Relocation Council.

SMITH P. B. (1992) 'Organizational behaviour and national cultures'. *British Journal of Management*. Vol. 3. pp39–51.

SNELL S. A., SNOW C. *and* DAVISON S. C. (1998) 'Designing and supporting transnational teams: the human resource agenda'. *Human Resource Management*. Summer. Vol. 37, No. 2. pp147–58.

SOLOMON C. (1996) 'Expats say: help make us mobile'. *Personnel Journal*. July.

SYRETT M. (1997) in L. Holbeche, *Motivating People in Lean Organizations*, Oxford, Butterworth-Heinemann.

TUNG R. (1998) *Selection and Training of Personnel for Overseas Assignments*. Cambridge, MA, Ballinger.

VERMA A., KOCHAN T. A. *and* LANSBURY R. D. (1995) 'Lessons from the Asian experience: a summary', in A. Verma, T. A. Kochan and R. D. Lansbury (eds), *Employment Relations in the Growing Asian Economies*, London, Routledge, pp336–57.

WARNER M. (1997) 'Introduction: HRM in Greater China'. *International Journal of Human Resource Management*. Vol. 8, No. 5. October. pp565–8.

WARNER M. *and* NG S. (1999) 'Collective contracts in Chinese enterprises: a new brand of collective bargaining under "market socialism"?' *BJIR*. Vol. 37, No. 2. June. pp295–314.

WONG S. (1998) *Emigrant Entrepreneurs: Shanghai industrialists in Hong Kong*. Oxford, Oxford University Press.

ZANKO M. (ed.) *Global Advantage through People: Human resource management policies in ten APEC economies*. Wollongang International Business Research Institute, University of Wollongang and Asia Pacific Economic Co-operation.

Developing International Management Teams through Diversity

Malcolm Higgs

Introduction

Globalisation and teamworking appear to be high-profile topics seen as priority issues by organisations as they move into the new century. It is increasingly common to find management books, papers and conferences including one or other, or indeed both, of these topics in some guise.

This growth in interest is a manifestation of an increasing belief that one of the major sources of competitive advantage for businesses is the effective management and development of people. Illustrative of this trend is the research reported by Sparrow, Schuler and Jackson (1994). Their report of a worldwide IBM study covering 2,000 organisations pointed out that the dominant view of participants was that an organisation's people provide the only realistic basis for achieving a sustainable competitive advantage. In a global setting the emphasis on managing and developing people invariably leads to consideration of the management of diversity and related challenges. Many researchers into globalisation identify the major challenges facing cross-border organisations as the ability to develop practices that balance global competitiveness, multinational flexibility and the building of a worldwide learning capability. Achieving this balance requires organisations to develop cultural sensitivity in their managers and an ability to manage and leverage learning to build future capabilities.

It has been suggested by many authors that teamworking provides an effective framework for meeting the need to achieve performance goals in organisations that require greater flexibility in responding rapidly to market challenges and opportunities. In looking at the dynamics involved in organisational learning and competitive success, the key role of effective teamworking is highlighted. More recently, researchers have produced evidence that demonstrates, in a commercial rather than 'classroom' setting, that diversity of team types within a team (using Belbin team roles as a framework) leads to more effective performance.

The integration of research into cultural diversity and teamworking provides a backdrop for considering the development and performance of international management teams.

Global organisations face a growing need to ensure that groups of managers from different nationalities work together effectively, either in permanent management teams or in project teams addressing specific business issues. However, many organisations have found that bringing groups of managers from different cultural backgrounds together in a team can in practice be difficult. The performance of such teams often fails to live up to expectations. Indeed, as regards the development of effective international management teams, it has been suggested that the following areas be considered:

⊕ identifying the nature and implications of national cultural differences within the team
⊕ establishing a basis for building understanding and awareness of national cultural differences and the ways in which they may be managed
⊕ formulating a framework for developing a high-performing team which takes account of cultural differences and leverages the diversity present in an international team.

Each of these areas is examined in more detail below.

Identifying the nature and impact of national cultural differences

Identifying a clear framework for analysing and understanding national cultural differences is a valuable starting-point, and frameworks of this kind have been developed by such researchers and consultants as Hofstede and Trompenaars. Although the merits and drawbacks of these frameworks are the subject of much discussion and disagreement, their use as helpful tools for examining the major issues is widely accepted.

For the purpose of developing this chapter, the author has selected Hofstede's model as a basis for illustration.

In his original work Hofstede identified four key dimensions that affect national cultural differences. These were:

- ⊕ *individualism/collectivism*: the extent to which individuals value self-determination, as opposed to having their behaviour determined by the collective will of a group or organisation.
- ⊕ *power-distance*: the question of involvement in decision-making. In low power-distance cultures, employees seek involvement and desire a participative management style. At the other end of the scale, employees tend to work and behave in a way appropriate to those who accept they will be directed within the terms of the hierarchy of the organisation.
- ⊕ *uncertainty-avoidance*: individuals' tolerance of ambiguity or uncertainty in their working environment. In cultures with a high uncertainty-avoidance, employees will look for clearly defined, formal rules and conventions to govern their behaviour.
- ⊕ *masculinity/femininity*: the dimension related to individual values. It is possibly the most difficult dimension to use within an organisational context, but in practice the difficulty is more to do with terminology and linguistics (see Hofstede, 1991). In highly 'masculine' cultures, dominant values relate to assertiveness and material acquisition. In highly 'feminine' cultures, values focus on relationships among people, concern for others and quality of life.

The findings of Hofstede's original research are often supported by the practical experience of organisations attempting to implement global HR policies. Research conducted in the early 1990s into Japanese financial organisations operating in UK markets produced evidence of experiences explicable in terms of Hofstede's framework. This research illustrated the impact of national culture on managerial style and beliefs, and the significance of a mismatch between managerial style and staff expectations. Researchers have also reinforced the significance of cultural characteristics on managerial style, although they do point out that the level of industrialisation in a country is a co-determinant of style.

Employing the Hofstede framework it is possible to identify differences in management styles, organisational preferences and motivation patterns. Table 1 summarises some aspects of cultural difference that can affect the way in which managers from different countries may behave and perform in a team. The table illustrates differences on the Hofstede dimension of 'uncertainty-avoidance'. From this it would appear likely that, say, a UK member (low uncertainty-avoidance) and Japanese member (high uncertainty-avoidance) of a management team would have significant differences in their initial perceptions and expectations both of team purposes and processes.

From this brief illustration it is, hopefully, evident that in order to develop effective international management teams it is necessary to create an environment that both acknowledges and values cultural diversity and that develops individuals' cultural awareness and sensitivity.

Establishing a basis for understanding cultural differences

All too often multinationals see the cultural diversity within their operations as an area of difficulty rather than as an opportunity to build competitive advantage. This point is well illustrated by an exercise in the early 1980s carried out by Laurent and Adler. International executives attending management seminars in France

Table 1
DIFFERENCES IN UNCERTAINTY-AVOIDANCE

Low uncertainty-avoidance	High uncertainty-avoidance
• Achievement	• Security
• Leader as facilitator	• Leader as expert
• Minimum rules	• Emotional need for rules
• Open-ended learning	• Structured learning

were asked to list the advantages and disadvantages of *cultural diversity* for their organisations. Although 100 per cent of participants were able to identify *disadvantages*, fewer than 30 per cent could identify any *advantage*!

Understanding the nature and value of cultural diversity is very often not well embedded within company thinking and practice. In many ways, organisational thinking in this area has not developed in line with the trend to globalisation. Phillips (1992) has commented on the apparent inability of organisations to develop managers with cross-border capabilities. David McGill of BP has also pointed out that 'Making someone aware of cultural diversity is something that has to start at day one when they join the company.'

The performance of international management teams may well be as much to do with the values of their organisations as with team-building and development processes. A leading academic in this field, Nancy Adler, provides some evidence for this in her analysis of organisational strategies for managing cultural diversity (Adler, 1980). This analysis is summarised in Table 2, which highlights the *parochial* response as the most common.

In addition to understanding cultural differences *per se*, it is important to identify the potential advantages and disadvantages that may be brought to a team by managers from different national cultures.

Table 3, taken from Hofstede (1991), provides an illustration of comparative contributions from differing cultural perspectives.

The consideration of diversity in international management teams requires us to do more than think about cultural differences. In a study in the early 1990s conducted by the Cranfield Executive Competencies group, which examined management teams on a pan-European basis, the observation was made that:

> To differing degrees, the same sort of problems is shared across different nation states. The skill is not to be blinded by national parochial differences. Attention should be given to those levers that are required to focus on attaining business goals.
>
> Kakabadse (1994)

Table 2
ORGANISATIONAL APPROACHES TO DIVERSITY

Type of organisation	Perceived effect of cultural diversity on organisation	Strategy for managing the effect of cultural diversity	Most likely outcomes of strategy	Frequency of perception and strategy
Parochial Our way is the only way	*No effect* Cultural diversity has no recognised effect on the organisation	*Ignore differences* Ignore the effect of cultural diversity on the organisation	*Problems* Problems may occur but will not be attributed to culture	*Very common*
Ethnocentric Our way is the best way	*Negative effect* Cultural diversity will cause problems for the organisation	*Minimise the differences* Minimise the sources and effect of cultural diversity on the organisation. If possible, select a mono-cultural workforce	*Some problems and few advantages* Problems will become less as diversity is decreased, while the possibility of creating advantages will be ignored or eliminated; problems will be attributed to culture	*Common*
Synergistic The combination of our way and their way may be the best way	*Potential negative and positive effects* Cultural diversity can simultaneously lead to problems and advantages for the organisation	*Manage differences* Train organisational members to recognise cultural differences and use them to create advantages for the organisation	*Some problems and many advantages* Advantages to the organisation will be realised and recognised; some problems will continue to occur and will need to be managed.	*Very uncommon*

This study highlighted the importance of focusing on the competencies required for effective performance, and for the effective development of these, in a team context.

Hofstede outlined a broad framework for building the competencies required for operating on a cross-cultural basis. This framework may be summarised as involving the:

Table 3
POTENTIAL COMPETITIVE ADVANTAGES OF DIFFERENT CULTURES

	Low	High
Power-distance	• Accept responsibility	• Discipline
Individual/ collective	*Individual*	*Collective*
	• Management mobility	• Employee commitment
Uncertainty- avoidance	*Low*	*High*
	• Innovation	• Precision
Masculine/ feminine	*Masculine*	*Feminine*
	• Efficiency	• Personal service
	• Mass production	• Custom-building

Source: adapted from Hofstede (1991)

⊕ building of awareness both of individuals' own cultures and the differences between national cultures
⊕ development of knowledge of the effect of cultural differences, and of the relative strengths and weaknesses of different cultures in a managerial context
⊕ building of skills in the areas of managerial cultural sensitivity.

Whatever the theory says, it is *practice* that influences organisational behaviour: it is through working on *real* problems and issues in a multicultural setting, using a structured framework, that skills and understanding are developed. It is therefore in this arena that the benefits of diversity may be realised. Such practical experiences (and studies of these) highlight the importance of developing skills in a *team context* and recommend their development in *actual teams* designed to:

⊕ build cohesion and consistency in teamworking
⊕ develop a shared vision and understanding
⊕ establish high-quality dialogue between members
⊕ establish feedback mechanisms to review and improve team processes.

Thus, in examining a possible framework for building effective international management teams, it is important to consider not only the factors associated with effective teamworking but also those associated with cultural diversity.

Developing a framework for building effective international management teams

Within a single national cultural framework, it has been identified that the issues relating to diversity in personal styles and behaviour are an important factor in effective team performance (see, for example, the work of Belbin, and Margerison and McCann). In examining a team task, Belbin demonstrated (within an experimental environment) the value for effective team performance of diversity in team role and style, and the Belbin team role model has accordingly been widely used within organisations.

The wisdom of such widespread use in an organisational setting has been challenged, given the lack of validation data outside the original experimental setting. However, although there are debates about the psychometric robustness of the Belbin instrument, many researchers and practitioners have argued for its pragmatic value as a team development tool; and even though the majority of the research work on the Belbin model has been carried out in the UK, the model is widely used for team development purposes on an international basis.

The debate about the Belbin team role model is one of many concerning the whole question of teamworking and its value for organisations. Indeed, the literature on teams and teamworking is extensive. The case made for the organisational effect of teams remains, however, open to question. Although much is claimed for teams in terms of performance benefits, there is still a dearth of rigorously researched evidence to support such claims.

Given the underlying assumption that teams do contribute towards organisational performance, there is a wealth of data on the factors that contribute towards effective teamworking. Much of this information is derived from group research and dynamics (one of the most widely researched areas in the social sciences). A review of a selection of the literature on teams has identified over 100 claimed effectiveness factors (Higgs, 1999). These factors map well onto the

Hackman and Morris (1975) model for examining group perform-ance. The key team factors that emerge consistently are input and process factors.

Input factors
- Skills of team members and the appropriateness of the skill mix.
- Clarity, mix and understanding of roles.
- Attitudes and expectations of team members.
- Mutual accountability.
- Nature and complexity of tasks.
- Organisational culture.

Process factors
- Nature of goals and purpose of team.
- Involvement of team members in formulating goals.
- Interaction of team members.
- Management and leadership style.
- Degree of commitment to goals and purpose.

Two comparatively recent studies have re-inforced earlier ones on the factors underpinning effective teamworking. One of these studies (carried out by the author), involving an examination of teams in a diverse range of multinational and UK organisations, identified the following factors as correlated with effective team performance:

- team balance
- leadership behaviour
- inter-team working
- overcoming hurdles
- autonomy
- shared understanding of goals
- recognition
- reward
- full-circle feedback.

In an earlier study, Higgs and Rowland (1992) identified key elements found to be determinants of effective management team performance in a major multinational's international project teams. These were:

- a shared understanding of, and commitment to, team goals and objectives

- clear and shared understanding of each team member's role and contribution
- recognition of the value of diversity in style, expertise and contribution
- effective pooling of knowledge and skills.

The factors emerging from an analysis of these and earlier studies indicate that a framework for developing effective international management teams needs to address:

- team purpose/charter
- objectives
- values
- team member roles
- teamworking processes.

Combining these requirements with cross-cultural considerations may be achieved by a framework that addresses both the 'What' in terms of content and focus of the teamworking and the 'How' in terms of style and working processes. Such a framework is summarised in Figure 1.

Building a team around the need to address hard and specific business issues provides a clear context for examining the cultural and process elements of performance. Being able to anchor all activities and developments to hard deliverables provides focus for developing

Figure 1
A FRAMEWORK FOR DEVELOPING INTERNATIONAL MANAGEMENT TEAMS (HIGGS, 1995)

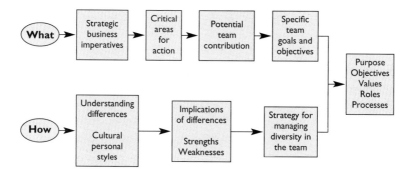

and applying understanding, and helps to provide a clear and unifying goal for the team. In practice, we have found that the achievement of the business-related result re-inforces the process understanding and learning that has taken place within the team.

Although the framework outlined above can be valuable in building a specific team, the overall issues reviewed in this chapter require a more concerted organisation-wide approach. For many organisations, the move to build multicultural management teams and to leverage the ensuing diversity represents a major change. As such, it may be worth viewing the process within the context of the change management framework (first proposed by Lewin – see Lewin, 1951). Figure 2 summarises a possible overall framework for building more effective multinational management teams using Lewin's model.

A case-study in building multicultural management teams

We have now seen that the development of an effective multi-national team requires both cross-cultural and team-building issues to be addressed. Although examples of effective strategies to deal

Figure 2
MANAGING THE CHANGE TO MULTICULTURAL TEAM WORKING (ADAPTED FROM LEWIN, 1951)

Unfreezing	Moving	Refreezing
Communication of issues	Action learning by solving real business problems in multinational teams	Design team selection processes
Development of awareness and understanding	Review and sharing of learning	Building teamworking processes
Top leadership commitment and example		International teamworking at many levels
		Recognition and reward

with cross-cultural and team development issues are clearly documented, published research into the development of multicultural teams appears scarcer.

This chapter provides a specific insight (by means of a brief case-study) into building a cross-cultural management team. Although many question case-studies as a basis for research, there are areas in which they can be of value, in particular for dealing with 'how' and 'why' questions which may lead to the formulation of issues that can be pursued by alternative methods. The validity of generalising from a single case-study has been (for example) an issue of considerable debate. However, this has to be set alongside the equally valid question of the extent to which generalisations may be made from a single experiment.

In presenting this case-study, the author recognises the above concerns and limitations. However, the intention here is to share observations of how one multicultural team developed and functioned, and, hopefully, to promote interest in further study and research into this area of team performance.

Background

Company X is a major multinational consumer goods company with an impressive record of growth and profitability. It is based in North America and, along with many multinationals, is aiming to implement a strategy of globalisation.

Following a strategy review two years ago, the company determined a range of core values to underpin their future growth. One of these was teamworking.

Each year the company conducts a worldwide attitude survey. In 1994 the survey indicated that teamworking was seen significantly less positively in European countries than in the rest of the world.

The president of the company established a task force of European country managers to identify the reasons for this difference and to recommend practical actions to improve teamworking in Europe. The author of this chapter was asked to act as a facilitator to this task force.

The team

The membership of the task force comprised the country managers of the Netherlands, France, Germany, Greece and the UK. All were experienced managers with Company X, with good performance records. Their careers had been primarily within the marketing function in a range of leading consumer goods companies.

Expectations of behaviour

The company is highly results-focused, and it both recruits and rewards highly motivated and achievement-oriented individuals. As one team member described it, the predominant corporate culture was one that 'honoured the individual hero'.

The existence of a dominant type of individual who succeeds within Company X was supported by the results of a Belbin team role analysis of some 80 European managers, which showed an extreme dominance of 'shapers' (see Figure 3). All members of the team had 'shaper' as their predominant Belbin role and, indeed, for all of them 'team worker' was the lowest role in their Belbin profile. This mix did not bode well for effective teamworking.

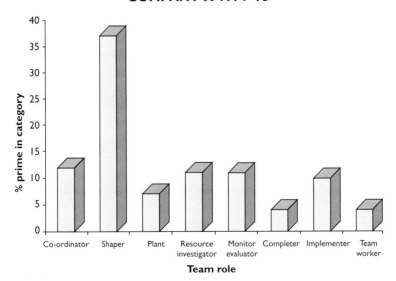

Figure 3
OVERALL BELBIN TEAM ROLE SUMMARY FROM COMPANY X 1994–95

Prior to the first meeting of the team, the author had developed a profile of expected behaviours and issues based on indications from Hofstede's work on cultural differences. (Scores for the five countries represented by the team members are shown in Table 4.)

Using these scores and Hofstede's descriptions, the authors developed the following hypotheses relating to the likely profiles of the team members:

⊕ **From the PDI scale**

The Greek and French country managers would be more likely to accept the need to address the issue raised by the president of Company X because of his position within the organisational hierarchy, although *he* may feel that it is incumbent on higher management to make final decisions on the issue. The managers from the UK, Germany and the Netherlands would be more likely to want to challenge the issue and have a good deal of influence on the ultimate decision.

⊕ **From the INV scale**

In the view of all country managers, with the exception of the manager from Greece, there would be a great likelihood of resistance to a strong focus on team involvement in decision-making at the expense of potential for individual contribution.

Table 4
COUNTRY SCORES ON HOFSTEDE'S SCALES

	PDI	INV	MAS	UAI
France	68	71	43	86
Germany	35	67	66	65
Greece	60	35	57	112
The Netherlands	38	80	14	53
UK	35	89	66	35

Key
PDI = Power-distance
INV = Individual/collective
MAS = Masculine/feminine
UAI = Uncertainty-avoidance

◉ **From the MAS scale**
The manager from the Netherlands would be likely to focus on the intrinsic value of teamworking in terms of building relationships. The other managers would be likely to raise issues relating to extrinsic reward in connection with teamworking.
◉ **From the UAI scale**
The French, German and, in particular, Greek managers would be concerned over precision in terms of reference, procedures and protocols in relation to the nature and scope of the task force's project. The managers from the Netherlands and the UK would be content to adopt a more open position and to work with few (or indeed no) formal rules and procedures.

Reflecting on what was known about the company culture and on the Belbin profiles of the individuals, it was further hypothesised that there would be:

◉ considerable competition between members
◉ conflict over the project goals and objectives
◉ strong resistance to spending time on process issues – the push for results would be high.

The process

Working from the above 'hypotheses', it was important to develop a process that addressed cultural differences, individual differences and team development. The timescale for the project was relatively short (some three months), and the number of occasions on which the whole team could meet was limited by forward commitments and the availability of team members.

It was decided to use the synergistic development model proposed by Nancy Adler (1980). This model proposes the following steps for building cultural synergy:

◉ Step 1: develop an understanding of cultural differences
◉ Step 2: examine the problem or issue from the different cultural perspectives
◉ Step 3: explore options and build ideas without working within any one particular cultural framework
◉ Step 4: review proposed ideas or solutions to test for cultural fit
◉ Step 5: implement solutions and monitor to evaluate cultural fit, modifying as necessary.

Although Adler's model was proposed as a framework for managing cultural diversity, it was felt that it could also apply to the personal diversity of team members.

The first step (understanding differences) offered a good fit with the literature on teams. In particular, Belbin pointed to the benefits of understanding the mix of styles in a team, and the limitations, strengths and weaknesses of a mix that does not offer the balanced range he describes. The value of reviewing styles and roles has been highlighted by a number of other authors, each of whom has a somewhat different team-role classification and model. Building on these thoughts, the overall process proposed was as follows:

Meeting 1
⊕ Review and discuss cultural differences.
⊕ Review and discuss individual differences.
⊕ Agree goals and method of working.

Meeting 2
⊕ Problem exploration.

Meeting 3
⊕ Idea generation and selection.

Meeting 4
⊕ Preparation of presentation to president.

Meeting 5
⊕ Review of process and learning.

Outcomes

The initial meeting was, as hypothesised, a fairly difficult and stormy affair. A number of the initial 'hypotheses' were borne out, and a number of surprises in outcomes were encountered:

⊕ The managers from the UK, Germany and the Netherlands challenged the findings of the original survey and the need to improve teamworking. The manager from France argued strongly that the team has to respond to, rather than challenge, the brief. Surprisingly, the manager from Greece aligned herself with the UK, Germany and Netherlands in challenging the brief.

⊕ The only manager to support and promote a significant increase in a team-based approach to decision-making in Europe was the manager from the Netherlands. The manager from Greece did not take the expected stance.

⊕ In discussing the problem faced (this was brought forward from step 2), the managers from the UK, France, Germany and Greece all raised issues related to the linking of financial reward and teamworking, whereas (as 'hypothesised') the manager from the Netherlands wanted to focus more on the intrinsic rewards and benefits of teamworking.

⊕ A lot of debate in the initial meeting focused on how the team would work. The managers from the UK and Netherlands were arguing in favour of exploring the issue within a loose framework, whereas the managers from Greece, Germany and France wanted to establish clear boundaries, terms of reference, reporting arrangements and allocation of accountabilities. This was very much in line with the initial 'hypotheses'.

Overall, as expected, the teams were strongly resistant to the proposed process, and stated that they could see little value in using time on discussing such 'flaky' issues when they were under pressure to produce results. However, they did eventually agree to try working through the process and engage in a discussion of Hofstede's framework and the Belbin team-role implications.

At the end of the initial meeting there was a clear and shared understanding of the project purpose and its goals.

The second meeting was less stormy than the first, although there was resistance to spending much time on exploring the problem from different cultural perspectives. The point was made that the culture of Company X was a more significant determinant of behaviour than national cultures. The need to discuss the different cultural perspectives did, however, emerge when considering the definition of teamwork and its importance to the business. The diversity in definitions and importance ratings was considerable, and is shown in Table 5.

Table 5

KEY POINTS IN TEAM MEMBERS' DEFINITIONS OF TEAMWORK

Country manager	Elements in definition	Importance (1 = low, 5 = high)
UK	Teamworking is a way of breaking down functional barriers and developing better ways of working.	4
France	Teamworking is a way for leaders to communicate effectively and to make the best use of people's skills.	3
Germany	Teamworking is about involving people in decision-making and using their skills to build improved performance.	3
Greece	Teamworking is what happens when groups of people meet in the same room.	1
The Netherlands	Teamworking is about building shared commitment to goals and helping and supporting one another.	5

A review of the range of definitions and importance ratings revealed some elements that reflected Hofstede's categories:

⊕ The French manager's definition reflected organisational hierarchy (high power-distance).
⊕ The definition from the Dutch manager reflected values associated with relationship and co-operation rather than assertiveness (low masculinity).
⊕ The German manager's definition emphasised involvement in decision-making (low power-distance).
⊕ The definitions from the UK and German managers emphasised performance as the overriding purpose. This reflected their relatively high scores on the masculinity scale.

A consistently surprising picture emerged from the Greek manager. It might have been anticipated that she would have rated the importance of teamwork at a higher level (given the low Greek score on the individuality scale).

Having seen the diversity of responses, the team agreed that the process proposed could be valuable and that they would work with it as long as it remained instrumental in helping them achieve the key results.

By the end of the second meeting the team had:

⊕ agreed a common definition of teamworking that was framed as follows:
A 'high-performing team' is a group of people who are:

  ⊕ inspired by the same vision and achieve their challenging goals through a co-ordinated use of their complementary skills
  ⊕ led by a respected and demanding leader who builds a culture in which open communication and respect between team members are encouraged and in which learning both from success and failure is encouraged.

⊕ agreed a common problem-definition, an objective for the task force and performance standards to which they all felt committed and for which they agreed to be mutually accountable
⊕ agreed clear roles and responsibilities – this was perceived as critical, given the limited number of possible meetings and the amount of background and research into the issue required between meetings
⊕ agreed to observe the process and established a set of 'ground rules' to enable them to deal with the interpersonal behaviours, given that they were all 'shapers' (in Belbin terms) and fiercely competitive and individualistic; they felt it was important that these 'rules' should ensure that they addressed and confronted differences in a positive and constructive way; and they recognised at this point that the Adler process model would be helpful to ensure they explored individual as well as cultural differences
⊕ established a framework for researching the issue with their colleagues; this framework identified different levels of team,

relative needs for improvement, the relationship of teamwork to business imperatives and the importance of action.

During the second meeting the team identified a need to check their input to problem-exploration with colleagues in each of their respective countries, and arranged to conduct a brief survey based on the model that had been developed.

The aim of the third meeting (based on the agreed adherence to the Adler model) was to generate ideas for dealing with the problem by seeking to create alternatives not necessarily rooted in any one participant's individual culture and framework. This meeting turned out to be extremely productive, and the discussion at the end established the participants' reasons for taking this approach, namely:

⊕ high-level team commitment to the overall project goals and acceptance of mutual accountability for their achievement
⊕ a greater level of respect for individual views and contributions
⊕ a recognition of the diversity within the team and of the potential value to the ideas-generation process of diverse perspectives
⊕ the existence of an agreed process to confront differences without being competitive or aggressive.

In addition, the team members stated that they were 'feeling good' about the extent to which they were making progress in a project that within Company X would ordinarily have run into difficulty and failed to deliver. This view was re-inforced by receiving information that other projects, established following the worldwide attitude survey, were behind schedule and unlikely to deliver the required results. Discussion of this last point led to a team view that they had really formed a cohesive group and had transferred their traditional competitive values from an individual to inter-team focus.

During the third meeting the move from idea-generation to selection was greatly aided by the team 'brainstorming' a set of selection criteria and then refining these through reference to the overall agreed objectives and the background data that they had obtained. The nature of the problem did not lend itself to a single solution. Rather, the team identified a range of actions necessary to address the core issue of improving teamworking within Europe. Importantly, the team identified as a significant evaluation criterion the likelihood of the action working in each of the national cultural environments. This led to further discussion of cultural differences, which was found valuable by team members.

The team members saw the fourth meeting as critical. At its start there was a lot of debate (often heated) about the extent to which the company president should receive a presentation that incorporated team learning or merely focused on the recommended actions. An intriguing point at this stage was that a number of members pointed to a need to consider the cultural background of the president (a North American) as a significant factor in determining the ultimate focus and shape of the presentation. This proved to be a helpful intervention and was seen by the team as evidence both of the value of the process they had undertaken and of their ability to function as a team in confronting and resolving conflict.

Perhaps the most significant aspect of this meeting was the discussion of who should make the presentation. Within Company X formal presentations to top management were perceived as significant opportunities for self-promotion. The making of such a presentation was both a high-profile event and one of which the quality and ideas are attributed directly to the presenter. The team recognised this as an issue and went through a process (which they subsequently described as 'revolutionary and counter-cultural') of initially offering the opportunity to each other. Ultimately they agreed to share the formal presentation among three members. This, they felt, would demonstrate evidence of changed behaviour and underpin their core recommendations.

The final meeting was, owing to time pressures, relatively short. The presentation to the president had been very successful, with many recommendations (some of which were challenging and contentious) having been accepted for implementation. The team saw this as a significant measure of success, and it led them to agree that they would continue to work (informally) together to monitor the implementation and thus be able to see the Adler model through to step 5.

Taking time to review learning from the process was seen as somewhat indulgent by the team and thus of questionable value. But in discussing this view the members recognised that they were ascribing 'traditional' Company X values to the process. Because challenging 'traditional' values (eg the culture of the individual hero) had been significant in developing their recommendations, they felt in the end that a reflection on the process and learning might be worthwhile. The review of the process, which they ultimately agreed to undertake, focused on two questions:

⊕ What had they learned about working together as a team?
⊕ What had they learned about the management of national cultural differences within Company X?

The learning about teamworking was tackled by identifying what they had done well as a team and what they felt could have been improved. The results of these deliberations are summarised in Table 6.

Further review and discussion of this summary led to the following conclusions being drawn by the team:

⊕ Teamworking can be effective only if there is a clear and shared purpose and set of goals that are clearly related to the needs of the business.

Table 6
TEAM PROCESSES AND LEARNING

Positive factors	Areas to improve
• Clear common goal • Good listening • Active participation • Honest and open discussions • Alignment on issue • No politics or 'hidden agendas' • Good teamwork or idea generation • Good spontaneous ideas • Building on ideas/contributions • Process checks and review on meeting • Flexibility in building structure • Preparation done between meetings • Willing to go 'off-track' – 'holiday from problem'	• Lower teamwork in analytical phases • Evaluating ideas too soon • Need to show respect for timing • Need to speed up/plan 'warm-up' process • Too polite/too much consensus – lack of controversy/challenge

⊕ It is essential that all team members accept and internalise accountability for achievement of the team's performance goals.

⊕ Differences in style and approach of individual team members should not be merely tolerated but seen more positively as a real potential strength.

⊕ Individuals should be aware of their own style; this information should be shared within the team and a clear process established to review and confront differences in a non-competitive and non-threatening way.

⊕ It is important that all team members clearly understand roles and accountabilities related to the overall team purpose.

The debate on learning associated with national cultural differences resulted in less clarity in the team's conclusions. Overall they agreed the following:

⊕ An appreciation of the nature and potential impact of national cultural differences is valuable.

⊕ Within Company X the effect of the corporate culture (one that focuses on the 'individual hero') is a more significant factor in influencing behaviour than national culture. Recruitment and selection processes, together with reward systems, were seen as ensuring that individuals recruited from different nationalities had values and characteristics more in line with corporate values and culture.

⊕ The Adler model is helpful in exploring cultural differences and generating effective cross-cultural solutions to problems. However, the model's value was seen as being equally (if not more) important in providing a framework for exploring and resolving *individual* differences.

⊕ At the end of the day, the team felt that cultural differences were less significant than their common 'buy-in' to the shared business problem.

Conclusions

This chapter set out to explore two issues – teamworking and national cultural differences – and their interrelationship in the context of developing cross-cultural teams. The limitations of case-studies as a vehicle of research are well established. However, the case presented here raises a number of points, some of which support previous findings and others that may well be worth further study and research. These may be summarised as follows:

- Goal clarity and shared purpose are important in building effective teamworking.
- There appears to be some evidence that the overall focus on results and the general organisational performance culture contributed to the performance of the team.
- Although the Belbin roles of team members were similar (they were all 'shapers'), members' understanding of the strengths and weaknesses of this lack of mix helped them to overcome limitations. This increased awareness and understanding was highlighted by Belbin as a basis for performing in the absence of a good role mix.
- Focusing on what the team share, in terms of business and performance needs, may have been more important than over-concern with national differences.
- Although some evidence emerged that supported Hofstede's framework for describing cultural differences, there were as many illustrations either of individual differences or corporate cultural influences that may have accounted for differences from the expected behaviours. Hofstede does, indeed, make the point that his framework presents a *general* cultural picture and does not necessarily predict individual behaviour.
- Understanding of cultural differences and working to resolve business problems and issues constitute a framework for improved effectiveness envisaged by both Adler and Hofstede.
- The influence of corporate culture on valuing and managing cultural diversity can be greater than individual or team action.
- The synergistic model proposed by Adler for managing cultural diversity may have broader applications, encompassing the management of individual stylistic and behavioural diversity.
- Although national cultural differences clearly affect behaviour, perceptions and approaches to problem-solving, it is equally evident that corporate culture has a significant influence. It would be valuable to establish the respective nature and strength of influence of these two factors.

The growing trend towards the globalisation of businesses is giving rise to a need for the development of effective international management teams. For many organisations this need entails thinking more clearly about cross-cultural issues, and more overtly and systematically understanding and valuing the benefits of diversity in international teams. Achieving this requires the integration of thinking and practice relating to teambuilding, and an understanding of the benefits of differing personal styles and behaviours. Although much can be achieved by working with specific teams, the truly successful global players are likely to be those that embed the change through integrated changes to selection, development, reward and recognition policies and practices. In doing this, the value of effective multicultural working can be captured at many levels in the organisation, and international teams, whether project-based or permanent, may reach high performance levels more rapidly and consistently. This can in turn help organisations build global capability and competitive advantage.

References and further reading

ADAIR J. (1986) *Effective Teambuilding*. Aldershot, Gower Publishing.

ADLER N. J. (1980) 'Cultural synergy: the management of cross-cultural organisations', in W. Warner Burhe and Leonard D. Goodstern (eds), *Trends and Issues in OD: Current theory and practice*. San Diego, CA, University Associates.

BELBIN R. M. (1981) *Management Teams: Why they succeed or fail*. London, Heinemann.

BLAKE R. R., MOUTON J. S. *and* ALLEN R. L. (1987) *Spectacular Teamwork*. New York, John Wiley and Sons.

CAMPBELL J. P., DAFT R. L. *and* HULIN C. L. (1982). *What to Study: Generating and developing research questions*. Beverley Hills, CA, Sage.

HACKMANN J. R. *and* MORRIS C. G. (1975) 'Group tasks, group interaction processes and group performance effectiveness: a review and proposed integration', in L. Berkowicz (ed.) *Advances in Experimental Psychology*, Palo Alto, CA, Psychological Press.

HIGGS M. J. (1994) 'Global HR management and cross-cultural issues'. *Cross-Cultural Management*. Vol. 1, No. 3. pp23–8.

HIGGS M. J. (1995) 'A case-study in cross-cultural teams'. Paper presented at EIASM Conference, October 1995.

HIGGS M. J. (1999) 'Teams and teamworking: what do we know?' Henley working paper series. HWP 9911.

HIGGS M. J. *and* ROWLAND D. (1992). 'All pigs are equal?' *Management Education and Development*. Vol. 23, No. 4. pp 349–62.

HOFSTEDE G. (1991) *Cultures and Organisations: Software of the mind*. Maidenhead, McGraw-Hill.

KAKABADSE A. (1994) 'Qualities of top managers: comparison of European manufacturers', Cranfield School of Management paper.

KATZENBACH J. R. *and* SMITH D. K. (1993) *The Wisdom of Teams*. Boston, MA, Harvard Business School Press.

LEWIN K. (1951) *Field Theory in Social Science*. New York, Harper & Row.

PHILLIPS N. (1992) *Managing International Teams*. London, Pitman.

SENGE P. (1990) *The Fifth Discipline*. New York, Doubleday.

SPARROW P., SCHULER R. *and* JACKSON S. (1994) 'Convergence or divergence: human resource practices and policies for competitive advantage worldwide'. *International Journal of Human Resource Management*. Vol. 5, No. 2. pp267–99.

TJOSVOLD D. (1991) *Team Organisation: An enduring competitive advantage*. Chichester, John Wiley and Sons.

TROMPENAARS F. (1993) *Riding the Waves of Culture: Understanding cultural diversity in business*. London, Economist Books.

Chapter 11

International HRM: an Asian Perspective

Sek-hong Ng and
Malcolm Warner

Introduction

This chapter attempts to portray the main themes and patterns of human resource (HR) practices in the workplace as they have evolved in Asia. People management has not developed evenly among Asian economies (by which we mean East and South East Asia, mainly in the Asia Pacific region). Right across these areas both *yin* and *yang*, light and shade, exist. At one extreme, we have found in some places explicit admiration of the Japanese employment system for its sophistication – perhaps now a little muted, given that country's economic difficulties. At the other extreme, 'sweatshop' conditions of low pay and alleged 'labour exploitation' are perceived as widespread within the region, especially among the newly developing economies, but also among the older, developed ones. Such a wide spectrum of workplace characteristics gives rise to what we shall call a 'dualism' in understanding Asian industrial relations (IR) and human resource management (HRM) practices, not only when comparing nation states with one another but also when attempting to explain dissimilarities within each.

We are cautious here about applying Western IR or HRM theories or models. We believe that such a superimposition of exogenous constructs often hinders rather than assists understanding. For instance, a key aspect of appreciating Asian human resources as practised by business enterprises and public organisations is the role performed by the State, especially in prescribing labour law and employment policies. However, the State is now no longer prominent in Western

HRM theorising, which is essentially individualist rather than collectivist in its values, as well as enterprise-centred and managerial in its assumptions.

In parallel with this, 'culture' looms large as a major shaping variable. Many Asian societies have a rich heritage and distinctive traditions. It has always been argued that such traditional values, philosophy, assumptions, customs and practices have led Asian workplaces to evolve harmonious ways of organising and of motivating people to perform, both individually and in groups. Asian culture, it is said, can instruct and inspire a distinctively Asian (as opposed to Western) approach to HRM, just as the Japanese system has, which, although dependent on an active State role, is nevertheless widely emulated outside Asia as an alternative to 'mainstream' Western prescriptions.

❝Japanese people-management has provided an exemplar for many❞

We shall not dwell at too great a length on the Japanese system here, for it has been covered extensively both in the academic and popular management literature. The three pillars of the Japanese IR system (lifetime employment, seniority-based rewards and enterprise unionism) have been documented in detail in a number of sources and are widely regarded as having played a major role in that country's economic success. Together with such indigenous innovations as just-in-time production techniques, quality circles and the like, Japanese people-management has provided an exemplar for many, and a supposedly viable alternative to the Taylorist management model, in spite of Taylor's significant influence on Japan (see Warner, 1994). But, faced with recession, Japan has had to reconsider many of its cherished HR practices. The practice of lifetime employment was never universal or rigid anyway (1999: 10), nor did the seniority system give automatic promotion (1999: 11). It is clear that all Asian IR and HRM systems are now having to adapt to business restructuring in their respective ways as a result of globalisation and its pressures on these economies.

Some shaping factors

Before looking at the patterns of HR practice and its diversity within Asia, it is useful to consider briefly some of the key factors that help to shape these practices and to explain both their intra-regional similarities and their variations. The three strategic variables are the:

- level of economic development
- role of the State
- 'culture' factor.

Each is examined below.

The economy and the 'late development' syndrome

To a large extent, the 'dualism' noted earlier can be explained by the experience of economic development within the region following the Second World War. This process has not been even, as mentioned above, and yet it appears that major parts of Asia have emerged as young, new economies from an earlier stage of pre-industrial under-development prior to the Second World War. The pre-war economies were mostly traditional and agrarian, either as colonies or dependent territories of European powers, or else, like China and Japan, as old and formerly dynastic states endeavouring to modernise.

'Late development' is hence a common theme among these Asian economies (see Dore, 1973, 1990), because most of them started large-scale industrialisation only after the Second World War. The Japanese model is said to have gained many advantages from being a latecomer because it was able to 'learn' a great deal from the West, both in terms of the benefits as well the costs of industrialisation.

These national economic development processes also coincided with an era of post-war decolonisation and, later, political independence. Ironically, much of the initial momentum for such changes was due in part to the missionary drive of nationalism, and in part to an infra-structure with a limited 'modern sector' built by and inherited from the colonial powers. This modern sector, usually controlling such activities as commercial and maritime trade, was the custodian of Western personnel and HR practices. Élitist and always distinctive as an 'enclave', its existence actually laid the basis of the 'dualism' of the economies now found in most of these young, newly independent nation states, some of which remained trapped in a relative state of backwardness and poverty until the industrial take-off achieved after the Second World War.

There has been rapid economic growth across the region since the late 1970s and early 1980s. Inspired by the economic success of post-war Japan, many Asian societies launched into a spectacular process of rapid industrialisation and economic progress which earned them a high international reputation, especially for those East Asian new industrial economies (NIEs) popularly labelled the 'Four Little Dragons'. The hectic pace of post-war industrial development has hence shifted them from an essentially agrarian background (eg plantation economies) into the modern world. Most began as producers of low-cost and labour-intensive manufactured goods, acting as the offshore production bases for capital from such industrially advanced economies as Europe and the USA. The new Asian economies grew rapidly in affluence and per capita income during the 1970s and 1980s.

Such advances enabled these late-developing economies to catch up with their Western counterparts. Starting in the late 1980s and continuing into the 1990s, the Asian NIEs, notably the Four Little Dragons, have become increasingly oriented towards the provision of tertiary-level services, including finance and banking, hotels and hospitality, retail and trading, transport and container port handling, telecommunications, property development and business services.

The restructuring of the young Asian economies, which has entailed a concomitant process of 'deindustrialisation' of varying degrees of intensity, has led to the relocation of factories, cutbacks and lay-offs of workers in the manufacturing sector, industrial unemployment and a subsequent retraining and labour employment agenda. These shifts have led to calls for labour market reform not only at the macro level but also at enterprise level, with significant changes and adjustments in workplace practices and arrangements. Labour-hiring flexibility, such as contract and part-time employment, has become popular as a Western-derived HR solution.

However, the success of East Asian economies has also been thought to point towards the apparent efficacy of an *Asian* capitalist ethos, which has alerted Western 'mainstream' thinking to a viable alternative way of managing people at work. Labelled by Dore a philosophy of 'welfare corporatism' (Dore, 1973, 1990), and benchmarked against the Japanese system, these East Asian businesses have practised an enlightened version of Confucian-inspired traditional paternalism, leading to a collaborative and non-adversarial attitude among the parties concerned – the employer and the employed.

With the probable exception of South Korea, such East Asian economies have therefore been able to sustain relative industrial peace and stability, with a low propensity for strikes or direct labour–management confrontation in the workplace (see Rowley, 1998). The inner logic of such apparent altruism is probably enshrined in Asia's heritage of traditional values and ethical prescriptions. However, its application to the modern workplace has been so instrumental in workforce stabilisation, motivation and performance commitment that it actually helps to inspire and instruct Western endeavours at reforming the workplace and people management within a newly espoused HRM framework (see, for example, Guest, 1995). However, the role of the State is also evident among these Asian economies in either amplifying or constraining the way in which Asian capitalism has excelled in the workplace.

The role of the State

The role of the State has been conspicuous in most of the Asian economies under review in prescribing a regulatory framework of administrative control and legal norms external to the enterprise.

Japan has had very strong State influence not only in adopting the German model of economic protectionism and central direction, but also in a regulated and non-*laissez-faire* approach to labour management. The level and nature of the State's intervention in the labour market and the employment affairs of private businesses have been important factors in shaping HR policies and practices among private-sector employers in many Asian countries, especially where minimum statutory standards are set. In Hong Kong and Singapore, both of which are now the world's bastions of 'free enterprise' activity, and which owe their colonial legacies to former British rule, the Employment Act (in Singapore) and the Employment Ordinance (in Hong Kong) emulate the British Contract of Employment Acts and Employment Protection Act (see Ng and Warner, 1998). Such laws have effectively established a statutory floor of employment rights for workers.

This body of legal prescriptions also has important effects on the personnel and HR policies within enterprises by providing them with 'standardised' employment benefits, especially in the case of small and medium-sized businesses, which lack sufficient resources to organise and administer an elaborate 'in-house' hierarchy of pay and benefits, but which look instead to statutory and official prescriptions for the 'going rate' when determining pay and other substantive terms regarding the hiring of personnel.

The Singapore and Hong Kong experiences (see Ng and Warner, 1998), where employment (standard) laws have been pivotal in private-sector employers' decisions about employment benefits and security, have apparently been emulated by other East Asian NIEs such as South Korea and Singapore, and even by later-developing economies, notably China, which are endeavouring to reform and modernise. Taiwan and South Korea each introduced a Labour Standard Act (Law) during the 1980s, largely along the lines of the Japanese Labour Standard Law, whereas in 1994 China enacted a parallel piece of legislation, the Labour Law, which came into effect in 1995 (Warner, 1997).

""There is a noticeable amount of 'legalism' espoused by employers adhering 'doctrinally' to the law""

The presence of the State and its governing of minimum conditions of labour standards and employment protection at the workplace – which would otherwise have been left in a situation of unregulated control by capital – have actually bred a paradoxical feature among enterprises, both large and small, in NIEs like Hong Kong. There is a noticeable amount of 'legalism' espoused by employers adhering 'doctrinally' to the law, no more and no less, paralleled by a workforce dependent upon the external lever of the State and the law for employment protection (Maeda and Ng, 1996).

Another key role of the State has been in regulating workplace relations at enterprise level. It has done this by laying down the law on industrial conflict, defining the permissible scope of freedom of association and, recently, ushering the application of human rights codes, such as the UN's promulgation on the Covenant on the Elimination of All Discrimination Against Women (CEDAW) into the employment arena. Previously, many East Asian NIEs were known for the restrictive, if not coercive, approach adopted by a paternalistic yet authoritarian State towards the control of strikes, workers' right to combine and labour agitation. However, State hegemony appears to have weakened in such places as South Korea and Taiwan since the late 1980s because of domestic pressures for political democratisation, in part nurtured by economic advances and the growing material affluence of these societies.

As a result, many of the State-prescribed external restrictions on the freedom to combine, bargain collectively and strike etc have been steadily liberalised. Enlightened administrations, staffed increasingly by middle-class and professional technocrats, have also been active in sponsoring the extension of equal rights in the workplace as norms – partly in order to meet the social standards prescribed by such international trade and economic forums as the World Trade Organisation (WTO) and the Asia Pacific Economic Co-operation Organisation (APEC).

The government, as representative of the public sector and as (always) the largest employer, has also become the pattern-setter of HR practices for both corporate and smaller workplaces in the private domain, especially among such former British colonies as Hong Kong and Singapore, both of which have both inherited a civil service with a reputation for good and stable pay, generous employment benefits and welfare, and career progression with job security (see Warner and Ng, 1999). These personnel practices, reminiscent of Japanese 'welfare corporatism', have led to (and helped to sustain) a loyal and self-disciplined workforce staffing their governments, in spite of decolonisation. In fact, it has been common for the civil service and key large-scale private enterprises (such as the British conglomerates, known as *hongs*, enfranchised public-utility suppliers and multinationals from abroad) to benchmark against each other regarding personnel decisions on, say, annual pay adjustment norms. Hence this kind of employer, both public and private, constitutes what labour economists have labelled the 'primary sector' in these Asian economies, as opposed to the 'secondary sector', which embraces, conversely, the smaller private businesses whose labour forces are less well off and less secure than their comparatively privileged counterparts.

The 'culture' factor

The popular explanation of East Asia's dramatic economic success falls back on a 'cultural' perspective. China and Japan (as well as the younger economies of Hong Kong, Singapore, Taiwan and even South Korea) have been categorised as 'Confucian' societies. Japanese and Korean culture may be distinguished from the Chinese in many respects but, as far as IR and HRM are concerned, all of these economies have emphasised harmony in the workplace, despite many periods of industrial conflict over the course of the twentieth century. They have earned a worldwide reputation of being able to cultivate a highly effective and solidaristic pattern of workplace and business management which excels in organisational commitment and performance (Hwang, 1995).

❝❝Asian capitalism offers a benevolent but prudent alternative to Western people-management❞❞

These East Asian managerial and work cultures have apparently espoused a new ethos of 'collectivism', fostered by their heritage, which helps to lay down norms of reciprocity, unspecified trust, and teamwork solidarity and dedication which are key to organisational performance, especially now in modern customer-oriented service industries. There is a belief that Asian capitalism offers a benevolent but prudent alternative to Western philosophies of people management, because it is rooted in Confucianism, which emphasises harmony and resilience.

In addition, these Asian societies are 'late-developing' and therefore able to learn from the West's know-how in science-based knowledge and technology – knowledge that has provided the core of modern industrialism (or post-industrialism). However, excessive and indiscriminate borrowing from Western institutions and arrangements is liable to conflict with the parochial and conservative psychology concerned with perpetuating Asia's own celebrated heritage. The 'boundary' conflicts between the 'local' and 'cosmopolitan' horizons are best illustrated by the lukewarm and occasionally hectic way in which human rights and equality norms governing pay and access to promotion etc were introduced to the labour markets of many of these Asian economies.

Despite this, Asian values and Western institutions have always been blended with varying degrees of success. A notable example always cited in Hong Kong is the incorporation since the 1980s of a customary year-end bonus, payable at employers' discretion – a traditional Chinese token of paternalistic benevolence and performance appreciation – into the Western-style Employment Ordinance. This provision, now a statutory or contractual entitlement, is widely known as the 'thirteenth month's pay'. This kind of prudent combination both of Western and Eastern practices frequently emerges in the workplace in multicultural settings like Singapore (eg calculating annual holiday schedules to take account of the various festivals of different cultures).

Even among the labour and employment reform that China has recently introduced to help modernise its economy (based on the 'market socialism' blueprint), this theme of cross-cultural synthesis appears largely applicable (see Child, 1994). This is because China has borrowed heavily from the Western workplace such devices and institutions as the individual labour contract, collective bargaining and agreement (adapted and relabelled the 'collective contract') and labour law. However, these emulations are not a direct replica of Western formulae *per se*, but are carefully and imaginatively repackaged, being extensively tailored to fit in with the nation's indigenous and socialist characteristics.

Perhaps the logic of assimilating Western institutions with an Asian flavour into the employment field of these societies is best exemplified by the so-called 'Asian approach' to trade unionism (see Thurley, 1988), inspired largely by the Japanese model of enterprise-based unionism. What it espouses in the workplace is a collaborative and non-adversarial approach to labour–management relations, enshrined in the Asian ethos of altruistic commitment and the collective awareness of an enterprise-based notion of 'commonwealth'.

''Asia's 'new model' unionism by-passes traditional class hostility''

Inasmuch as Asia's 'new model' unionism is open to consultative participation and partnership with enterprise management, it by-passes traditional class hostility and the 'us-and-them' attitude that divides labour and capital in Western economies. This Asian perspective greatly values harmony and co-operation, so that the industrial antagonism and intensive conflict that have accompanied Western-style unionism and collective bargaining can be marginalised to the point of irrelevance.

An Asian pattern of HR management and diversity

Following this preliminary look at some of the key factors affecting HR and people-management practice in Asian workplaces, it may be useful to examine the pattern of HR activities and provisions within the region, as well as the internal variations of such a pattern. As noted earlier, the 'dualism' theme is pivotal in any appreciation of Asia. Not only may most Asian economies be defined as dualistic economies, with both modern and traditional sectors, but also Asia (and notably East Asia) appears to have crystallised into a dualism in terms of economic development – between economies that on the one hand are highly industrialised and economically affluent and those on the other that are still trapped in the poverty of under-development.

We can group these Asian economies into two clusters (which we shall call Clusters A and B). In Cluster A, we find developed economies and their advanced sectors, with Japan at the core, and new entrants such as Hong Kong, Singapore, South Korea and Taiwan.

By contrast, Cluster B contains developing economies and sectors, embracing the majority of Asian economies, both old and new, although countries as diverse as China, Indonesia, Thailand and the Philippines (and others) are rapidly modernising. In many of the latter countries it is likely that people-management has remained problematic, limiting the productivity of those economies' human resources and therefore posing a constraint on their development.

The two clusters of Asian HR and employment patterns, then, underpin the following overview of the region. It is clear that the level of economic development, the role of the State and the 'cultural' factor affect each cluster, although in differing proportions.

Cluster A: The developed economies and sectors

Cluster A embraces those relatively developed economies along the Asian Pacific fringe, including Japan and the East Asian NIEs.

Some have relatively large populations – eg Japan (127 million) and South Korea (47 million); others' are relatively small – eg Hong Kong (6.8 million) and Singapore (3.2 million), and even Taiwan (22 million). Most of these economies are maritime, having established a sizeable external trade sector, and are hence amenable to a cross-border diffusion of Western assumptions, norms, protocols and practices. Such a 'cosmopolitan' character helps explain the relative prominence of foreign multinational corporations (MNCs) as standard-bearers of modern, scientifically based and technocratic people-management methods. Gross domestic product per capita in Asia Pacific ranges from US$27,181 in Singapore (greater than Japan's US$25,129) in the top echelon down to China's US$779 in the bottom, although purchasing power parity would boost this latter figure perhaps by several times (see *The Economist*, 1998).

> **"These apparently successful Asian economies share a common heritage derived from Confucian culture"**

However, these apparently successful Asian economies share, in terms of their national character, a common heritage derived from

Confucian culture, as noted earlier, with which the Chinese system is doctrinally associated. Yet the Confucian body of classic teachings and ethical prescriptions has informed not only the practice of 'Chinese capitalism' but also the 'paternalistic' orientation of 'welfare corporatism' in Japan (Dore, 1973 and 1990), which has in turn inspired a new class of family-business entrepreneurs and professional managers in South Korea (Lawler *et al*, 1998) and Taiwan (Chen, 1997).

The legacy of these Confucian values is therefore noticeable in the workplace among these Asian economies, shaping key personnel practices that emphasise trust, reciprocity and the endurance of work-based relations, especially altruistic loyalty to the firm. Examples are the enshrined norms of 'life-time employment', allegedly typical not only of Japanese welfare corporations (see Dore, 1990) but also Chinese family businesses. Network hiring is another example, although the practice appears to have been modernised, corporate employers now laying less emphasis upon the inclusivity of closely knit kinship ties and instead seeking to recruit and select their core personnel (especially managerial staff) from either occupational (professional) contact networks or school-based communities (notably, the alumni networks of the senior management echelons) in sourcing university graduate trainees and novice executives.

There are, in addition, other ways of stimulating motivation and commitment that have evolved within Asian custom to the point where they have been added to the statute book as legal entitlements. Two kinds of statutory provision in Hong Kong with roots in traditional Chinese practices are worth noting:

- the designation in law (Employment Ordinance) of the Chinese Lunar New Year bonus as a statutory year-end payment (mentioned earlier), now known as the 'thirteenth month's pay'
- the extension of the paternalistic practice originating in pre-war Shanghai textile mills whereby long-serving staff were awarded an *ex gratia* lump-sum payment for their loyalty. This has inspired the formalisation of an employment benefit norm: the long-service payment available to those who retire without a pension, a statutory provision in Hong Kong since the latter half of the 1980s.

The dualistic criteria of age and seniority are still basic, if not essential, requirements for many employing organisations, private and public, in allocating higher-level responsibilities, pay increments, promotion and other advancement opportunities among employees. Such a premium placed upon age and length of service (assumed to be indicative of loyalty) is perhaps consistent with the traditional image of Asia as a society deferential to age. However, the importance in the workplace of age is swiftly giving way to performance criteria.

In Singapore, for example, the National Wage Board has propagated the notion of the variable wage component as a key element in the pay structure of business enterprises keen to improve their flexibility and productivity in the use of manpower. This variable wage component (payable as a bonus and dependent upon such factors as the company's performance and profitability and upon the individual's performance) enables an employer to adjust the reward packages of his or her staff without affecting basic salary levels. Even public-sector employment norms and practices are also increasingly performance-oriented. An example is provided by the Hong Kong civil service, which has recently announced a comprehensive plan to overhaul the personnel system of the public sector. The aim of the reform is to convert the civil service bureaucracy into a leaner, more flexible and cost-effective organisation by introducing new key features like 'flexi-hiring' (especially 'fixed-term' contract hiring) and performance pay, while lowering correspondingly the numbers of core staff retained on a permanent and pensionable basis.

"Asian values of altruism remain instrumental in contributing to workplace stability"

Although the growing concern for performance control and the pressure to adopt austerity measures that arose from the Asian currency-cum-financial crisis in 1997 could have induced corporate bureaucracies to 'downsize' in emulation of their Western counterparts, Asian values of altruism were and remain instrumental in contributing to workplace stability and harmony. These values have generally been sustained in spite of sporadic labour–management confrontation resulting from the trauma of painful economic adjustments.

However, a dilemma encountered in many of the austerity-driven cases concerns the trade-off between pay cut and staff (personnel) cut. Evidently, where a pay cut is seen as helpful for preserving jobs, those on the shop floor always prefer such a measure as a less painful option. Similarly, other 'stop-gap' arrangements like short-hour working, job-sharing and even part-time hiring have been widely adopted throughout the region, and with tacit approval from employees anxious to keep their employers afloat.

This spirit of mutuality, forbearance and tolerance has tended to prevail among a variety of workplaces, large and small, private and public, during these testing times in East Asia, and in South Korea, Hong Kong and Singapore (where the National Wage Council of Singapore actually promulgated a State policy of levying an economy-wide pay cut in 1998 in order to help the nation recover its global competitiveness).

Up to now, the trauma of the 1997 Asian financial upheavals has not, in spite of its impoverishing effects on wealth, income and employment, touched off any large-scale worker unrest in any East Asian economy, although not every workplace in East Asia is always acquiescent and docile (for instance, strikes in South Korea have been frequent, and sometimes violent). However, spontaneous actions of worker militancy have been conspicuous by their absence in smaller establishments. Here, Asian trade unionism appears to have played a role of growing strategic importance as an industrial partner to employers and as a political partner to governments in the area of labour and employment, which is likely to become a more contested ground for social actions. This is particularly the case as the governments of these Asian nations are progressively democratised, at a time when their previously buoyant economies are trapped in the doldrums – for instance in South Korea and Hong Kong, where labour movements have endeavoured to consolidate their new political influence as the 'independent' voice articulating the interests and expectations of the 'working class'.

Union challenges, although devoid of large-scale worker militancy, have nonetheless put formidable pressure on private-sector employers

– notably large corporate businesses – to handle with better care and discretion their personnel and HR decisions on downsizing, lay-offs, pay pauses and wage or salary cuts and the like. Disclosure of information and prior consultation with either the trade union or elected worker representatives (like those elected to the consultative staff councils or joint consultative committees) has not been entirely without problems, as illustrated by a series of corporate announcements of austerity measures to help save labour-cost overheads in Hong Kong throughout 1998 in the aftermath of the Asian financial crisis.

Although Asian workers and their unions may have appeared to defer heavily to public authority during this latest region-wide 'drama' of economic austerity, relief provisions (essentially, unemployment benefits and vacancy creation, as well as retraining and re-employment services) and employers' restraint in taking action adverse to labour interests must be put in the context of Asia's HR and labour relations:

- First, Asian labour psychology, with its dependency of those at grassroots level upon 'authority', is consistent with the established imagery of Asian paternalistic assumptions and Confucian prescriptions.
- Second, the present crisis is of such magnitude that it is evidently beyond the scope of private resources to cope without the State's intervention.
- Third, the unions' behaviour in response to the crisis suggests a preference for lobbying the government to intervene centrally rather than dealing directly with employers in the workplace. To a large extent this is because Asian unions basically lack the organised power and industrial strength to challenge employers' domination of the workplace.
- And yet, fourth, the extension of grassroots democracy and electoral politics, witnessed largely since the close of the 1980s within Asia, has in part devolved to labour unions a formidable power base that enables them to bargain effectively with the State for a better deal on public policies of employment and labour protection (as it has, for instance, in South Korea).

The Asian financial-cum-currency upheavals of the late 1990s have reshaped the pattern of human resources and labour relations in Asia, especially where the shock of prolonged recession has caused business enterprises to halt their expansion abruptly and suffer an agony of consolidation, downsizing and even business withdrawal and closure. Although such a recession 'syndrome' may simply be a transient phenomenon (at least, one hopes so), Asian HRM practices have as a result been concerned almost entirely with an austerity agenda: how to save, hive off or discharge manpower as human resources in surplus.

Flexible employment devices such as part-time hiring, fixed-term labour contracts, outsourcing and subcontracting have become conspicuous and widespread, alongside employers' apparent readiness to resort to salary and wage cuts and to renege on welfare and fringe-benefit provisions (even where these may be contractual, like the thirteenth month's year-end pay practised in Hong Kong). However, in an economy glutted with oversupply and plagued with weak demand, even a concerned government cannot somehow limit employers' downsizing, scaling-down, laying-off and downwards wage-adjustments, as the army of the unemployed swiftly expands.

Asian governments have responded to the labour market impasse of unemployment and downward wage drifts by publishing 'guidelines', in a prudent and non-compulsory approach to advise employers and employees on the best practices, desirable procedures and protocols to follow. Painstaking attempts have been made to avoid any 'hard' approach, ie legal enactments or enforcements. Such a non-punitive and non-coercive approach in regulating a labour market in disarray is, however, consistent with the paternalistic ethos of Asian governance of the workplace, family and key social institutions.

In some leading Asian economies, noticeably the affluent city states of Singapore and Hong Kong, the government as a public-sector employer frequently plays the role of trendsetter against which large private-sector corporations habitually benchmark their pay, benefits and employment practices (see Ng and Warner, 1998). In particular, the periodical (annual) civil service pay hike announced by the government, as in the case of Hong Kong, emulates a literal 'incomes policy' norm that is widely followed by large private-sector employers in the subsequent period. Reciprocally, government also conducts annual pay surveys by polling a sample of leading private enterprises about their pay adjustment decisions in order to compile a database on the key pay trends of the wider labour market. This has enabled government to harmonise civil service pay as an established policy with private-sector levels in the market.

Hence, even in places such as Hong Kong and Singapore, where a minimum wage law has not been in place and industry-wide collective bargaining has hardly been conspicuous, employing organisations are unlikely to design and devise their pay policies and HR practices in isolation. Instead, strategic references and comparisons are characteristically drawn against analogous arrangements elsewhere, such as in other firms belonging to the same local industry.

"Smaller and medium-sized enterprises are still enshrined in traditional clanship and ethnic-based communities"

Although large corporate employers appear to have formalised this type of business-cum-personnel networking through their own interest and representative organisations such as employers' associations and chambers of commerce, the smaller and medium-sized enterprises appear to have relied more upon their own fraternities of trade associations, which are in most cases still enshrined in traditional clanship and ethnic-based communities. It is probably relevant, in such a context, to make reference to the concept of a 'dual labour market' while discussing the diversity in HR practices that exists among enterprises in these affluent young Asian economies. 'Primary sector' employers are preponderantly the large public and private bureaucracies, including the civil service, public enterprises, MNCs, the British 'noble house' (*hongs*) and their business conglomerates, and the modern and aristocratic (Chinese) family businesses and so on. Co-existing alongside this 'primary sector' is a 'secondary sector' of smaller employers who are basically local capital operating the medium-sized and small business enterprises.

We can see that the level of economic development is more advanced in the above examples (from Cluster A). The role of the State is surprisingly active, given the *laissez-faire* ideology of say, Hong Kong and (to a degree) Taiwan, and the 'culture' factor is very influential across the board.

Cluster B: The less developed emergent economies and sectors

Common both to older Asian countries such as China (with a massive population of over 1.2 billion and consequently a huge workforce) and younger Asian nations such as Indonesia (208 million) which are still backward in socio-economic terms, are the twin problems of massive poverty and low income, and a relatively huge agrarian sector, where the impact of new technology has not been even and productivity erratic and low. Economic reforms and restructuring to rationalise and modernise key aspects of their economies, like hardware and infrastructure provisions, education, and HR and managerial skills, as well as 'marketisation' to liberalise competition, have been noticeable on the State agenda of almost every nation in this league since the latter half of the 1980s. These policies have been pursued with varying degrees of rigour, leading to differing levels of success. By far the most conspicuous results have been achieved in mainland China (see Child, 1994).

China began her spectacular process of modernisation with a novel, yet hybrid, formula of 'market socialism' in the early 1980s. This change-over has been largely engineered by the State. The pervasive theme of its employment agenda has been a consistent attempt to discard the personnel system of the pre-reform era of 'democratic centralism' of centralised and permanent allocation to the employing units, and to institute in its place a nascent labour-market (see Warner, 1995).

''The Communist party and the labour ministry have withdrawn from a direct role''

A pivotal workplace device has been the use of 'labour contracts', Western-inspired and adopted nationwide since the mid-1980s (see Warner and Ng, 1999). Defining the duration of the contract helps to delimit the period of employment and hence displaces, by implication, the celebrated and enshrined norm of 'life-time employment'.

Parallel wage system reforms have also been in process since the latter half of the 1980s as the State's centrally administered pay grade hierarchy withered away, giving way to enterprise-specific wage adjustment processes. Performance-based pay has also been popularised recently, either to supplement or to substitute the pre-existent system of seniority pay. At the same time, both the Communist party and the labour ministry have withdrawn from a direct role, leaving these matters to be dealt with by enterprises at their management's discretion.

However, such an appearance of conversion to a Western-style HR and personnel system should not be overstated (see Warner, 1997). The emergent pattern of economic and labour relations in post-reform China also features 'dualism', with a boundary commonly drawn between on the one hand the sector predominated by the multinationals and capital investment from overseas (generally labelled as the foreign and overseas-funded sector) and on the other an essentially 'home' sector of State-owned enterprises (see Goodall and Warner, 1997). The latter, the larger foreign-funded enterprises, mostly MNCs, hitherto admired as the pattern-setting employers, are the principal firms practising HR policies borrowed from the West, as is the case in many other Asian countries.

Although China is a special case on account of its size, other Asian economies have also been burdened with a substantial State-owned industrial sector and a public bureaucracy (for example, Indonesia). Each has an employment model involving rigid employment practices that has set the norm for labour practices and HR allocation in the urban economy. China had the so-called 'iron rice bowl' (*tie fan wan*) model, with lifetime employment and cradle-to-grave welfare. In such countries labour market flexibility has been lacking in these parts of the urban economy (China, Indonesia, Vietnam); there has been a top-down State-sponsored trade union centre (the above-cited nations plus, until recently, Taiwan); and there has been a lack of free collective bargaining (most Asian countries).

"Trust and reciprocity have always been cherished"

HR practices are less structured and formalised both in the less developed economies of Asia and their enterprises (involving the mass of the population and workforce in the region) and in the secondary sectors of the more developed ones (involving relatively fewer workers). Instead, the binding nexus in the workplace appears to be the personalised relations between the employer and the employed, the manager and the managed, as well as between the individual and his or her peers. Within the umbrella of the ethnic Chinese and, wider still, the Confucian cultures that pervade almost every society in East Asia, such informality and emphasis placed upon personal ties, trust and reciprocity have always been cherished as the source of what has been labelled by industrial sociologists 'spontaneous and normative consensus' (Fox, 1974). However, the price to pay for affording and maintaining this type of workplace informality, reputed to be a source of in-built flexibility in Asian capitalism, is that the bulk of modern HR and personnel management techniques have remained relatively underdeveloped and rudimentary in these places.

In contrast to their bureaucratic large-scale counterparts in the modern primary sector, smaller and medium-sized workplaces typically lack a systematic and coherent infrastructure of procedures and norms for handling employment and personnel matters, whether in the Little Dragon economies (Hong Kong, Singapore, South Korea or Taiwan) or even Japan, let alone in smaller Sino-Foreign Joint Ventures in China or their equivalents in Indonesia, Malaysia, the Philippines or Vietnam (Burma being regarded as a 'pariah' State). Established arrangements for the conduct of performance appraisal and benchmarking exercises (such as job evaluation) are conspicuous by their absence in these smaller and less bureaucratic nations among the East Asian NIEs, either in the developed economies or the less developed ones.

These employers have remained sceptical about formalising their workplaces with legal and codified norms and etiquette governing equal access to pay and employment opportunities (especially across the sex 'divide'), nor are they amenable to such ideas as minimum wage and maximum work hours, compulsory dialogue with labour unions or procedures to recognise the latter for collective bargaining purposes. Indeed, trade unions are either very thin on the ground or, if State-sponsored, largely 'transmission-belts' of government policy. Apprehensive about the restrictive effects and extra burden of labour cost overheads associated with the global labour and employment standards set out by the International Labour Organization (ILO) and the like, small and medium-sized businesses have found an effective lobby against national governments and legislative assemblies in East Asia enacting, or continuing to enact, labour legislation suspected by such businesses of having already eroded their competitiveness. In some cases, new legislation that has extended gender equality and compulsory union recognition procedures has exempted firms below a certain size from their statutory requirements.

"Labour protection has emerged again as a social issue"

Yet legal exemptions and non-regulation by the State have also left behind a normative vacuum, laying open potential gaps for 'exploitation' by unscrupulous employers among the smaller and less standard-conscious 'sweatshops', for which these East Asian NIEs, especially less developed ones like Indonesia, Thailand, Vietnam and so on, were heavily castigated at the beginning of their post-war industrialisation during the 1960s and 1970s. In fact, 'labour protection' has emerged again as a social issue in spite of the modernisation of East Asian workplaces (including both large and smaller enterprises) over the last two decades of economic and social advance, because many of these firms are subcontractors of MNCs promoting famous 'brands' in Western markets, such as Nike. These recent industrial predicaments are largely the outcome of the labour market's segmentation in many of the East Asian NIEs, resulting in a caste of peripheral workers vulnerable to low pay and other exploitation.

In addition, HR and personnel practices in East Asia have always had to confront the ghost of Asia's colonial past in struggling to reconcile expatriate and local differences with sensitivity. The formerly privileged employment position of the expatriates (mainly European) has been responsible for sustaining a dual system of employment and personnel provisions both in the civil service and the private sector (today, the larger Joint Ventures and MNCs). Such employment dualism, in-house for the bureaucratic 'primary-sector' employing units, has basically corresponded to and helped to sustain an implicit 'class' system.

A post-independence localisation policy was primarily intended as a lever against the disadvantages that would previously have denied local candidates access to opportunities comparable to those of their foreign counterparts. However, with the advent of greater global trade and the arrival of the MNCs and foreign capital, most Asian economies (including the formerly closed economies of China and Vietnam) have again begun to liberalise the entry of foreigners (especially those from Europe, Japan and the USA) into the upper layers of their labour markets.

In Cluster B, then, the level of economic development is lower and came later than in Cluster A. The role of the State, particularly in the larger economies, is more prominent, and the 'culture' factor is now as influential as – if not more influential than – ideology, especially in the case of China.

Concluding remarks

To sum up, we have attempted to present the complexity of IR and HRM practices in Asia Pacific with an essentially 'broad-brush' approach. We divided the range of practices into two sets of HR-related institutions and behaviour, namely those in the more developed economies and sectors (Cluster A) and those in the less developed equivalents (Cluster B). The former include the Big Dragon, namely Japan, and the Little Dragons, such as Hong Kong, Taiwan, Singapore and South Korea; the latter term covers China as the largest (and, if you will, the New Dragon) but also medium-sized ones such as Indonesia and smaller ones such as Vietnam. We have also examined the SME enterprise sector, which, although it includes both developed and less developed countries, has a common set of features.

In order to understand the complexity of people management in the Asia Pacific region better, we have argued that account must be taken of the level of economic development, the role of the State and the 'culture' factor, among other variables. These factors differentiate the Asian HR-related models from those outside the region. Most of these countries have 'neo-authoritarian' regimes, but with varying degrees of strong government. There is the so-called 'Asian Model', apparently defying the 'end of history' hypothesis (see Fukuyama, 1992).

We conclude that, in the light of the evidence we have presented, it is clearly naïve to superimpose Western models of HRM on this wide range of economies, institutions and behaviour.

References and further reading

CHEN S.-J. (1997) 'The development of HRM practices in Taiwan'. *Asia Pacific Business Review.* Vol. 3, No. 4. Summer. pp152–69.

CHILD J. (1994) *Management in China during the Age of Reform.* Cambridge, Cambridge University Press.

DORE R. (1973) *British Factory–Japanese Factory.* London, George Allen and Unwin. Reprinted, with an afterword, by University of California Press, Berkeley, CA, 1990.

THE ECONOMIST. (1998) *The World in 1999.* London, Economist Publications.

FOX A. (1974) *Beyond Contract: Work, power and trust relations.* London, Faber and Faber.

FUKUYAMA F. (1992) *The End of History and the Last Man.* New York, Free Press.

GOODALL K. *and* WARNER M. (1997) 'Human resources in Sino-foreign joint ventures: selected case studies in Shanghai compared with Beijing.' *International Journal of Human Resource Management.* Vol. 8, No. 5. October. pp569–94.

GUEST D. E. (1995) 'HRM, trade unions and industrial relations', in J. Storey (ed.), *Human Resource Management: A critical text*, London, Routledge, pp110–41.

HONG KONG SPECIAL ADMINISTRATIVE REGION GOVERNMENT, CIVIL SERVICE BUREAU, GOVERNMENT SECRETARIAT. (1999) *Civil Service into the 21st Century: A consultation document on civil service reform.* Hong Kong, Printing Department. March.

HWANG K. (1995) 'Integrated summary', in K. Hwang (ed.), *Easternization: Socio-cultural impact on productivity*, Tokyo, Asian Productivity Organization, pp1–13.

KAO H. S. R. *and* NG S. (1997) 'Work motivation and culture', in D. Munro, J. F. Schumaker and S. C. Carr (eds), *Motivation and Culture*, New York, Routledge, pp119–32.

KAO H. S. R., SINHA D. *and* NG S. (1994) 'Introduction', in H. S. R. Kao, D. Sinha and S. Ng (eds), *Effective Organizations and Social Values*, New Delhi, Sage, pp11–21.

KASSALOW E. M. (ed.) (1996) *National Labour Movements in the Postwar World*. Howolulu, Northwest University Press (1993), and East-West Centre Press.

LAWLER J., SIENGTHAI S. *and* ATMIYANANDANA V. (1998) 'HRM in Thailand: Eroding traditions', in C. Rowley (ed.), *Human Resource Management in the Asia Pacific Region: Convergence questioned*, London, Frank Cass, pp170–96.

LEGGETT C. (1992) 'Trade unionism, industrialism and the State in Singapore', in E. K.Y. Chen, R. Lansbury, S. Ng and S. Stewart (eds), *Labour–Management Relations in the Asia-Pacific Region*, Hong Kong, Centre of Asian studies, University of Hong Kong, pp54–71.

MAEDA M. *and* NG S. (1996) 'The role of the State and labour's response to industrial development: an Asian "drama" of three new industrial economies', in I. Nish, G. Redding and S. Ng (eds), *Work and Society: Labour and human resources in East Asia*, Hong Kong, Hong Kong University Press, pp167–97.

NG S. (1995) 'Labour and employment', in J. Y. S. Cheng and S. S. H. Lo (eds), *From Colony to SAR: Hong Kong's challenges ahead*, Hong Kong, the Chinese University Press, pp197–225.

NG S. *and* LEE G. O. M. (1998) 'Hong Kong labor market in the aftermath of the crisis: implications for foreign workers'. *Asian and Pacific Migration Journal*. Vol. 7, No. 2–3. pp171–86.

NG S. *and* PANG C. (1997) 'Structuring for success in China: critical organisational and HR issues'. Hong Kong, *The Financial Times*.

NG S. *and* WARNER M. (1998) *China's Trade Unions and Management*. London, Macmillan.

NG S. *and* WRIGHT R. (1998) 'Hong Kong', in M. Zanko (ed.), *Global Advantage through People: Human resource management policies and practices in ten APEC economies*, Wollongang, International Business Research Institute, University of

Wollongang and Asia Pacific Economic Co-operation, pp135–205.

NG S., STEWART S. *and* CHAN F. (1997) *Current Issues of Workplace Relations and Management in Hong Kong*. Hong Kong, Centre of Asian Studies, University of Hong Kong.

ROBERTS B. C. (1964) *Labour in the Tropical Territories of the Commonwealth*. London, the London School of Economics and Political Science.

ROWLEY C. (1998) 'Introduction: comparisons and perspectives on HRM in the Asia Pacific', in C. Rowley (ed.), *Human Resource Management in the Asia Pacific Region: Convergence questioned*, London, Frank Cass, pp1–18.

THURLEY K. (1988) 'Trade unionism in Asia countries', in Y. C. Jao, D. A. Levin, S. Ng and E. Sinn (eds), *Labour Movement in a Changing Society: The experience of Hong Kong,* Hong Kong, Centre of Asian Studies, University of Hong Kong, pp24–31.

VERMA A., KOCHAN T. A. *and* LANSBURY R. D. (1995) 'Lessons from the Asian experience: a summary', in A. Verma, T. A. Kochan and R. D. Lansbury (eds), *Employment Relations in the Growing Asian Economies*, London, Routledge, pp336-57.

WARNER M. (1994) 'Japanese culture, Western management: Taylorism and human resources in Japan'. *Organization Studies.* Vol. 15, No. 4, pp509–34.

WARNER M. (1997) 'Introduction: HRM in Greater China'. *International Journal of Human Resource Management*. Vol. 8, No. 5. October. pp565–8.

WARNER M. *and* NG S. (1999) 'Collective contracts in Chinese enterprises: a new brand of collective bargaining under "market socialism"?' *BJIR.* 37, 2. June. pp295–314.

WONG S. (1988) *Emigrant Entrepreneurs: Shanghai industrialists in Hong Kong*. Hong Kong, Oxford University Press.

ZANKO M. (ed.) (1998) *Global Advantage through People: Human resource management policies and practices in ten APEC economies*. Wollongang, International Business Research Institute, University of Wollongang and Asia Pacific Economic Co-operation.

Afterword

Plenty of evidence over the last 25 years has pointed to the fact that managers from all professions, including HR, have been pursuing an obsessive search for 'How-To' solutions to their business and people problems. 'Fadism' and 'short-termism' have never been more popular, particularly in the Western world, leading to a worrying reduction in the thinking capability of managers. The production of 'one-best-way' approaches and instant solutions based upon all-encompassing models has become an industry in itself, particularly in the USA and Europe.

This book deliberately set out not to provide such approaches, or to chase the 'Holy Grail' of a fully integrated model of SIHRM. The field is constantly evolving, and the wide variety of cultures and sub-cultures, both within organisations and nationally, makes it almost impossible to develop such all-encompassing models. Instead, the IHR professional needs to be able to think through and develop approaches suited to his or her organisation, its business goals, culture, environment and competition. This requires deeper thinking at a macro- and micro-level when constructing policies and practices for international people management and development. The more effective examples are often contingent in nature, rather than prescriptive, and have been developed taking into account organisational and cultural issues.

The chapters of this book provide a series of perspectives and insights, of experiences and frameworks, that HR professionals can use to aid their thinking.

Such thinking will help to advance the IHR profession beyond its often fallacious image of dealing solely with expatriate management. To achieve this advance we need to develop the professionalism and capability of people working in IHR, especially in understanding the functioning of their businesses in a global context. This understanding will provide the basis for better integration of IHR into the strategic management of the business.

We hope this book has aided that understanding.

Professor Pat Joynt
Bob Morton
October 1999

Index

accountability, personal 69
adaptability, cultural *see* cultural
    adaptability
adding value, focusing HR on 70, 72,
    81
    on an organisational level following
        merger or acquisition 67
    on a personal level 61
advertising, cross-national 102–103,
    104, 113
agility and flexibility in organisational
    capability 12, 46, 75–6, 80–81,
    121, 207
    lack of, loss of 51, 54
agility of thought with which to
    attack problems 69
Alitalia (and KLM), comparisons with
    8–9
American workers abroad *see* expatriate
    workers, from the USA
Amoco, comparisons with 70
Apple (corporation), comparisons with
    55, 57
appraisal(s), systems of/for 8, 57, 100,
    122, 173
    360-degree feedback and 6
    see also performance measurement
Asian economies and economic
    development 4, 235–255
    cultural factors in 240–242,
        244–5, 247, 249
    recession (1997–8) in 245–8
Asian perspective on international

HRM *see* global HRM, from an
    Asian perspective
assessment centre(s) 96, 107–109,
    113
    BA's General Manager Programme
        108–109
assessment of candidates for
    international posts 87
    cross-cultural 110–112, 113
    see also psychometric assessment of
        managerial competencies
AT&T, comparisons with 5
Australian managerial attitudes 190
Avon, comparisons with 75

'balanced scorecard', the 7
benchmarking 7
benefit programme(s) 36
best-practice considerations 27, 28,
    31, 62, 77, 118
    diffusion of responsibility for
        implementing 31
    disseminated by government
        agencies 248
Boeing, comparisons with 15
British Telecom (BT), comparisons
    with 7, 101
business acumen for HR professionals
    67–70
business credibility, as a key to global
    success 63, 83, 201
business credibility factors 63, 70,
    81

business culture *see* organisational
culture
Business Intelligence Unit (BIU), the
6–7
business partner, the HR manager as
global 59–84
business process re-engineering *see*
process re-engineering

capability of an organisation *see*
organisational capability/
capabilities
career management in/by international
HR 10, 144–155
careers and career development in
general 36, 157, 175
case-studies 4–9, 27, 108, 218, 229
British Airways' graduate General
Manager Programme 108–109
Cadbury Schweppes' clinical risk
factor assessment 96–8
'Company X's' building
multicultural management
teams 218–229
EMI Music's skills database
tracking systems 99–100
Ericsson's international
teamworking methodology
199–202
'GloCorp' 4–5
Procter & Gamble's 'Visor' 15–17
S.W.I.F.T.'s critical success factor
mind-set 93–5
teamworking in an international
engineering company 195–6,
197
change, efforts at organisational 7, 53,
72–3, 80, 116, 156–7
forces for (political, technological,
economic, socio-demographic)
157–8
see also innovation; leadership, in
change management
China, domestic economic factors in
235, 238, 240–241, 243,
250–254
international attitudes towards
124–5, 181–2
CIRIA, comparisons with 8
Citicorp, comparisons with 56
clinical risk assessment of managerial
competencies 93, 95–8, 99, 113

Cadbury Schweppes' accelerated
development programme 96–8
Coca-Cola, comparisons with 60, 101,
133, 150
Colgate-Palmolive, comparisons with
23
collaboration: effective working
together 10, 46, 62, 65, 67, 95,
198
collective bargaining *see* organisational
dialogue, traditional
communications, importance to global
HRM of 10, 59, 68, 94, 157,
167–8, 176, 190, 194, 199
sustaining across cultural
boundaries 156–177, 190
communication skills 55, 194
community-building 68, 69
compensation/reward(s), and non-cash
benefits 130–131
appropriate 10, 36, 54, 55, 62, 80,
204
disparities in senior 135
domestic policy for 117
international 115–142, 185
international strategy for 117,
126–131, 136–8, 185, 223
linked to performance (to minimise
costs) 133, 136, 158, 251
obtaining and interpreting data on
international 137–8
the transnational solution to
117–118, 121, 122–6
competencies, core business 12, 140
see also international manager,
competencies required in an
competition, as promoter of internal
solidarity 50
global 10, 60
computerisation, importance to global
HRM of 59
see also technology, the role of in
global HRM
conflict management and negotiation
68, 69
consultants, the role of 7
continuous development,
organisational 1, 24
co-ordination of people management
activities 3
corporate culture *see* organisational
culture

corporate governance, comparative
128–131, 133, 136
corporate social architecture *see*
organisational culture
costs, reduction in 2, 25, 27, 53, 116,
123
credibility of an organisation *see*
business credibility
cultural adaptability of the
international manager 95, 96–8,
194
assessment of 96–8, 111
cultural clusters 169–170
cultural differences and boundaries 6,
7, 8–9, 39–46, 52, 57, 62, 67,
94, 156–177, 182, 187–191,
208–214, 221
awareness of/empathy towards 87,
183, 184, 194, 208, 210–214
between the UK and the USA
168–9
'doers' and 'be-ers' defined in terms
of 42
effects of 4, 8–9, 42, 44–5,
187–191, 240–242
extrapolation from
Hofstede's/Trompenaars'
research into 164–172,
189–190, 209–210
gaining added value from 9, 78–9
Hofstede's/Trompenaars'
dimensions of 160–164, 168–9,
171, 189, 209–212, 220–221,
223–4, 230
organisational management to
utilise 40, 41, 66, 78, 87,
176–7, 183, 207–231
social architecture/environments
39, 41–2, 46, 52
supposed attitudinal and
behavioural implications of 42
sustaining communications across
156–177
US research into 39–45
culture, definitions of 41–2, 160–172
curiosity: a desire for new experiences
69
customer care considerations 7, 13,
20–24, 30, 59, 72, 78, 187,
200

database of people's skills and

competencies *see* skills database
tracking system(s)
decentralisation, de-layering and/or
downsizing 46, 53, 65, 128,
187
decision-making, effects of
internationalisation on 4, 67,
73, 187, 189, 191, 196, 220
Deutsche Telekom, comparisons with
67
development, personal *see* personal
development
Digital (Corporation), comparisons
with 5
digitalisation, importance to global
HRM of 59
discrimination, control of 40
Disney theme parks, comparisons with
20–24, 80
distance, effects of 4
distribution, increased speed of 2, 15
diversity, cultural *see* cultural
differences and boundaries
diversity, management of *see* cultural
differences, organisational
management to utilise
diversity of operational environments
3, 4, 6, 73, 78, 142
diversity of personal background(s) 3,
44–6, 66, 134, 210, 222
positive attitude towards 87, 210
domestic operation of foreign firms 2,
3, 4, 10, 125
drivers of success 5, 29, 35–6, 61,
74
Dutch managerial attitudes 220–225

e-commerce, the effects of 1
see also Internet
employee relations, as an HR priority
157, 233–4
effects of culture on 167–175,
233–4, 240–242, 252
from an individual's viewpoint
162–7
empowerment of employees 5, 73,
158, 191
equal opportunities considerations 40,
103
Ericsson (Sweden), comparisons with
7, 199–202
ethical standards, global 62

executive search (head-hunting)
        100–102
expatriate workers 119–121, 151–5
    from the EC/EU 2
    from the USA 2, 29, 66
    in the EC/EU (as 'guest workers') 2
    research into success or failure of
        90, 153
    see also foreign companies in the
        UK; foreign nationals,
        employment and management of
external influences on the
        international people manager 4

financial aspects of an international
        assignment 138–140
first to/in market, association of
        competitive advantage with
        being 1–2, 12–13
flexibility, organisational see agility
        and flexibility in organisational
        capability
flow of resources through an
        organisation 65, 66, 70–71
foreign companies in the UK 2
    number of workers employed by 2
foreign nationals, employment and
        management of 2, 3, 4, 10, 87,
        90, 104, 121, 125
'Four Little Dragons', the 236,
        243–250, 252, 254
France, market preferences in 15–17
France Telecom, comparisons with 67
French managerial attitudes 43, 190,
        220–225
French shareholding attitudes 128
Fuji and the 'invasion' of Japan by
        Kodak 26

gap analysis 7–8
GE (General Electric), comparisons
        with 5, 7–8, 27–8, 72, 80,
        190–191
German managerial attitudes 43, 190,
        220–225
German shareholding attitudes 128
Germany, market preferences in
        15–17
global business leaders, competency
        clusters needed by 67–70
global business partner, HRM as the
        63, 66–7

global enterprise system, the 71
    partnering in 82–4
global HRM, comparison of practices
        within 4, 151–5
    development of a strategy/
        perspective towards 14, 19, 29,
        33, 52–7, 62–3
    differences from domestic HRM 4,
        122
    examples of and insights into 4,
        8–9, 10, 62–70
    existence and development of 4, 35,
        41
    from an Asian perspective 233–255
    optimisation of 65, 70–71
    research into 4, 10, 61–2
    sustaining a strategy for 14, 34
    the seven Cs of 10
    'Think global, act local' 14 19,
        29–32, 33, 35, 121
globalisation of business 1–4, 10,
        14–32, 33, 35, 40, 59, 63–70,
        71, 131–5, 146, 179, 207, 230,
        234
    and 'localisation' 15–17, 29–36,
        46, 65, 66, 73, 74, 125
    forces driving 15, 33–4, 46, 63–4,
        71
global organisation, the see
        organisation, the global
global performance advantage (GPA)
        63
global stakeholders 67–8, 74
    HR orientation towards 68–9, 83
government agencies as employers
        248–9
    of expatriates 3
graduate recruitment, international
        101, 103, 104, 106–107,
        108–109, 113, 194
Greek managerial attitudes 220–221,
        223–5

head-hunting 100–102, 106
Heineken, comparisons with 56
Hewlett Packard, comparisons with
        55, 57, 72
high-speed transportation systems,
        importance to global HRM of
        59
high-tech industries in relation to
        traditional industries 2

Hitachi Credit, comparisons with 8
homeworking 176
    reliance on 50
HR strategy of an organisation 39, 41
    the Asian pattern in relation to
        diversity 242–254

IBM, comparisons with 29–31, 101,
    150
IHRM *see* global HRM
IKEA, comparisons with 191
improvisation, creative 69
Indonesian managerial attitudes 43,
    251
industrial relations (IR) *see* employee
    relations
influencing skills 68, 69
information systems (IS) 61, 62, 71,
    82, 84
information technology (IT) 7, 61, 71,
    82, 84
    and competitive advantage 6, 25,
        61
innovation 7, 28, 50, 51, 78, 80, 118
integration of corporate activities on a
        global basis 29–36, 65, 67,
        70–71
integration of people management
        activities 3, 4, 66
Intel, comparisons with 12–13, 191
intelligence, as a source of competitive
        advantage/added value 61, 63,
        120
    mobilisation of organisational 62–3
internal perspective on financial
        effectiveness/productivity 7
international career, issues raised by
        taking up an 145–151, 152–3,
        154
    management of an 151–5; *see also*
        international manager *entries*
    options (empire, colonial,
        professional, peripheral,
        expedient, fringe) 146–151,
        152, 154
    see also financial aspects of an
        international assignment
international division of a (domestic)
        corporation 66
international HRM *see* global HRM
international management teams, a
        case-study in building 217–229

development of through diversity
        of 207–231
    framework for building 214–217
international manager, attracting and
        engaging the 88–9, 100–103
    competencies required in an 10,
        90–100, 183
    design of assignment around the
        93, 98–9, 113
    Peiperl's (1998) survey of the 183
    selection of the 88, 93–100,
        107–112
    socialisation of the 90–91
    sourcing the 88, 103–107
    the changing purpose of the
        91–2
    the development (and/or training)
        of the 92–3, 195
    the support structure for the 95–6,
        126, 147
    types/categories of 76–7, 89–90,
        91
international team(s) *see* team(s)
        entries
international teamworking *see*
        teamwork(ing) *entries*
Internet, Dell's strategy 75
    recruitment via 104–106, 113, 194
    the effects of 1
intranets, for achieving clarity of
        communications 75
Italian managerial attitudes 43, 190

Jaguar (North America), comparisons
        with 80
Japanese companies, employment
        systems in 233–4, 242–4
    in the UK 2, 209
    outside Japan 182
Japanese managerial attitudes 43, 190
job security 54, 234, 244, 246, 250,
        251
Johnson & Johnson, comparisons with
        55, 57

KLM/Alitalia, comparisons with 8–9
knowledge, as a political/power issue
        186
    association of competitive
        advantage with 1, 6, 33
    eliciting and the creation of new 6,
        26, 28, 33, 34, 71, 77–8

international transference of 1, 28, 77–8, 82, 89, 141
knowledge management (KM) 6–7, 77–8, 186, 198
knowledge-sharing 5, 20, 26–8, 33, 67, 186, 198, 202, 216
  and the 'not invented here' syndrome 26–8, 79
Kodak and the Japanese market 26

leadership 6, 83, 192–5, 215
  competencies for global 69–70, 76
  competencies for international team 183–4, 192–5
  development processes 55, 56, 57, 193–5
  in change management 68, 69
  'virtual' 201
learning of/by individuals 7, 69
  as an aspect of cultural behaviour 45
  double-loop 80
  enthusiasm for 69
  few opportunities for 50
learning of/by the organisation 33, 67, 78, 207
  in global terms 34, 207
leverage wielded by an organisation *see* organisational leverage
line managers, responsibilities of 6, 14, 82–4, 100, 164, 166, 168, 174
localisation as opposed to globalisation *see* globalisation of business, and 'localisation'
logistics, as a core global strategic force 72

management teams, international *see* international management teams
manager, the international *see* international manager, the
'manager-as-coach' profile for executives 126
marketing strategy, and globalisation 18–19
Mars, comparisons with 56
maturity, as an element of personal effectiveness 69
McDonald's, comparisons with 60, 133, 150
migration(s) of the labour market 40

mind-set required for managing internationally 3, 76, 84, 92–3
  ability to adapt emphasis in 4, 95, 96–8
  Cadbury Schweppes' accelerated development programme 96–8
  polycentric 98
  S.W.I.F.T.'s critical success factor 93–5
mismanagement, effects of 9
motivation, factors in 6, 42, 78, 118, 123, 140, 204
  lack of/reduced 77, 110, 183
Motorola, comparisons with 60, 78, 101, 125
multiculturalism, as a source of competitive advantage 9
  conscious and subconscious awareness of 159
  within a single workforce 159
  within the USA 40
  within what used to be the Soviet-dominated bloc 40

Nabisco Foods, comparisons with 6
needs of individual employees in relation to motivation 6
network hiring in Asia 244
networking, global/international 10, 59, 62, 68, 92
  organisational 46, 48–9, 52–4, 55–6, 78
new industrial economies (NIEs) of Asia *see* 'Four Little Dragons', the
Nike, comparisons with 64, 253
non-financial rewards 36
non-profit organisations as employers of expatriates 3
Nortel, comparisons with 8

organisation, as 'a bundle of capabilities' 12, 13, 32, 35
  as a political 'system' 43, 46, 49
  as a 'system' for imposing authority 43
  the 'centralised hub' model of 121, 122, 127, 140
  the communal 51–2, 54–5, 56–7
  the co-ordinated federation model of 119–121, 122, 127, 140, 141
  the fragmented 50–51, 54, 55, 56

the global 14–32, 64–81, 115–142, 181–2

the hierarchical or role-formalising 43, 46

the international 181–2

the lean 2

the mercenary 49–50, 53–4, 56

the multinational (= decentralised federation) model of 66, 118–119, 127, 140, 141, 181

the 'pro-foreign' 149, 150

the seamless 1, 3

the 'shamrock' (= core/internals + periphery/externals) 148

the theory of the 12

the transnational 117–118, 121, 122–6, 127–8, 141, 181

the 'virtual' 1, 56

organisational architecture *see* organisational structure

organisational capability/capabilities 12–14, 32, 33, 35–6, 61, 75, 82, 83, 115, 123, 141, 207

as following organisational strategy 12–14, 19, 32–5, 74

assessment/measurement of 13–14, 33–4

identification of the required 33–6

transference across an organisation for global success 61–2

organisational culture 7, 9, 10, 12, 39–57, 71, 78–9, 118, 160, 215

aligned with performance management systems 80

as a source of competitive advantage 9

as different from national/local culture 8–9, 10, 19–23, 39–46, 136, 160

conflict in 52

development and preservation of 9, 41, 78–9

relationships within, models of 47–52; *see also* sociability; solidarity

organisational dialogue, changes in 156–7

to bring groups to closer understanding 174–5, 176

traditional, including collective bargaining 156, 241, 251, 252

organisational diversity *see* diversity of operational environments

organisational form and/or philosophy *see* organisation *entries*

organisational goals, balance of long- and short-term 7

clear and measurable 50

shared 83

organisational leverage (ie size and reach) 20, 25–6, 33, 34, 57, 65, 70–71

as an element in recent major mergers 25

organisational procedures 12

imposed by corporate centres of excellence 50

organisational resourcefulness as an element of global leadership 69

organisational stability 71, 79–80

organisational strategy/policy 9, 10, 12–14, 19, 22, 30, 36, 52, 62, 73, 79, 136

achieving consistency yet allowing flexibility in 22–5, 33

delivery of global 32–5, 68, 72, 73–4, 81, 141

determination of what is core/non-core to 19–21, 22, 23, 33

nationally and globally oriented 30, 34, 36, 71, 73, 81, 141

organisational structure 9, 36, 43, 45

as related to globalisation 14, 17–19, 30, 41, 46, 71, 82, 131–2

as traditionally following strategy 12

different attitudes of managers towards 43

interdependence/reciprocity as important to 46, 140

outsourcing, reliance on/use of 50, 82, 84, 200, 248

overseas operation of parent-company firms 3, 125–6

ownership of companies *see* corporate governance

PAG *see* 'performance advantage group', the

partnership, as an ideal for business success 59, 61, 84

the role of HRM in 63, 65, 81–4
pay *see* compensation/reward
people, as a resource 2, 76, 79, 207
people management, development in
    Asia of 233–242
    training in 3, 4
people management policies in general
    3, 137, 140
    successful 3, 167
    unsuccessful 3, 173
people management skills,
    development on an international
    basis of 2, 3
    necessary combination of 3, 137,
    165–6, 173
people–technology interface, the
    62–3, 84
PepsiCo, comparisons with 56, 101
'performance advantage group' (PAG),
    the 62–3, 65, 67, 70, 72–84
performance measurement 53–4, 56,
    80, 136
performance-related pay *see*
    compensation/reward(s), linked
    to performance
personal development 207
    360-degree feedback and 6
    see also careers and career
    development
personal effectiveness 68–9
personality tests/profiling 111–112,
    174
    the Myers Briggs® Type Indicator
    175
    the Perception and Preference
    Inventory (PAPI) 111–112
personnel policies *see* people
    management policies
Philips, comparisons with 56, 122,
    123
problems of international
    management, increased 4
process redesign 7
process re-engineering 7, 120
promotion 54
Procter & Gamble (P&G),
    comparisons with 15, 23, 78
psychological contract, the 10, 39,
    52–3, 55, 164
    different perceptions of 162–7,
    173, 174
    research into 107, 164

psychometric assessment of managerial
    competencies 93, 95, 98, 108,
    110–112, 113

reasoning tests 111
recruitment and selection, factors in
    international 87–113
    for compatibility 55, 57
    for customer-oriented capability
    13, 22–3
    for global HRM capabilities 10,
    87, 90–100, 194
    media and advertising 102–3
    of the best in their field 56, 76
    see also graduate recruitment;
    Internet, recruitment via;
    selection philosophies,
    competing
Reebok, comparisons with 64
religious affiliations as part of cultural
    background 40, 41
remuneration *see* compensation/reward
reward *see* compensation/reward
risk (factor) analysis/assessment *see*
    clinical risk assessment
role-playing 7
Russian managerial attitudes 190

sales strategy, and globalisation 18
selection philosophies, competing 88,
    91–100
seven Cs of global HRM, the *see*
    global HRM, the seven Cs of
shareholding and company ownership
    see corporate governance
Shell, comparisons with 32, 150
skills database tracking system(s) 99
    EMI Music systems 99–100
    relating to expatriates 105
sociability, as an analogue of corporate
    cultural relationships 47–52,
    53, 57
    definition: friendship groups 47
    levels of 48–52
solidarity, as an analogue of corporate
    cultural relationships 47–52,
    53, 57
    definition: intermittent association
    for a common purpose 47–8
    levels of 48–52
Spanish managerial attitudes 190
Sprint, comparisons with 67

stability of a business *see* organisational stability

stereotyping, as an aspect of cultural behaviour 45, 159
  as something to avoid 39

stress management, as a required capability 194, 195

Swedish managerial attitudes 43, 190

talent, attracting and developing and retaining global 61, 71, 76–7, 82–3

team(s), Belbin role model of 208, 214, 219, 222, 223, 225, 230
  building 36, 188, 192–4, 198, 211, 217–229, 231
  considerations of status within 187, 193
  cultural differences within 9, 180, 181, 182, 183, 187–191, 204
  defusing conflict within 197
  development of 6, 46, 192, 198–9, 207–231
  supporting role of HRM for international 192, 194, 198–9, 202–203
  types of international 180–181, 208
  'virtual' 180–181, 185, 192, 198, 203–204
  see also international management teams; teamwork(ing)

team goals, achieving 197
  setting 36, 198, 215

'team room', the 199

team strategy 14

teamwork(ing), and innovation 51, 78–9
  barriers to international 184–191
  enabling international 192–5, 208; *see also* team(s), supporting role for HRM
  international 179–204, 207, 208, 221–9

key factors in effective 215, 228
  skills/competencies required for international 182–4, 192–5, 198–9, 212–213, 215
  360-degree feedback and 6
  see also team(s)

technology, the role of in global HRM 10, 61–3, 73, 77, 126, 199

360-degree feedback 5–6
  design and implementation of a system for 6
  effectiveness of 6

trade union(s) 156–7, 242, 246–7, 252
  the 'Asian approach' to 242, 251

training and development, oriented towards customer care 13
  oriented towards marketing shared norms 55

UK managerial attitudes 190, 220–225

UK shareholding attitudes 128–130

Unilever, comparisons with 24–5, 56, 124–5

USA, social/ethnic patterns within the 40

US managerial attitudes 43–4, 119, 120, 190

US shareholding attitudes 128–130

Virgin firm brand, positive equity in the 24

virtual organisation, the *see* organisation, the 'virtual'

virtual teams *see* team(s), 'virtual'

visa issues and considerations 107

Volvo Car Corporation, comparisons with the 195

W. H. Smith, comparisons with 5

workers abroad *see* expatriate workers